materialist feminism
the politics of discourse

Thinking Gender
Edited by Linda J. Nicholson

Also published in the series

Feminism/Postmodernism
Linda J. Nicholson

Gender Trouble
Judith Butler

Words of Power
Andrea Nye

Femininity and Domination
Sandra Bartky

Disciplining Foucault
Jana Sawicki

Beyond Accommodation
Drucilla Cornell

Embattled Eros
Steven Seidman

Erotic Welfare
Linda Singer

materialist
feminism
AND THE
politics of
discourse

rosemary hennessy

ROUTLEDGE
NEW YORK/LONDON

Published in 1993 by

Routledge
An imprint of Routledge, Chapman and Hall, Inc.
29 West 35th Street
New York, NY 10001

Published in Great Britain by

Routledge
11 New Fetter Lane
London EC4P 4EE

Library of Congress Cataloging in Publication Data

Hennessy, Rosemary.
    Materialist feminism and the politics of discourse / by Rosemary
Hennessy.
      p. cm.
    Includes bibliographical references (p.   ) and index.
    ISBN 0-415-90479-X (cl.)   ISBN 0-415-90480-3 (pbk.)
    1. Feminist theory. 2. Marxist criticism. I. Title.
HQ1190. H46 1992
305.42′01—dc20   92-9689
                                              CIP

British Library Cataloguing in Publication Data

Hennessy, Rosemary
    Materialist Feminism and the Politics of
    Discourse.—(Thinking Gender Series)
    I. Title II. Series
    305.4
    ISBN 0-415-90479-x
    ISBN 0-415-90480-3 (pb)

For Molly and Kate

Contents

Acknowledgments

This book could not have been written without support and encouragement of various sorts, from diverse quarters, over many years. Because the first phase of the project was a dissertation produced out of a time of great upheaval in English departments nationally, and at Syracuse University in particular, its passage through institutional channels was far from smooth. As a result, the support it did receive was crucial and taught me much about the politics of discourse. For their willingness to serve as directors, for their incisive readings and critical advice, I am especially grateful to Robyn Wiegman and Steven Mailloux. I also want to thank Linda Alcoff, Thomas Yingling, and Dympna Callahan who gave my ideas their time and useful commentary. For his contribution to the intellectual ferment and ideological discomfort out of which this phase of the book was produced, I want to acknowledge Mas'ud Zavarzadeh. Although he did not see the project through to completion, he extended immeasurably its political reach.

Financial aid from several sources helped provide the precious time I needed for writing and research. Part of my work on Foucault was funded by a Syracuse University Faculty Senate Research Grant in 1987. In 1991 a New York State United University Professors New Faculty Development award from the University at Albany provided the resources for a summer spent on revisions.

Sections of this book have appeared previously in an essay published in *Rethinking Marxism*. I want to thank the editors of this journal for their interest in my work.

The materialist feminism I argue for here has been shaped by the solidarity and critique of several friends and collectives. Many of the ideas that found their way into this book are indebted to my work with Rajeswari Mohan whose bold thinking, rigor, and incisive readings have always inspired me and whose critical support through collaborative projects and difficult times I value highly. I also owe a special thanks to Fred Fiske for years of unqualified endorsement of my intellectual pursuits, despite their costs and often disruptive outcomes. At Syracuse University long hours of debate, writing, and struggle with The Student Marxist Collective (Amitava Kumar, Minette Marcroft, Raji Mohan, Bob Nowlan, Ron Strickland, Mark Wood) helped shape my thinking on innumerable facets of postmodern marxism and collective work. Hypatia: The Graduate Group of Women's Studies taught me invaluable lessons in feminist praxis, and the Feminist Theory Colloquium (1989–90) offered a useful forum for discussing many of the issues I grapple with here. Thanks are also due to several colleagues at the State University of New York at Albany who generously read the manuscript or parts of it and offered encouragement—Ruma Chawla, Helen Elam, Jill Hanifan, Deb Kelsh, Cy Knobloch, Steve North. The Feminist Theory Group at SUNY Albany was a challenging testing-ground for materialist feminism. I want to acknowledge especially those who participated in the session on my Foucault essay: Lil Brannon, Judith Fetterley, Claudia Murphy, Marjorie Pryse, and Joan Schulz. Discussions and collective work with Teresa Ebert have spurred my thinking on many issues; her critical solidarity in negotiating what it means to be an oppositional intellectual has often affirmed my faith in feminism. The students at SUNY Albany in the courses I offered in 1990 and 1991 taught me a great deal about feminist pedagogy and the function of theory in postmodern culture.

I owe a very special debt to Linda Nicholson who pursued the manuscript for the Thinking Gender series; she has been a staunch friend and mentor and a magnanimously supportive editor. I am also grateful to Maureen MacGrogan, my editor at Routledge, for her endorsement of the project and patience with its production.

Finally, I want to acknowledge Chrys Ingraham who more than anyone has fortified my understanding of feminist practice. She read and commented on each of the chapters; our countless conversations and debates thread their way through all of the ideas here. Her renegade wisdom and humor, fierce commitments, and keen theoretical insights have been my most valuable resources.

My daughters, Marian and Katherine Hennessy-Fiske, to whom this book is dedicated, lived through the many years I was writing it with love and forbearance, and I thank them for that. I hope that witnessing my labors has already persuaded them to persevere and take risks in their own work for social justice and will encourage them always to believe that failure is impossible.

Introduction

One of the foremost issues—perhaps even *the* issue—western feminism faces in the nineties is the impact of the general crisis of knowledge on its historical subject. This crisis of authority has intensified anxiety around the category "woman," an anxiety which has to a greater or lesser extent haunted bourgeois feminism from its inception in the form of questions about the woman—or women—feminism speaks for. In some instances, questioning feminism's claim to speak for all women has led to fears that dismantling the identity "woman" may well lead to the dissolution of feminism itself. At the same time, the myriad forms of violence against women, the persistent worldwide devaluation of femininity and women's work, and the intensified controls over women's sexuality and reproductive capacities are daily reminders of the need for a strong and persistent feminist movement. Surely feminist critique of the systematic oppression of women is still necessary, perhaps more now than ever. The challenge is to find ways to anchor feminist analysis in our recognition of the continued brutal force certain social totalities like patriarchy and racism still exercise, at the same time acknowledging that the social construction of "woman" is never monolithic. Over the past decade materialist feminist theory has been in the forefront of the effort to take up this challenge.

In the late 1970s materialist feminism emerged from feminist critiques within marxism. Working in critical engagement with the formation of the New Left in Britain and France especially, materialist feminist work contributed to the development of theories of patriarchy and ideology, elaborating more specific understandings of the relation between the operation of power in the symbolic order and in other material practices. Annette Kuhn, Anne Marie Wolpe, Michele Barrett, Mary MacIntosh, and Christine Delphy were among the initial promoters of "materialist feminism," favoring that term over "marxist feminism" on the basis of an argument that marxism cannot adequately address women's exploitation and oppression unless the marxist problematic itself is transformed so as to be able to account for the sexual division of labor. With its class bias, its emphasis on economic determinism, and its focus on a history exclusively formulated in terms of capitalist production, classic marxism in the seventies had barely begun to analyze patriarchal systems of power. At the same time, there was a marked tendency in most feminist theory to conceptualize woman in essentialist and idealist terms. In this context, materialist feminism provided a historically urgent ground from which to launch a critical counterknowledge to both feminism and marxism.

By the early eighties a small but growing body of materialist feminist theory from across diverse national boundaries was making use of the insight that subjectivity is discursively constructed to analyze the intersections of gender and class. These analyses served as a powerful critique of mainstream feminism's appeals to individual rights or to a universalized notion of "women's experience," but for the most part they gave priority to the social construction of gender. This tendency to focus exclusively on gender has blunted materialist feminism's effectivity in many areas of oppositional political struggle, however, and in this respect aligned it with much mainstream western feminist work. Over the past twenty years, the voices of women who have found themselves outside the boundaries of that mainstream—women of color, lesbians, working-class, and "third-world" women—have pressured feminism to question the adequacy of a generic "woman" and a gender-centered feminist inquiry. These knowledges draw from (and contend with) the discourses of the postmodern avant-garde which have also rewritten the subject-in-difference by calling into question the empiricist self. The materialist feminism that is circulating in the nineties—in the work of Norma Alarcón, Evelyn Brooks-Higgenbotham, Teresa Ebert, Teresa deLauretis, Donna Haraway, Chandra Mohanty, Toril Moi, Mary Poovey, Chandra Sandoval, and others—has grown out of and been shaped by both of these critiques of identity. Increasingly, materialist feminist analyses problematize "woman" as an obvious and homogeneous empirical entity in order to explore how "woman" as a discursive category is historically constructed and traversed by more than one differential axis.

At a historical moment when the pressures to address difference are often formulated in terms of a logic of inclusion or contingency, when imperatives to abandon systemic thinking and "overarching totalities" in our analysis exert their force from the left and from the right, materialist feminists need to insist on one of the strongest features of feminism's legacy—its critique of social totalities like patriarchy and capitalism—without abandoning attention to the differential positioning of women within them. As a multinational military industrial complex systematically expands its network of exploitative relations of production and consumption, patriarchal and capitalist relations become even more securely imbricated. Witness the growing violence against women in the periphery by corporate research, the increasing sexualization of women internationally by an all-pervasive commodity aesthetics, and the intensified contestation over woman's body as the site of reproduction in the "first world" and of production in the "third world." At the same time that capital's colonization has become more wide-reaching and insidious, oppositional struggles are increasingly confined to regional and isolated sites. As this strategy of localizing extends to many cultural registers and becomes a common mechanism of crisis management, materialist feminists need to attend critically to its effects on the conceptual frameworks which structure our concepts.

This book is not an overview or a genealogy of materialist feminism. It does not offer an introduction to materialist feminism or plot out its organizing concepts. It is, instead, an argument for and within a materialist feminist problematic that takes as its particular focus the problem of the subject—more specifically, the discursively constructed subject. This focus leads me to explore some of the theoretical and political issues that materialist feminism's appropriation of the concept of a discursively constructed subject has raised: whether and how it matters which theory of discourse we work with, for instance, or whether a discursively constructed subject is coherent with feminism's emancipatory aims. Throughout I argue for materialist feminism as a way of reading that need not shrink from naming social totalities in order to address the complex ways in which subjectivities are differentiated. And I present this argument by way of several conceptual—which is to say theoretical, historical, and political—issues it raises for the question of who feminism speaks for.

In naming this nexus of issues "the politics of discourse," I took the risk of invoking a phrase that, in some circles at least, has become almost a cliché. It seems to me, however, that for all of the invocations of "politics" in studies that have addressed the "discursive construction of the subject," we still have very few rigorous theoretical formulations of exactly what these terms mean. This is even more the case when they are combined with another word, also lately in vogue, "materialism." The title, then, is a way of insisting that we cannot shy away from concepts like "politics," "discourse," or "materialism" simply because they are last year's fashion, and now are no longer "hot" or "fresh." Instead we need to continue the hard work of explaining and rewriting them.

Materialist feminism is engaged in this rewriting. Like other reading practices, its ways of making sense of the world *make* sense; that is, materialist feminism affects what gets to count as "reality" through the assumptions it valorizes and the subjects it produces. It is in this sense a discourse that has a definite politics. Even as it takes as its particular focus the elimination of patriarchal power, the assumptions on which materialist feminist theory rests have been forged out of appropriations from an array of discourses—postmodern, marxist, liberal humanist, anticolonialist, anti-racist. In the following chapters I examine how this focus is affected by the various and often contesting discourses materialist feminism appropriates and the issues raised by its appropriation of concepts. Throughout I suggest that the task of redefining who feminism speaks for is intimately bound up with how the discursive construction of the subject is conceptualized. This means, in part, that the various theories of discourse we appropriate and how we articulate them into a feminist critical framework have an effect on the sense we *make* of the world—on our feminist politics and the reality it transforms.

I approach this general issue of the politics of discourse by way of several problems. Chief among them is the problem of social analytics—that is, how *the social* is conceptualized in the various theories materialist feminism draws from— and the accompanying question of how to understand the materiality of discourse and of history. The standpoint from which and for which I argue is a much more emphatically postmodern marxist feminism than much recent work in materialist feminism has been willing to embrace. However, to my mind taking the risk of situating materialist feminism's *materialism* more firmly within a postmodern marxist problematic has two crucial positive consequences. It avails feminism of a framework for developing a more rigorous theory of the materiality of discourse— including materialist feminism's own discursivity—and it opens a productive avenue for rethinking feminism's subject.

Implicit in the organization of the book is the assumption that in order for materialist feminism to be a powerful critical intervention in the reformation of the hegemonic subject in the postmodern moment, we have to attend more rigorously to the materiality of knowledge. This means, in part, that we have to inquire into the processes whereby feminism appropriates and reformulates its concepts. If feminist inquiry is not to be a re-enactment of the dominant pluralist paradigm, it needs to make visible the contesting interests informing new knowledges and disarticulate their salient features from analytics that often subvert the aims of feminism's political agenda. In order to foreground the materiality of feminism as a mode of reading, we also need to situate the various facets of a materialist feminist theoretical framework in relation to other contesting materialisms.

For the reader primarily interested in the *feminism* of materialist feminist theory, these efforts may seem belabored "detours" through various marxisms and post-marxisms. Anticipating these objections, I want to emphasize that *materialist* feminism dismisses sustained inquiry into these discourses which also claim to be materialist at the risk of reifying its own historicity. While the extent of my critique of post-marxism in the first two chapters could be improved upon— and no doubt will be in the continuing work of others—if we are going to take seriously the notion that discourses have a materiality, we cannot shrink from rigorous critical assessments of the theoretical paradigms we draw our concepts from.

In order to relate the crisis of feminism's subject to the re-formation of subjectivities in the larger culture now, I begin chapter 1 by situating materialist feminism in the discursive field where it primarily circulates, that is, the postmodern academy. The crisis of knowledge in the academy is increasingly being understood in terms of forces that extend much more broadly than the invasion of postmodern theories. Provoked by pressures as wide-ranging as shifts in U.S. hegemony and demographics, the technological revolution, and the installation of a service-based economy now in recession, this "crisis" is a struggle over the distribution of wealth and the reimagination of civic identity. Feminism has been one of the primary new knowledges fomenting this crisis, at the same time it has been affected by and helped manage it. The reconfiguration of what and how we know has provoked feminism's critical assessment of who it speaks for, and helped us reimagine the feminist subject as a highly differentiated one, positioned across the multiple axes of race, class, gender, and sexuality. At the same time that feminism's critical edge has been honed by the array of new knowledges loosely identified as postmodern, its relationship to postmodernism has also been contentious. Many postmodern theories have threatened to recuperate feminism's oppositional force. Examining the social logic implicit in the postmodern theories we appropriate—particularly those claiming to be materialist—can enable feminists to assess the extent to which a particular theoretical framework may subvert or enhance feminism's political objectives.

I inaugurate this process of "disarticulating" postmodern materialism in chapter 1, through a critique of the social logics in the work of Foucault and Laclau and Mouffe. Each has important concepts to offer materialist feminism, and yet each frames these concepts within a social logic of contingency, a framework that I argue undermines feminism's critique of patriarchy. Disarticulating some of these concepts—the notion of discursive practice, is one—from a contingent social logic is a first step toward rearticulating them within an alternative *systemic* conception of the social. Theories of ideology post-Althusser are to my mind a very useful instance of systemic analysis for feminist theory now. Conceptualizing discourse as ideology allows us to consider the discursive construction of the subject, "woman," across multiple modalities of difference, but without forfeiting feminism's recognition that the continued success of patriarchy depends upon its systematic operation—the hierarchical social relations it maintains and the other material forces it marshals and is shaped by. It is, moreover, a mode of analysis that is coherent with feminism's commitment to the elimination of exploitation and oppression.

In chapter 2 I turn to the problem of the materiality of discourse as it has been formulated in the work of several post-marxists: Foucault, Kristeva, and Laclau and Mouffe. Each of them has devised materialist theories of discourse which have been extremely influential, particularly for feminist theory, in configuring relations between language and the social. I pay particular attention to Foucault because of the tremendous impact his conception of discourse has had on materialist feminism. Reading Foucault in relation to Kristeva, whose work is usually seen as quite distinct from his, brings into relief certain shared features of their analytics and demonstrates once again "the politics of discourse"—in this case, how the framing of concepts in social theory has a bearing on larger social arrangements. As part of their project of putting forward a conceptual outline for radical democracy, Laclau and Mouffe's materialist theory of discourse is also relevant to feminists. Their understanding of the formation of a democratic plurality gives a great deal of prominence to political movements, including feminism, and is increasingly being appropriated by materialist critics of culture.

Reading these three theories against each other makes visible unexpected similarities in their analytics: in the relationship between the discursive and the nondiscursive, in their ways of understanding the disruptive "unthought" of culture, in their notions of the body. It underscores the potentially useful ways of conceptualizing the social construction of difference they make possible as well as those they block. Reading them in relation to each other also foregrounds the conservative implications of their theories of discourse, an issue often overlooked in materialist feminist appropriations of their work.

My rewriting of the materiality of discourse for feminism begins with an assessment of feminist standpoint theory in chapter 3. Although not without its shortcomings, this body of work now comprises one of the major feminist contributions to the rearticulation of the subject. It offers a very powerful critical framework for explaining the relationships among knowledge, power, and subjectivity. In this regard, standpoint theory supersedes many of the impasses of liberal and postmodern feminism. However, one of its intractable issues is an often contradictory allegiance to both a discursively constructed subject and an experiential self. The theoretical problem that underlies this contradiction is standpoint theory's failure to explain the material relation between the discursive (feminist critique) and the nondiscursive (women's lives). Drawing critically upon developments in postmodern marxist theory, I argue that understanding discourse as ideology offers a way out of this impasse.

A theory of ideology makes it possible to explain the complex ways social reality is shaped—through the overdetermined relations among mechanisms for making sense, distributing resources, dividing labor, and sharing or wielding power. If we acknowledge, for instance, that discursive struggles over woman's reproductive body in the U.S. now have less to do with women's "choice"—or even with abortion per se—than with the maintenance of a social order in which the few still benefit from the work of many, where power and resources are distributed on the basis of wealth not human worth or need, and women are generally devalued, we can begin to make sense of the contest over abortion from the standpoint of those who are already most affected by the legislation of women's bodies—the thousands of poor women who are also disproportionately women of color. We need critical frameworks that can address these issues and explain the complex ways in which the social marks of difference do not serve as indices of plurality but rather as guarantors of inequity. The causal logic underlying a theory of discourse as ideology makes it possible to acknowledge the systematic operation of social totalities like patriarchy and racism across a range of interrelated material practices. These totalities traverse and define many areas of the social formation—divisions of labor, dimensions of state intervention and civil rights, the mobility of sites for production and consumption, the reimagination of colonial conquest, and the colonization of the imagination. If feminism as a mode of reading is to confront and explain the highly differentiated positioning of "woman" across densely mediated social practices like these—those spanning the sexualization of the female body in the west and the feminization of colonized peoples, for instance—it cannot relinquish systemic analysis.

Drawing upon elaborations of Gramsci's concept of hegemony, postmodern marxist theories of ideology afford a way to understand the current crisis of feminism as itself an enabling condition for transformative change. As a counterhegemonic discourse, materialist feminism can provoke and make use of ideological crisis by reading the fault-lines in the texts of culture symptomatically. Symptomatic reading is a practice which makes sense of the gaps in narrative coherence as signs of the dis-ease that infects the social imaginary. Unlike neoformalist notions of the slippage of signification, however, it historicizes these gaps and reads them as displacements of the broad-ranging contradictions upon which late capital depends. And in so doing it supersedes them with an alternative explanation of social relations. In these respects, it is a form of ideology critique with tremendous potential for materialist feminism.

Understanding feminist practice as ideology critique provides a way to rethink the feminist standpoint not as an experiential ground for knowledge but as a critical practice. In chapter 4 I develop the implications of this notion of standpoint for feminist history. I read several feminist histories by way of a discussion of the discourse of *the new* and its function in helping to manage the symbolic anchors of the social imaginary through times of cultural crisis. Continuing the theme of situating materialist feminism in relation to Foucauldian and French feminist problematics, I examine in some detail two variants of recent feminist work that in different ways offer a "history" of the new woman: the New Woman's History, much of it informed by Foucault, and a group of readings of Freud's *Dora*, heavily inflected by French feminism and psychoanalysis. In reading history as narrative, I give particular attention to the relation between history and theory, the extent to which efforts within feminist history to rewrite the category "woman" are impeded by a lingering empiricism, and to the ways the new feminist history has collaborated with the conservative face of psychoanalysis in managing the current crisis of feminism's subject.

Reading these histories of the new woman from the standpoint of ideology critique has a bearing on how feminists understand their interest in and renarration of "woman." Central to my argument for reading history as ideology is the claim that history, as one of the narratives of a culture, is always an intervention in the present. The political importance of feminist reconstructions of the new woman— either from the late nineteenth century *or* from the late twentieth century—is how they help to shape the ideological uncertainty surrounding "woman" now. From the standpoint of ideology critique, then, feminist history is inextricably bound up with feminist theory and the question of identity. How feminist histories theorize "woman" has a tremendous effect on who feminism speaks for. To the extent that it can disrupt the hold of an identity politics which continues anxiously to trouble and tame the radical potential of feminist thought, a more fully materialist feminist narrative holds much promise.

As the struggle over how to reimagine the boundaries of social plurality continues into the twenty-first century, feminism offers a crucial and necessary critical standpoint. Inserting the social subject—including feminism's own subject—into the historical contest over meaning and resources, materialist feminism also reclaims one of the strongest features of feminism's legacy—its analysis of social totalities—and articulates it with some of the most important insights of postmodernism. Without forfeiting feminism's specificity, materialist feminism fosters the alignment of a feminist standpoint with other political movements. The creative tensions in this collectivity coupled with an insistence on historicizing help keep materialist feminism vital and open to history. This historicity has taught us that feminism's vision of democratic possibility is always *provisional* because continually subject to critique. It is in recognition of the constructive power of this ongoing double-move between solidarity and critique that I offer my arguments for materialist feminism here.

1

Materialist Feminism in the Postmodern Academy: Toward a Global Social Analytic

I

In the past two decades or so a "crisis" has occurred in western knowledge across a broad range of disciplines as the basic assumptions of the social sciences and humanities have been called into question. Recently the more dramatic aftershocks of this upheaval have shown some signs of abating as the academy proves capable of accommodating discourses subversive of the humanist and empiricist foundations of western tradition. One index of this adjustment is the re-formation of curricula, as knowledges which challenge western civilization's stories about itself are not only welcomed but increasingly considered *de rigueur*.[1] While the academy manages this disruption, the forums in which its effects are being debated have widened. As local newspapers from Albany to Austin and national magazines like *Time, Newsweek,* and *The Atlantic Monthly* invite their readers to contemplate the implications of college curriculum reform, it becomes clear that the assimilation of new knowledges in universities is not simply a matter of cultural updating. The growing activity of the corporate-financed National Association of Scholars and the restrictive funding policies of the National Endowment for the Arts and Humanities are indicators that the crisis of authority in higher education is a very public and high-stakes battle over how meanings and social categories are to be secured. The spreading ripples of this disruptive event make very visible that the production of knowledge in universities is a densely mediated activity, affecting, if only indirectly, the formation of meaning and value—the very fabric of culture in the west.

Critics inside and outside universities are quick to attest that feminism has helped to produce this decisive moment in western culture. As a set of discourses born out of modernity, feminism has long called into question the master narratives of western knowledge, delineating the contradictions between their democratic ideals and their exclusionary effects. Increasingly more "at home" in the academy, feminism is still, nonetheless, distinguished as an emancipatory movement whose interests exceed academic enclaves. Any history of feminism will demonstrate that one effect of this wide-ranging circulation has been a long-standing and productive questioning of the subject of feminism itself.

From its inception, feminism as a political movement and a way of making sense of the world has forged its objectives through, against, and in the face of challenges from within its ranks over who feminism speaks for. While these challenges have been unevenly addressed and sometimes even ignored, in the past decade they have come to dominate feminist discussions in the academy, cutting deeply into assumptions of solidarity, testing appeals to sisterhood to reckon with the differences between women, within "woman." Although these debates over difference have incurred a great deal of uncertainty about how exactly to understand the subject of feminism, in all of their difference feminists invariably insist that knowledge is politically organized.

Dubbed the political conscience of postmodernism, feminism is increasingly pointed to on the academic left as a model for the articulation of a new subject of knowledge. In part, this authority derives from the relationship to the academy that has shaped feminism's history over the past twenty years. Feminism in the university is defined by its constitution as a network of practices that tests the very boundaries of the institution, ranging over Women's Studies, feminist theory, and the women's movement (Rooney, "Discipline," 16). The "internal" debates over who feminism speaks for, (which for all of their divisiveness have also honed feminism's oppositional edge) can be ascribed, at least in part, to the fact that feminism circulates so widely if unevenly beyond the academy.

Certainly feminism is not unique in this respect. Other political movements have also gathered their strength in the university from similar extra-academic networks. And it is the use to which this loosely shared history is put that will, perhaps, determine feminism's future in the academy. I think it is fair to say that feminism's potential as an oppositional discourse in the university rests upon its ability to articulate a radical political critique that takes into account its intersection with other political movements. As many feminists recognize, the degree to which feminism is allowed—or, more rarely, encouraged—in the university is to a great extent the effect of how much the discourse of "women's liberation" has been absorbed by the hegemonic culture. The challenge for feminists working in the academy now is to forestall similar efforts to absorb and domesticate feminism in the name of "women's inclusion" or the latest professional fashion. This means we will have to continually insist on feminism's radical oppositional stance in critical solidarity with other political discourses and against the myriad daily efforts to suppress movement toward critical democracy.

Unlike many postmodern discourses, feminism grounds its critique of western knowledge in an emancipatory agenda.[2] To what extent this agenda is neutralized, sabotaged, or strengthened in the current crisis of knowledge is one of the pressing questions for feminists now working in academic institutions increasingly redefined by the postmodern condition. For almost two decades now feminists have grappled with the political implications of the intersection between feminist and postmodern critiques of difference.[3] Feminist deconstructions of the binary oppositions which shape the dominant representations of difference (man-woman, culture-nature, reason-body) certainly intersect with postmodern critiques of western metaphysics and are indicative of the extent to which both have been produced out of longstanding contradictions within modernity. In his now often cited essay "The Discourse of Others: Feminists and Postmodernism," Craig Owens puts feminism at the forefront of the postmodern debate for precisely this reason, posing it as the vanguard of a new and more politically sharpened postmodernism.

More recently, critiques issuing from neo-marxist, post-colonial, and materialist feminist positions have undertaken a more aggressive remapping of the postmodern which—to use Teresa Ebert's terms—distinguishes between ludic and resistance postmodernisms.[4] Whereas ludic postmodernism signals an emphasis on the mechanics of signification, with language understood as a formal system of differences, resistance postmodernism is concerned with the politics of the production and maintenance of subjectivities, that is, with language as a social practice. As Ebert indicates, feminist discourses align with postmodernism on both sides of the divide. Those like Ebert, Henry Giroux, Linda Nicholson and Nancy Fraser have emphasized the ways in which feminism can criticize and extend postmodernism—by asserting the primacy of social criticism and by rewriting postmodernism's attention to signification in order to attend to the ways social difference is historically and hierarchically constructed. Resistance postmodernism insists that social totalities like patriarchy and racism *do* continue to structure our lives and for this reason critical analyses cannot afford to turn away from them. Feminist critiques of the limits of ludic postmodernism increasingly raise the possibility that an emancipatory movement requires normative grounds and closure. Claiming normative grounds means that critique of the binary oppositions which structure meaning is not aimed at dispelling difference, for difference will always shape culture, but at redefining the systems of value, the divisions of labor, and the allocations of resources the social construction of difference helps determine. This feminist position endorses a claim that feminists have long made—that the texts of culture (including those that seemingly renounce the norms imposed by narrative closure) are invariably invested with value. And in doing so, feminist proponents of a resistance postmodernism also insist that holding on to normative grounds does not mean embracing master narratives or totalizing theories. But it does mean *rewriting* them.[5]

Building upon a critical articulation of postmodernism and marxism by British socialist feminists, materialist feminism in the U.S. is just beginning to address these issues and to formulate a strongly materialist and feminist resistance postmodernism. In doing so materialist feminism intervenes in the crisis of knowledge now by offering a way to make use of postmodern notions of the subject in conjunction with a theory of the social which is congruent with feminism's political goals and which reinforces its critical edge across a broad range of discourses and institutions. The pages that follow situate materialist feminism in relation to its encounter with other materialist and postmodern discourses. Several concerns shape my delineation of this discursive field and my own position within it. One of them is how the gradual recentering taking place in the humanities in the wake of this immense cultural upheaval threatens to erode feminism's *potential* as a transformative political discourse. I stress "potential" here as a way to signal that feminism, even in its more emphatic affiliations with postmodernism, is an ensemble of discourses, some of which line up quite neatly with the more reactionary aspects of postmodernism and traditional humanism, while others enhance those features of postmodernity and modernity that undermine hegemonic knowledges and the subjectivities they produce. Central to this concern is *how* a discourse focused on the politics of the production and maintenance of subjectivities understands the materiality of language and the social. As a newly emergent critical cultural studies begins to define a space from which the disciplining of knowledge can be critiqued, how the social is imagined and how the "logic" of its configuration intervenes in reality, become crucial components of that critical margin. Feminist theory radically informs this nascent critical cultural studies in the U.S., effecting what counts as "theory," its relation to critique and culture, and its effectivity as an intervention in the formation of subjectivities. In negotiating the insistence on pluralism from the university and the culture at large, as well as the pressures toward textual play or mere local analysis from ludic postmodernism, feminism as a critical discourse needs to attend vigilantly to the knowledges it appropriates and its own rearticulations: the terms of value and difference in these narratives and the social logics they propose.

This work extends the crisis of authority to the critic's own situation, making the requirement to own one's positionality much more than a matter of claiming an identity—white western woman, lesbian, academic—or aligning with a particular marginalized group. Because the relationship between social analytics and social identities is not a simple one, however, the argument I initiate here doesn't directly confront the problem of identity until chapter three. By addressing the issue of positionality by way of the question of how the social is imagined in a theory, I hope to situate my own position—the materialist feminism I speak from and for—within a larger project which circumscribes the responsibility of the oppositional intellectual in the west. This is the critical effort Stuart Hall has called "the alienation of advantage." In his words:

> the vocation of intellectuals is to alienate that advantage that they have had out of the system, to take the whole system of knowledge itself and, in Benjamin's sense, attempt to put it at the service of some other project ("Emergence of Cultural Studies," 18).

Taking a system of knowledge and putting it at the service of some other project entails confronting the materiality of that system—in its economic, political, and discursive dimensions—and learning how to make sense of the world for other ends. At the very least this new mode of sense-making requires sorting out the knowledges we rely on—postmodern, marxist, feminist—to discern how they are unevenly, at times perniciously, supportive of unfair advantages, including our own as intellectuals.

Materialist feminism is distinguished from socialist feminism in part because it embraces postmodern conceptions of language and subjectivity. Materialist feminists have seen in postmodernism a powerful critical force for exposing the relationship between language, the subject, and the unequal distribution of social resources. From several vantage points postmodern theories have critiqued the liberal humanist individual, disclosing its status as the self-evident origin of meaning to be a function of an epistemology of the sign which relies upon a relation of equivalence between the signifier and the signified. As Derrida demonstrates, rather than acquiring its meaning from reference to a preordained signified, the meaning of any sign is a constant slipping, a non-identity between sign and signified.[6] Within this logic, the authority of signification rests not on its reference to a pre-existent reality but on its differential properties. The subject, accordingly, can be seen as a construct of language, not an essential entity, no longer/not ever anchored in its fullness by reference to an Absolute Signifier (God, Reason, Science, Man), but in its status as textual difference dispersed across a range of signifying relations. The deconstructionist notion that there is no meaning outside the text has been challenged and re-written by postmodern materialists who make use of deconstruction's critique of logocentrism to de-naturalize language as a referential system. From a materialist vantage point, deconstruction helps make visible that the "real" is not given or unalterable. Like a text, it is socially constructed and "differential" and therefore open to radical change (Morton and Zavarzadeh, "Nostalgia," 52). While postmodern critiques of signification in themselves do not guarantee an oppositional politics, they do open up the subject to language and difference. In this way they make available ways of thinking that feminists grappling with the problem of feminism's own monolithic subject have found useful.

How language is conceptualized in its relation to the social is probably the most heavily contested, troublesome, and fruitful area of postmodernism for feminists now. At the same time that the postmodern reconception of subjectivity provides an immensely powerful critique of the political interests sheltered within western metaphysics, emphasis on the slippage of signifiers in many postmodern theories of subjectivity often merely celebrates a fragmented, dispersed and textualized subject. Postmodern discourses that stress the play of signification and difference or rejoice in the diffuse contingency of social arrangements promote social analytics that discourage or forestall explanation of these conditions. By refiguring the self as a permeable and fragmented subjectivity but then stopping there, some postmodern discourses contribute to the formation of a subject more adequate to a globally-dispersed and state-controlled multinational consumer culture which relies upon increasingly atomized social relations.[7] In the "age of information," cybernetics, instantaneous global finance, export processing zones, artificial intelligence, and hyper-realities, an atomized socius affords an increasingly fluid and permeable capital its products, its work force, and its new markets. To the extent that some postmodern knowledges situate their permeable and fluid subjectivities, their "new" identities within *noncausal, dehistoricized* frames of intelligibility, these theories can be readily recuperated for capital's rapidly re-forming and diffused horizons. As a result, for all that they demystify certain structures in an "old order," some postmodern challenges to the humanist self have also made it possible for the interests this "old order" shelters to reassert their claims in new "po-mo" guise. I will elaborate more fully later on the particulars of this recuperation in several postmodern theories of discourse. For now, however, I only want to indicate in a general way that it is precisely this potential for postmodernism to serve as the vehicle for merely updating the symbolic order, legitimizing the continued unequal distributions of power and privilege in the formation of "new" subjects, that feminists interested in the oppositional potential of the postmodern critique of liberal humanism need to be on guard against.

In framing the problem of the crisis of the subject in these terms I am drawing upon another distinguishing feature of materialist feminism—its interest in marxism as a problematic which explains social relations causally. In marxism's social logic, crises are understood as systemically produced and unevenly linked to a broad network of relations and to other crises. Of course, it is precisely because of its causal theoretical framework that marxism's historical materialism has had a contestatory relationship to many postmodern discourses. One of the consequences of that contest has been the articulation of neo- and post-marxisms: reformulations of the social logic of historical materialism that draw upon post-modern critiques of science and the subject as well as the political discourses of a range of emancipatory movements, feminism among them. Developments in theories of ideology over the past twenty years, both with and against postmodern ways of thinking about language and subjectivity, have argued vigorously that a reductionist and determinist marxism in which social arrangements are driven by the economy and social change is brought about by the proletariat is no longer feasible. This work has drawn upon postmodern theories in order to formulate the ways in which the relationship between language and subjectivity is crucial to an understanding of social change. Materialist feminist theory has both emerged out of and helped shape this engagement between postmodernism and marxism.

In this context, the often uncritical appropriation of postmodern theory by materialist feminist scholars deserves attention and raises a host of questions:

what is at stake in the differences among postmodern critiques of marxism—post and neo—in relation to feminism? What exactly constitutes the materialism of materialist feminism and how is this problematic important to feminism's political aims? How is materialist feminism related to the materialism of various marxisms and postmodernisms? Before exploring these questions, I want to stress at the outset that raising the call for a feminist critique of post-marxist theories does not dismiss their usefulness to materialist feminism. On the contrary, through critique, concepts developed in the work of materialists like Foucault and Laclau and Mouffe, whose engagements with marxism lead them ultimately to reject it, can be disarticulated from their post-marxist problematics and rearticulated within a more thoroughly oppositional and politically effective framework. One of the aims of the following chapters is to argue that this practice of disarticulation-re-articulation which critique enacts offers a feminism committed to broad-reaching emancipatory change and interested in the usefulness of certain postmodern discourses for that project a powerful strategy for *rewriting* the theoretical texts we encounter.

In the face of postmodern and post-marxist arguments against theory as a "master narrative," it is increasingly important for feminists to come to terms with the difference between theory as a mode of intelligibility and theory as a totalizing or master narrative. Theory is generally understood to be inquiry into the grounds, assumptions, and conditions of knowledge or social arrangements. Postmodern critiques of theory (those of Derrida, Lyotard, Baudrillard, Fish, and others) join forces with various empiricist conceptions of theory in equating theoretical inquiry with metanarrative—that is, a narrative which stands outside the object of analysis. Metanarrative escapes the critical gaze to the extent that it constitutes an (invisible) outside frame which establishes the terms of coherence for an empirical account. As I will discuss in more detail later, understanding theory as ideology dispels the distinction between metanarrative and narrative. From the standpoint of ideology, no theory is outside the discourses of culture. As ideology, theory is one of many cultural narratives. It inquires more directly than others into the conditions of possibility of knowledge, but it does not for that reason claim the status of metaphysical truth or provide any fixed "outside" frame for knowledge. While there are differences among the ways various theories understand these "conditions of possibility," all theories are ways of making sense and as such have a materiality in that they help shape the formation of social subjects as well as what comes to count as the "real" or the "truth." Understanding theory as ideology also means that theoretical discourse or an analytic framework is not a cognitive process or a set of logical axioms. Taking their place among the texts of culture, "theoretical narratives" circulate within the highly mediated field of discursive struggles over social meanings and resources. Moreover, theories themselves can be considered to be the effects of struggles over what meanings are allowable and endorsed as truth at any given time. That is, theories have and can acknowledge their own historicity. Investigations into the conditions of possibility which make certain meanings allowable and which also acknowledge their own historicity are not fixed metanarratives or totalizing theories but theoretical practices.

As the academy weathers the major challenges to the disciplinary structure of the humanities and social sciences inaugurated by the discourses of poststructuralism and postmodernism, it is urgent that feminists continue to claim theory as a crucial component of our political practice. Interrogating the politics of knowledge productions, theory monitors this crisis and continually makes space for—even foments—the storms that belie any imposition of a fixed and oppressive coherence. As a critical practice, theory issues from the cracks and seams in the coherence of culture's regimes of truth, forcing the system of knowledge out of its "proper" disciplinary boundaries, and inquiring into the conditions of possibility that define them. In these ways theory intervenes in what comes to count as the real. By insisting that in any historical moment modes of intelligibility are closely tied to economic and political practices, materialist feminists can develop these powerful oppositional and transformative features of theoretical discourse in the service of feminism's commitment to the end of exploitation and oppression.

II

The crisis of knowledge in the academy now can be understood broadly as the overdetermined effect of shifts in economic, political, and ideological arrangements in the west over the past fifty years. Among them are the development of a service-based economy, especially in the U.S., and the accompanying displacement of industrial production to the "third world," the increased emphasis on consumption as crucial for capitalist growth, and the revaluation of the "third world" and rapidly shifting socialist bloc as potential markets. With the realignment of markets after World War II, the United States overtook Britain's claims to "imperial preference" through free trade policies, an expanding corporate internationalism, control over aid societies devoted to "third-world development," and a system of monetary transactions built around the U.S. dollar—all of which contributed to the development of a multinational economy.[8] As capital entered its late phase, neo-imperialist economic arrangements controlled by western finance and protectionist trade arrangements were modified.[9] These economic rearrangements have been in turn affected by the growth of the increasingly pervasive administering and regulating apparatus of the corporate state.

The extension of corporate/state interests to new areas of social life affects the academy at many levels.[10] For state universities and community colleges state control is most overt, their priorities and "missions" often directly dictated by state policies and budgets. But "private" universities are less overtly but often even more financially tied to the state in the form of government contracts and grants for scientific and technological development. Such funding directly fosters a mutual alliance between capital's expanding markets and academic institutions which serve as centers of research and development. In this way universities across the U.S. are a vital "raw materials resource" for the development of multinational capitalist production, a vast reserve of scientific information often tailored to the needs of the military-industrial complex. The university is also one of the primary institutions where subjects are produced, and in the late twentieth century this means subjects equipped for a growing service-based economy and consumer culture. Most western universities now are schools of professional training. The subjects they produce are for the most part skilled technocrats who will go on to become the new middle strata of managers and professionals.

Through its commitment to the liberal arts core, the university has traditionally enacted a key component of the formation of subjects by acculturating a broad range of students to an ideal of the "cultivated citizen" (Robinson, 361). In the process it also produces good consumers desirous of the commodities offered in the marketplace.[11] A major requirement of the cultivated citizen is that she not "see" the historical conditions that make possible her position in the world. One of them, for example, is the relation between the service/consumer economy she supports and the "feminized" industries which supply the products for her work, now increasingly displaced to a "developing third world."[12]

Under industrial capitalism the entrepreneurial subject—humanist individual and agent of choice—was a necessary support for a social organization that required the worker "freely" exchange his or her labor on the open market. However, this subject has become less adequate under late capitalism where the state's intensified regulation of commodity exchange and labor and pervasive intervention into the once "private" sphere blurs the boundaries of individual "freedom." A decentered, fragmented, porous subject is better equipped for the heightened alienation of late capitalism's refined divisions of labor, more readily disciplined by a pandemic corporate state, and more available to a broad nexus of ideological controls.[13] These ideological controls are enmeshed in the explosion of information which is one of late capitalism's distinguishing features. The development of computer technology and telematics is a dramatic instance of the ways in which economic, political, and ideological arrangements are overdetermined. Economically the growth of computer technology has intensified capital's reach, proliferating opportunities for investment, speeding up shifts in production, and refining divisions of labor. The accompanying fragmentation and dislocation of communities and the increasingly anonymous corporate structure have made the operations of exploitation in the age of information ever more insidious even as inequalities between women and men, minorities and dominant racial and ethnic groups, have intensified. As the terms of economic power veer more and more toward control over information, knowledge is being stripped of its traditional value as a product of the mind, making it a commodity in its own right whose exchange and circulation helps multiply new divisions of labor and fractured identities. Politically, the "ruling class" is being reconfigured as a composite conglomerate of corporate leaders, high level administrators, and heads of professional organizations. An accompanying reinscription of the bourgeois "self" as a more complex and mobile subjectivity, inextricably bound up in myriad circuits of communication, is unfolding in multiple cultural registers. One of them is the academy.

The crisis of knowledge in western universities now is symptomatic of the bourgeois subject's inadequacy to this extensive transformation in relations of production. Nowhere is the effort to retool more pronounced than within the humanities, premier legitimator of the bourgeois self. This updating process is occurring not just through the dissemination of postmodern theories, but also through pressures on the humanist self issuing from an array of political discourses. The most visible recuperation of this pressure is taking place in multicultural and diversity programs. The debate over multiculturalism and human diversity courses on U.S. campuses now indicates the ways in which the crisis of authority in universities (which in English departments at least was long associated exclusively with the displacement of literary study by postmodern theory) actually entails a much more far-reaching struggle over subjectivities. The movement for multicultural education emerges out of the same historical moment that produced postmodern theory. Both are the effect of a crisis of the subject; both are efforts to rearticulate the self as a subject-in-difference. While postmodern theory has been associated with an effete intellectual "avant-garde," multicultural studies has been seized upon as a much more palatable, even if potentially contentious, required knowledge for new times. While I support the ways in which multicultural studies rewrites the universalized Eurocentric subject of humanist knowledge, I would also argue that the new knowledge it offers also needs critical attention from its supporters, attention that is vigilant to the many subtle ways in which university reforms can rewrite and suppress the oppositional force of counterhegemonic knowledges.

Courses on multiculturalism and human diversity definitely have a subversive edge, as the right has recognized. They extend what counts as "culture" beyond the narrow boundaries of the traditional canon of great works; they underscore that knowledge is never objective but always entangled in humanly constructed values; and they are interdisciplinary, intermingling knowledges from discrete fields—English and Art History, Sociology and History. The very *inter*-disciplinarity of their approach, however, often forestalls questions about the disciplining of knowledge and the "difference" that makes. To the extent that diversity courses attend to cultural differences without questioning how difference organizes knowledge and how this organization is in turn imbricated in larger social structures, they can serve as one of the academy's most skillful crisis *management* strategies. By exposing students to "different" cultures, these courses can quell the pressure put on what counts as culture by the influx of "minorities" into college campuses and the U.S. population generally.

Of course, like any institutional practice, courses in multiculturalism or diversity can be taught in oppositional ways, offering students access to critical knowledges that question the social and historical conditions of multiculturalism. Often, however, they are not. Too frequently learning about human diversity means celebrating or appreciating "difference" rather than acquiring the critical frameworks to understand how and why social differences are reproduced. In its liberal manifestations, multicultural studies helps to re-form the cultured liberal self into a more porous subject who is open to difference. This "openness" too often means that the student can see and even honor cultural difference, but does not have to examine, change, or be responsible to the economic and political power structures difference is entangled within. Not the least of the benefits of the newly acculturated subjects these courses produce is the formation of a professional service corps capable of successfully conducting business in a multi-national sphere.[14]

The hazardous task for feminists, particularly in the humanities, where the proliferation of these new knowledges proceeds most rapidly, is to offer a critical rewriting of inquiries into difference and their effect on the reconfiguration of the subject now. Materialist feminists have argued that claiming the powerful critique of difference developed in the discourses of resistance postmodernism can advance the development of *critical* cultural studies. Focusing attention on the prior questions that establish what counts as the study of culture, *critical* cultural studies directs attention to precisely those features of cultural study that are frequently occluded in the diversity movement.[15] The critical self-consciousness that characterizes critical cultural studies is most evident in its emphasis on the relationship between knowledge and power, particularly the ways the disciplining of knowledge is implicated in the formation of social subjects. The crisis of authority in literary study has been in part an effort to manage the explosion of questions about precisely these issues. While some of the postmodern discourses that have rocked the foundations of the liberal humanist tradition have been used to merely update literary study into textual study, others have addressed the power/knowledge relations of that tradition, often parallelling and coinciding with feminist and anti-racist challenges to western epistemology. Together these critical discourses set in motion a whole array of questions about the once obvious and sacred components of the "culture" literary study took as its object: what constitutes literature as opposed to other texts of culture? In teaching students how to read and write are we indeed disciplining them and to what ends? How does our work in teaching the texts of culture itself participate in much larger social arrangements? In confronting these and other questions, critical discourses within the discipline of English have irrevocably made difficult any simple pursuit of literary study, displacing this once-obvious emblem of culture with inquiry into the processes whereby reading and writing in their broadest sense continually remake social relations.

In breaking from the disciplinary boundaries of English in order to confront some of its taken-for-granted assumptions, critical cultural studies becomes *trans-*

disciplinary. Unlike interdisciplinary studies, it does not merely draw from an array of disciplines but rather inquires into the histories of the organization of knowledges and their function in the formation of subjectivities. In other words, critical cultural studies aims to make visible and put into crisis the structural links between the disciplining of knowledge and larger social arrangements. This critical component of cultural studies draws upon an array of discourses that conceptualize the texts of culture as historically constructed, traversed by power relations, and constitutive of social value. Chief among them is feminism. Partly because of its history as a critical practice within the academy and within literary study in particular, but also because of its ties to political movements outside the academy, feminism has already had a tremendous impact this *critical* component of cultural studies.

One of the ways this impact has been registered is in analysis of gender. Gender has increasingly become a respectable object of scholarly inquiry in both the humanities and the social sciences, and it features prominently in courses on diversity. The outpouring of conferences and publications and the number of sessions devoted to considerations of gender at major conferences across the disciplines in the past five years, as well as the inclusion of courses on gender in reformed curricula, attest to its legitimation as an object of inquiry. Feminists need to question the ideological work being done through this new category of study, especially when feminist studies programs within the same institutions that proudly tout courses on "gender" often have to scramble for funding and basic resources like office space, staffing, and equipment. The disciplining of feminism as "gender studies" contributes to the substitution throughout the academy of a more innocuous and ostensibly "inclusive" signifier, "gender," for the more explicitly political one, "feminism." This strategy is only one instance of the many ways in which feminism's critical standpoint gets repressed even as the academy claims that it is accommodating feminist interests.

Certainly the emergence of gender as a category of analysis has had enormously useful effects on denaturalizing identity and is not to be discounted. But establishing gender as an area of inquiry in its own right has an effect similar to that of other regional divisions of knowledge into area specialties, including "Women's Studies." Substituting the social category "gender" or the identity "woman" for the set of discourses constituted by feminism mutes the interestedness and potential collective power posed by feminism as a critique of the systemic inequities wrought by capitalist patriarchy. The recuperation of feminism in the academy is not an even process, however, and is undoubtedly not done simply by changing the name of one program. As Evelyn Torton-Beck has observed, the containment of feminist work within traditional disciplines has made the "feminist scholar" more respectable, in part because he or she remains within departmental boundaries and control. At the same time, autonomous Women's Studies programs and departments continue to strike fear into institutional administrators, and the pressures of professional credentializing often compel censorship of the word "feminist" in any public forum even by those working most avidly in Women's Studies (Torton-Beck, 22).

Nonetheless, the incipient feminism of both gender studies and Women's Studies is often tamed by their autonomy and ghetto-ization. Disciplinary or "program" segregation reinforces an exclusively regional emphasis in much feminist praxis. According to this logic, women's history or culture is made discrete from studies organized around other identities that also threaten the hold of prevailing knowledges—for example, Africana and Caribbean studies, Gay and Lesbian studies, Hispanic or Native American studies. In replicating the ideological segmentations in the larger culture, this division of knowledge makes invisible the social arrangements that link the histories and struggles of various groups and so dampens the potential for the production of a collective oppositional subject. A feminism which, as Monique Plaza has put it, is committed to "questioning its own contradictions . . . revealing the cunning, pernicious ways of oppression even inside our own struggle" (4) cannot *complacently* locate itself under the categories of "gender" or "Women's" Studies without some cost to the effectivity of its emancipatory political agenda. This is especially the case for a feminism that acknowledges the ways that its agenda has been pressured by other social movements.

Perhaps the key word in this wild assertion of mine is *"complacently."* Given the current conservative climate, and the uneven—often meager—interventions of feminist and anti-racist knowledges into the academy and the dominant culture, it is certainly still too early and too dangerous in the short-haul to call for the elimination of programs organized around single coordinates—gender, race, sexuality. (The unquestioned absence of "class" from this catalogue, especially in the U.S. academy, is of course significant.) But in shifting the focus and also the signifier of Women's Studies to Feminist Studies we can perhaps begin to mark out the goal of superseding single coordinate programs organized around identities—women, African-Americans, gays and lesbians—with programs in cultural studies organized around critical discourses or standpoints.

Certainly, feminism's asymmetrical relationship to the dominant culture poses problems for western academic feminists like myself who want to pursue the "alienation of advantage" Stuart Hall refers to. It seems to me that the least—and at times perhaps also the most—we can do is to make this unevenness more visible in all of its historicity. And this means rewriting feminism for and in the postmodern moment, confronting its contradictory positionality under late capitalism and in relation to an array of oppositional critical knowledges. Because materialist feminism locates its theoretical object and its frame of inquiry in history and understands its project as revolutionary praxis always subject to revision from the disruptive force of its own historicity,[16] it seems to my mind a most empowering feminist discourse. As I will elaborate in the following chapters, however, if materialist feminism is to maintain its radical force, it needs an analytic that can rigorously account for some of its key concepts: the social, the material, discourse, woman, history.

III

The uses and consequences of knowledges rest in part on the theories of the social they assume and the subjectivities they enable. Both inside and outside the academy knowledge is produced out of contesting modes of *reading* "society." Understanding "the social" as a category implicit in diverse and competing knowledges implies that it is a shifting construction, one that is historically produced and reproduced in the texts of culture. To say that the social is a shifting construction, however, is not to argue that it is simply a dispersed plurality of practices that can only be understood in terms of particular techniques and policies—as post-marxists and neo-pragmatists contend. Nor need it mean that any theory of the social is a metadiscourse. But it does mean that "the social" as a category of knowledge historically contributes to the production of material life. This assertion assumes a particular problematic—historical materialism—in which "the social" as a way of structuring how we make sense of the world is understood as ideology.

Ideology is the array of sense-making practices which constitute what counts as "the way things are" in any historical moment. Ideology helps produce and is in turn produced by the economic and political arrangements in a given social formation. As a discursive category, the social becomes meaning-full within the frames of intelligibility, the ideological practices, through which meaning is constructed. The "logic" of the social—or the structures by which social relations are made intelligible—informs every cultural narrative. What counts as the "social" affects whether and how we make connections among activities of various sorts—work and culture, laws and trade. What constitutes the "social" in a culture's stories affects (and is in turn affected by) its distribution of resources and power, categories of value, terms of inclusion and exclusion. In that they construct what is considered to be the real and the subjectivities that perpetuate the prevailing relations of production, the social logics implicit in the narratives of culture have a tremendous political force.

Understanding the practice of meaning-making as ideology implies that this activity is the effect of struggles over resources and power that are played out through the discourses of culture and the modes of reading they allow. The texts in which these discourses circulate are not just written documents, of course. They are all of those social productions that intervene in the process of sense-making by being *made* intelligible. Reading, then, is the ideological practice of making a text intelligible. And as such it is much more than simple deciphering. It is the necessary and inescapable process of *making sense* by negotiating the discursive materiality of one's lived reality. Once reading is understood in this way, the difference between reading and writing collapses. Both are activities of *making* sense—of and through the systems of difference available at any historical moment.

In the academy now the dominant mode of reading is eclecticism. Eclecticism uncritically links explanatory frames without making visible the contesting assumptions on which they are often premised. Underlying this easy mingling of contesting problematics is a pluralist social logic in which the production of knowledge is seen as consensual.[17] Such a social logic underlies many "new," "postmodernized" narratives which use terms like "discourse," "subject," and "positionality" but without engaging the assumptions upon which these concepts are founded. By appropriating contesting discourses uncritically, an eclectic mode of reading collaborates with more obviously conservative neo-formalist reading practices in that it treats knowledges as self-evident rather than situating them within a set of historical coordinates. The sort of uncritical appropriation which characterizes eclecticism also suppresses differences among the problematics upon which various (postmodern) knowledges draw. That is, eclecticism can occlude the materiality of language (the ways the production of the social real in language shapes and is in turn shaped by divisions of labor and formations of state) as well as its historicity (the ways meaning is the effect of social struggle).[18] Stopping short of addressing the materiality of discourse, eclecticism shares much in common with additive revisionist criticisms which correct the faults of a universalizing humanism merely by including "minorities," and both often underlie the pluralist approach to cultural diversity.

In contrast to eclecticism, ideology critique is a mode of reading that recognizes the contesting interests at stake in discursive constructions of the social. It does so from a committed position within a social analytic whose legitimacy is argued for not on the grounds of its scientific Truth but on the basis of its explanatory power and its commitment to emancipatory social change. Having foregrounded the contesting interests informing the problematics in which discourses are framed, ideology critique appropriates them through a process of disarticulation-rearticulation. As I will elaborate in chapter 3, it is through this process that ideology critique makes visible the historicity of the discrepancies in the textual production of concepts and rewrites these concepts within a social logic whose horizons are also extended as a result of the critique.

The social logic of ideology critique depends upon what I call a *global analytic*. I use the metaphor of "globality" here in order to refer to two distinct yet interdetermined registers of social relations: the worldwide (global) reach of capital's markets, and a (global) mode of reading systemically. As I will elaborate in detailing the global features of a post-Althusserian social analytic, the relation between these two domains of the social—and by extension, between these two concepts of globality—is more than merely metaphoric. The structure of multinational capitalism with its dense grid of information and highly refined international divisions of labor cannot in itself account for the complex ideological

processes through which various insertions into its global economy are represented and reproduced. Current analyses of the global culture of postmodernism
have made the instability of these processes quite visible.[19] Without denying this
instability, a global analytic insists on the political usefulness of delineating
relations among the various domains of even this highly complex social organization—among ideological processes, economic, and political arrangements that
together constitute the social "totalities" that profoundly affect our lives.

A global analytic posits the social not as a fixed or unified structure, but as an
ensemble of relations in which connections between cultural, economic, and
political practices are overdetermined. Global analysis understands the social in
terms of systems and structures of relations. In other words, globalization is a
feature of relational thinking. In this respect it is distinct from "totalization." As
a unifying strategy, totalization generalizes a logic of the whole from that of a
particular region in order to produce a unified or total structure; it is, in this sense
a mode of regionalism written large. Regional modes of reading have a similar
effect in that they close off ways of explaining relations between spheres of social
production. As critiques from many quarters have emphasized, a totalizing social
logic cannot account for its own discourse, an issue of particular concern for
feminists now who are grappling with the twin problems of how feminism can
claim its authority and who feminism speaks for. While it attends to social
totalities, a global analytic is a systemic, not a totalizing, critical framework.

IV

The recent attention to discourse in cultural studies, often drawing upon some
version of the work of Michel Foucault, has been in part an effort to address the
ways the subject is constructed in language without being trapped within analytics
which close both language and the subject off from history. However, much
feminist appropriation of Foucault for literary and cultural studies has been
eclectic—either adding Foucauldian concepts of discourse or power onto a feminist analysis or appropriating them along with concepts from other (contesting)
problematics without questioning the political/ideological effects of their accompanying frameworks or the effect of their eclectic conjunction on feminism's
political aims.[20]

A critical reading of Foucault's social analytic in conjunction with the collaborative work of Ernesto Laclau and Chantal Mouffe foregrounds features these
two post-marxist theories of discourse share and makes visible the ways their
social analytics affect certain of their concepts which materialist feminists have
appropriated. Both make important contributions to elaborating a materialist
understanding of the subject and of language from a standpoint which goes
beyond traditional marxism. In so doing both overcome some of marxism's
impasses. Both dismantle the monolithic marxist conception of social agency
as "class" subject and offer ways to understand the discursive production of

subjectivity. In this respect, they also open up socialist feminism's knotty attempts to relate patriarchy and capitalism. The articulation of a postmodern understanding of the subject with the emancipatory aims of radical democracy has made Laclau and Mouffe's work seem, like Foucault's, (whose notion of power/ knowledge they draw upon) a compelling instance of resistance postmodernism.[21] And yet, as I will argue, the concept of the social informing both of their projects ultimately is at odds with a feminism committed to the end of exploitation.

Part of the appeal of Foucault's social analytic, especially for feminists in the U.S., is its resistance to "theory" understood as a totalizing system and more often than not signified as marxism. Foucault's explicit comments on marxism present an ambiguous position, however. At times he reads marxism as a cognitive system grounded on claims to rational truth and continuous with the epistemological configuration associated with the emergence of the human sciences in the eighteenth and nineteenth centuries (*Order of Things,* 261–62). Consequently, he asserts, marxist theory cannot be subversive of the unifying structures of "bourgeois" thought. However, at other times he argues that it is impossible to write history without using a whole range of concepts directly or indirectly linked to Marx's thought.[22] At issue in determining Foucault's stance on marxism is not his explicit statements, however, but an epistemological and political problem: what are the ideological consequences of Foucault's construction of and departure from the marxist problematic, particularly in gauging the effectivity of their comparative social analytics for feminism?

It is important to stress that Foucault's critique of marxism is a reading, and like all readings it is interested. That Foucault often reads marxism as a fixed and totalizing theory rather than a discourse whose horizons are open to historical change is both one of the enabling conditions of his critique and one of its blind spots.[23] Because he understands the logic of contradiction as fixed in a totalized theory of the social—where power relations are determined from the top (the ruling class) down according to the laws of capital—Foucault closes off recognition of the ways marxism has historically been rewritten, including the contributions of his contemporaries, most notably Louis Althusser and members of the Frankfurt School.

The ideological boundaries of Foucault's "departure" from marxism are made more visible once we recognize, as Foucault himself acknowledges, that it is a departure that in many ways never quite leaves. The specter of marxism haunts Foucault's texts, marking its presence, ghostly fashion, by its absence. As Stanley Aronowitz has indicated, it is not as a series of abstract propositions that the new history Foucault proposes has significance, but as a dialogue with Marx and Hegel (*Crisis,* 313). And it is in part because of this submerged dialogue within his work that Foucault's contributions to a materialist theory of discourse can be so usefully disarticulated from his regional social logic and rewritten within a global one.

Like many postmodern theories produced in France in the seventies, Foucault's dialogue with Hegel and Marx culminates in an analytic that rejects the dialectic and reason. Vincent Descombes has commented that Foucault's rejection of the dialectic, particularly in his archaeology, shows how the production of reason involves the expulsion from the common space of all that refuse submission to a unified identity, all that is negatively denoted as difference, incoherence, unreason. While "an expanded reason toughened by dialectical logic . . . would have made short work of accommodating this negative," Foucault maintains that "reason, originating in a division between itself and its other, cannot return to this origin" (115). However, Foucault's Nietzschean critique of reason cannot escape logic per se. The discourses of postmodernism may prevent the adoption of a unifying theory from which insights about society and culture can be deduced. But historical or philosophical analysis cannot proceed without any rational framework at all. The fragments of history do not speak for themselves. The narrative frame of the historian, however discontinuous, is always bound up with ordering (Aronowitz, *Crisis,* 304–5). Foucault's critique of reason does not dismiss rationality and intelligibility altogether; it only substitutes the rationality of differences and incommensurability for the rationality of identity (ibid., 319).

The question is, then, what is the effectivity of this rationality of incommensurability? Foucault claims that the "sterilizing constraints of the dialectic" inhibit analysis of the specific terms necessary to think struggle (*P/K,* 144, 164). His reading of contradiction assumes that as a concept it is inextricably linked to a totalized understanding of the social:

> If one accepts that the form—both general and concrete—of struggle is contradiction, then clearly everything which allows the contradiction to be localized or narrowed down will be seen as a break of a blockage. But the problem is precisely as to whether the logic of contradiction can actually serve as a principle of struggle. (Ibid., 143)

In part because of the political uses to which marxism was being put both in the Soviet Gulag and in post-1968 France, Foucault's reading of contradiction and the dialectic skirts the question of whether the dialectic can be thought in a nontotalized social logic and what is lost—or gained—in abandoning it. The answers to this question are suggested, however, by examining Foucault's alternative.

Foucault's analytic shifts the terms of coherence for the social so that it is not conceptualized as a totality governed by a fixed unifying principle, nor as a system whose principles of organization shift over time, but rather as a network of alliances. In this scheme the social is an unstable set of relations in perpetual disequilibrium, formulated in terms of a diagram or map rather than a system (Deleuze, 36). The implications of Foucault's social logic can best be seen in the conception of power that defines his topology. It is, first of all, a notion of power which offers several very important contributions to the materialist problematic. It makes available a way to examine how power is exercised concretely and in detailed ways no one had ever attempted to ascertain (Gordon, *P/K,* 115–16). It also advances the critique of humanism and intervenes in discussions of language and subjectivity among poststructuralists and marxists by considering power as a positive and discursive force rather than the property of an individual or a group. In addressing the discursive operations of power, Foucault refuses poststructuralist analyses "couched in terms of the symbolic field" in favor of the social domain of signifying structures. As he puts it, the point of reference shifts from "the great model of language (*langue*) and signs to that of war and battle" (*P/K,* 114). For Foucault, power does not originate in a privileged place—that of the sovereign, the ruling class, or the state. And in this regard, his work is both a corrective and a development of other materialist theories. While Foucault does not deny the existence of class, he illustrates it in a totally different way, as "innumerable points of confrontation, focuses of instability, each of which has its own risks of conflict, or struggles" (Ibid., 115–16). This micro-analysis of the circulation of power within institutions opens up Althusser's rather opaque conception of the distribution of power through ideological state apparatuses. A negative representation of power as juridical and repressive is replaced with a notion of power working through positive technologies.

In recasting power in positive terms as subjugation through the discourses of truth rather than in negative terms as repression or sovereignty, Foucault abandons what he calls a deduction of power from its center for an ascending analysis. But in the process several problems arise, problems which can be seen in the tension between the metaphors of "network" and "hierarchy" in his methodology. Foucault asserts that when he says power establishes a "network through which it freely circulates, this is true only up to a certain point." But what is this point? In his discussions of power in *Power/Knowledge* this point seems to be the place where the metaphor of "network" is forced to give way to a metaphor of "hierarchy": "one must rather conduct an *ascending* analysis of power," he says, "starting, that is, from its infinitesimal origins" (ibid., 99). Foucault posits this hierarchical paradigm in order to prevent a reading of the circulation of power as "a sort of democratic or anarchic distribution of power through bodies" (ibid.). But the circulation of power is also contained at some points in his argument by what looks very much like a global analysis. The following is one example:

> I believe that the manner in which the phenomena, the techniques and the procedures of power enter into play at the most basic levels must be analyzed . . . but above all what must be shown is the manner in which they are invested and annexed by more global phenomena and the subtle fashion in which more general powers or economic interests are able to engage with these technologies. (Ibid.)

This is an argument for analysis that can make connections on several levels—from the operations of power in the most specific conjuncture to broader, more general interests. There is also an implicit notion of systemic correspondences between and among these levels, between particular exclusionary practices and "global mechanisms and the entire State system" (ibid., 101). Foucault does contend that the "general design" of the multiplicity of force relations that comprise power "is embodied in the state apparatus, in the formulation of the law, in the various social hegemonies."[24] But despite these acknowledgements of the ways in which power works systemically, the focus of his analysis is nonetheless emphatically on the particular. While his "methodological precautions" present the local instance as a point of entry into analysis of a "complex strategical situation in a particular society" that theoretically extends to the global level, in fact, his readings almost never reach this far (*HS*, 93). Whether the focus is medical practices, the history of sexuality, or the penal system, the ceiling of the ascending hierarchy of social arrangements is invariably institutions within a particular social formation. This limit is bound up with his denunciation of a logic of causality and has enormous implications for the effectivity of his theory of power.

Relations between local strategies and global arrangements in Foucault's analysis are only articulated through vague metaphors of causality: terms like "support," "prop," or "conditioning." He does acknowledge that no local center could function if it did not eventually enter into an overall strategy and that no overall strategy could achieve comprehensive effects without support from precise and tenuous relations serving as its "prop" and "anchor." But this tenuous causality is overwhelmed by the insistent focus on local tactics unconnected to the "strategic envelope" that makes them work. *IMPORTANT*

The shortcomings of this commitment to the contingent and the local can be gauged by the kinds of knowledge it allows. First of all, a contingent social analytic is necessarily a descriptive one. As several feminist critics of Foucault have already indicated, this descriptive analytic requires normative neutrality. Without a normative frame for distinguishing the acceptable from the unacceptable, it is impossible to consider any sort of systemic social arrangements like patriarchy, capitalism, or white supremacy, not to mention explaining the relations among them, except as they are manifest in the most local institutional practices. But to do this is to strip the conceptual frame in which they are couched of its systematicity. Secondly, Foucault's social analytic makes it difficult to explain the workings of power in terms of antagonistic relations between oppressor and oppressed.[25] And it certainly makes difficult—if not impossible—any formulation of a relationship between the materiality of a discourse like sexuality and the materiality of nondiscursive practices—a problem I will return to in the following chapter. While Foucault's political objective seems to be an effort to make available a much more specific logic of power for struggles excluded from a left party politics bound by a rigid class analysis, the regionalism of his analytic—despite its contributions to a conjunctural analysis of the operations of power—ultimately disempowers these diverse struggles. I say "ultimately" because the refusal of causal explanation discourages any way of making the broad-reaching connections between oppression and social struggle which transformative social change depends upon.

In arguing for causal explanation I am considering social logics as ideological practices, not as reflections of empirical truth. From this understanding, differences among social logics are not just cognitive, but political. At stake in the struggle over how to understand social arrangements is the relationship between meaning-making and the distribution of social resources—in other words, the *social effects* of modes of intelligibility. Foucault's denunciation of causality, his emphasis on the local and the descriptive, are dictated by his anti-hierarchical concept of power. Like other postmodern discourses, this logic of incommensurability and disconnection confirms a plural social space. Without a hierarchical understanding of power, the oppositional subject of this analytic can only function in very specific, micro-instances, her oppositionality always undermined and overscored by power's slipperiness. A social logic that aims to confront the widespread and complex workings of patriarchy needs to be able to link seemingly disparate social arrangements; if that logic is to be marshalled for an emancipatory political movement it needs a theory of power which can allow for both collective social agency and radical change.

That Foucault's work has offered feminists very useful concepts is undeniable. But this usefulness is severely curtailed by the roadblocks his local analysis raises for a materialist feminism grappling with the ways "woman" is discursively constructed across various modalities of difference. Foucault's social logic cannot explain the relationship between the social construction of difference and power in any systemic way, nor can it allow for any necessary relation between the multiple registers in which the modalities of difference circulate. It cannot explain, for instance, relationships among the proliferation of discourses on sexuality, shifting family alliances in the west, and the demands of empire. Foucault's emphatic regionalism forestalls any possibility for understanding how the emergence of feminism and the category of the "independent woman" in social formations in the industrialized west is inextricably bound to colonial expansion and the reconstruction of an "other" woman "elsewhere." The effect of uncritically appropriating this social logic is to encourage the obviousness of particular segmentations of both "history" and "woman." Foucauldian feminist readings of the operations of power in a particular social formation—medical practices on women in nineteenth-century Britain or constructions of feminine sexuality in the Renaissance—can suppress inquiry into the global power relations these local arrangements sustain. Merely adding on "gender" while otherwise accepting the Foucauldian social analytic wholesale certainly does not remedy this problem, either. It merely implies that the circulation of power strategies around the construction of a gendered subject can be examined without having to make visible any *necessary* connection between these strategies and others. Not uncoincidentally, uncritical feminist appropriations of the Foucauldían analytic reproduce a feminist subject whose regionalism (as white, western, middle-class, or heterosexual) many feminists—sometimes the very same feminists—are now vehemently questioning. This regionalism is less a function of attention to identities per se than of the social analytic through which identities—like woman—are defined.

V

Laclau and Mouffe's *Hegemony and Socialist Strategy* employs postmodern philosophy, particularly the work of Derrida and Foucault, to launch a critique of historical materialism that refutes marxism as a form of essentialism. The theoretical terrain they occupy is explicitly post-marxist: critiquing marxism's class subject, its vision of the historical course of capitalist development, and utopian notions of communism. Rejecting what they see as marxism's monistic effort to capture history, they nonetheless work within the debates of marxist theory to draw out a concept of hegemony which they claim was obliterated by a monolithic image of "Marxism-Leninism." Hegemony forms the backbone of their proposal for democratic pluralism. As they see it, hegemony represents a logic of contingency and articulation. As such, it dissolves the bulwark of economic determinism by allowing various forms of social protest to overflow the boundaries of class (86). It is a paradigm based on the notion that social movements—like feminist, anticolonial, ecology, and youth advocacy groups—rather than political parties have the potential to transform civil society (Aronowitz, "Socialist Strategy," 2).

In many respects their project shares much in common with Foucault's, and like his it has some affinity with the aims of materialist feminism. Both set out to supersede the class subject of marxism by devising an analysis which does not depend upon a transcendental subject but instead "can account for the constitution of the subject within a historical framework" (*P/K*, 117). The radical democracy Laclau and Mouffe call for seizes upon postmodernism in order to pursue and deepen the democratic project of modernity by abandoning the abstract universalism of the Enlightenment, an essentialist notion of social totality, and the myth of the unitary subject (Mouffe, "Radical Democracy," 44).[26] However, if their suggestions for rethinking agency are to be useful to a materialist feminist theory—and I think they potentially are—the logic of the social that informs them must be examined critically.

Laclau and Mouffe's argument for an alternative to orthodox marxism's notion of the social is premised on the claim that the social is an indeterminate space that has no essence in itself. Rather, everything rests on how its organization is conceived. In orthodox marxism, they contend, there is a fundamental ambiguity in how the organization of the social is understood. The texts of Luxembourg,

Kautsky, and others indicate that the concept of hegemony emerged as a response to this ambiguity and the form it took: a theoretical and political fissure between marxism's economic determinism and various political affirmations of the limits of that logic. In their reading, as economic fragmentation proved increasingly unable to constitute class unity in social struggles throughout the early part of the twentieth century, marxism's logic of a determining infrastructure failed to provide an adequate foundation for political struggle. At the same time, marxism's political analysis was unable to offer social agency any *necessary* character. In the texts of the Second International and after, economic determinism constituted marxism's primary theoretical narrative; here class identities are constituted on the basis of relations of production. But this story was supplemented by another, political, narrative in which the tasks of a bourgeois class no longer able to fulfill its role are taken over by the working class. The concept of hegemony as it emerged out of the discourses of the Leninist tradition embraces the resulting split between the class nature of political action and the historical agent carrying it out (49). In its circulation in the texts of this period, hegemony marks a tension between the *class* agency of economic determinism and the actual political development of a democratized *mass* whose alliances exceeded the parameters of a strictly defined proletariat. This tension suggests a logic of indeterminacy quite at odds with the orthodox marxist logic of necessity. Thus, the concept of hegemony, as they read it, has two faces: an authoritarian one in which the class nature of every political demand is fixed *a priori* and the interests of any class are accessible only to an enlightened vanguard--the party--and a democratized one in which the democratic demands of the masses are the primary motor of history (59).

While Laclau and Mouffe's analysis has the virtue of challenging a reductive identification between social agents and social classes, and locating that challenge within the theoretical terrain of marxism, the aim of that effort is to do away once and for all with the function of economic forces in the shaping of social identities. In the process of formulating the theoretical tensions out of which the concept of hegemony emerges and claiming it as the organizing concept for a new radical democracy, Laclau and Mouffe virtually eliminate economic forces from the social organization. In their absence the political—as it is articulated discursively—becomes the primary arena of social change, defining both the desire of the masses—for democracy and liberty—and the surplus of the organized structures of society.[27] The effect is that "the identity of social agents ceases to be exclusively constituted through their insertion into the relations of production, and becomes a precarious articulation among a number of subject positions" (58). The word "exclusively" here signals both a misreading of Althusserian marxism's understanding of production and hints of some allowance for economic forces in their theory. But, in fact, for Laclau and Mouffe the category "class" is riven not only from any *necessary* link to economic arrangements, but from *any* link to them at all.

Laclau and Mouffe cast the tension between determinism and contingency within marxism as a conflict between two contradictory logics of the social: the logic of mediation and the logic of articulation. In the logic of mediation the social and its components comprise necessary instances of a totality that transcends them. This is the paradigm of economic determinism in which the relation of agents and political tasks is lodged in a prior concept (class or relations of production). In the logic of articulation social organization is contingent. This means that relations between the fragments of the social don't derive from a prior concept like class or production but have to be determined out of their own particularity. This is the logic of hegemony. According to Laclau and Mouffe, the incompatibility between these two logics underscores the essentialist construction of social agency as class in the discourse of marxism from the Second International on. This incompatibility can only be resolved, they claim, by firmly situating social theory within the logic of articulation.

Like Foucault, they present this alternative logic in opposition to a conception of marxism as a totalizing discourse. By constructing their critique of marxism in terms of an opposition between democratic and authoritarian versions of hegemony, Laclau and Mouffe close off the possibility of an alternative (global) analytic within the marxist tradition. As a result, the organization of their critique of marxism side-steps the radical potential of the work of Althusserian and post-Althusserian marxists as well as Althusser's own critique of marxism's totalizing logic of expressive causality and his alternative proposal of a logic of structural causality.

When Laclau and Mouffe do address Althusser's contributions, they do so in the context of their formulation of the concept of articulation and outside their genealogy of the contradictions in marxist discourse. One effect is that their reading of Althusser occludes the ways his conception of the social as mode of production addresses the tension between the contingent and the necessary in marxist theory by maintaining a domain for the contingent within a logic of causality. This tactic also obscures the ways in which post-Althusserian marxist theories have dismantled economic determinism and a reductive notion of class by reformulating agency in terms of the discursive construction of the subject across a range of positions.

Laclau and Mouffe's "blindness" to the radical potential of Althusser's concept of overdetermination occurs in part because they read the incompatibility between Althusser's concepts of "overdetermination" and "determination in the last instance" as a rehearsal of the dichotomy between the logics of articulation and mediation. The problem here is not that they charge Althusser with economism, a critique that has issued from many quarters, but the use they make of it. For they use it as the basis for separating the logic of overdetermination from production, concepts which are mutually imbricated in Althusser. This separation has the effect of equating "production" with economic activity and "overdetermination" with the symbolic. Reducing "production" to the economic sphere reinforces the vestiges of a base-superstructure model in Althusser's theory and makes it seem to be a totalizing perspective. Moreover, this equation reformulates Althusser's argument that the social is overdetermined into the assertion that "the social constitutes itself as a symbolic order" (100, 98). Through this sleight-of-hand, the logic of overdetermination is made categorically distinct from the logic of mode of production. And it is in this reified form that it serves as the founding concept for Laclau and Mouffe's post-marxist alternative (104–5). Here "discursive formation" is substituted for mode of production and "discourse" for ideology.

Constructing the social and the logic of overdetermination in this way produces another version of regionalism.[28] This analytic cannot *explain* the relation between economic forces—like the formation of new markets through colonization, shifting centers of production, or the development of new technologies—and the re-formation of subjectivities. Nor can it explain the relation between political alliances, state formations, and the development of disciplinary techniques. Failing that and instead privileging the political sphere does the work of ideology by obscuring several features of late capitalism. Among them are the shifts in exploitative economic arrangements to spaces outside western centers of production—a dislocation that tends to render them less visible to western eyes—and the effects of this adjustment to the extraction of surplus labor on the very atomization of political relations in the west which Laclau and Mouffe attend to.

Although in the final pages of their book Laclau and Mouffe assert that every project for radical democracy implies a socialist dimension, and that it is necessary to put an end to capitalist relations of production in order to realize this socialism (178), their project never directly addresses how the extension of political equalities will accomplish this or in what ways it will entail social transformations that are not just political and discursive. In this respect, their social logic conforms to their own definition of a reform movement: it is a program for transforming relations *in* production (157).

While both Foucault and Laclau and Mouffe extend our understanding of the discursive construction of subjects in ways I will detail more specifically in the following chapter, their social logics do not and cannot explain the connection between discursive and nondiscursive social practices. For feminists that means that their theories cannot explain the relationships among events like acts of violence against women, the feminization of poverty, and denigrating representations of femininity. They claim that any social movement organized in response to the subordination of women would only form alliances with other social movements—for example, gay and lesbian or anticolonialist movements which also, of course, include women—by means of an articulating discourse of equality and rights. Materialist feminist attention to patriarchy as an organizing social arrangement, however, is aimed precisely at shifting from this limited notion of power as rights and liberties to a much more pervasive concept of the operation of power across economic, political, and ideological arrangements.

The theory of power which accompanies Laclau and Mouffe's notion of the social as an open indeterminate space also poses problems for feminism. For Laclau and Mouffe, power is a function of political arrangements, a matter of relations of subordination, oppression, and antagonism. Subordination, as they see it, is an organization of social relations in which one agent is subject to the decisions of another. Oppression takes place in those relations of subordination which have transformed themselves into sites of antagonism. This transformation of subordination into antagonism is a process whereby the discourse of subordination is rearticulated in terms of a struggle against inequality. Throughout the various complexities of this theory, power is primarily presented as a matter of discursive struggle over equal rights. While the democratic impulse of distributing power equally among the people lies at the heart of emancipatory movements like feminism, socialism, or anticolonialism, any notion of power that ignores the relationship between equal rights and the ways divisions of labor or allocations of resources effect social equality re-enacts the liberal project of political reform. Here "rights" and political equality are extended in one sphere even as the relationship of this enfranchisement to the unequal redistribution of resources in another sphere is ignored.

In this respect, it is not accidental that the political movements Laclau and Mouffe treat in their analysis are for the most part western: ecology and peace movements, feminist, anti-nuke, gay and lesbian activist groups. Feminist reconsiderations of the discourse of equal rights in our own history and the theory of power it depends upon attest to its limits. Materialist feminists especially have pointed out that the discourse of political equality is often unevenly articulated within one social formation, empowering some women at the expense of others, and that the systemic workings of power are invariably not dismantled by campaigns aimed solely at the redistribution of political liberties. In order to further these explorations we need a social logic which is not confined to one region of the social alone but which can explain the often contradictory relationship between the distribution of resources in one sphere and another.

VI

A postmodern marxist social analytic can supersede the shortcomings of post-marxism's insistence on the local and contingent while still including within its framework some of the most radical features of postmodernism's critique of the subject and of epistemology. In this respect it is a useful problematic for materialist feminists to claim. This "usefulness" should not be taken to imply that postmodern marxism is "outside" of feminism, however. On the contrary, developments in marxist theory post-Althusser have been provoked by feminism, at the same time the formulation of materialist feminism in the past twenty years has been deeply indebted to marxism post-Althusser

A postmodern marxist social analytic begins with Althusser's argument for understanding the social by way of the concept "mode of production." I want to emphasize that to argue for theorizing the social in terms of mode of production, however, is not to lapse into idealism. An idealist social theory is a totalizing one; it posits the possible forms in which the social can be realized as deduced from an objective, pre-existent general structure. In contrast, an Althusserian argument for conceptualizing the social in terms of mode of production derives its postmodern edge in part from an alliance with antifoundationalist critiques of idealist epistemology. Postmodern marxism rejects the necessity for grounding its authority in an appeal to any absolute truth—a transcendental guarantee of "rightness"—whether God, Reason, Science, or any master discourse. But instead of denying truth claims altogether, it affirms that claims to truth are historical and inescapably inscribed in theoretical frameworks. At the same time, postmodern marxism argues for a materialist understanding of epistemology based on the effectivity of knowledges as ideology, and it critiques theoretical skepticism for bracketing off the social consequences of truth-claims along with metaphysics.

The revolution in language that marked the postmodern crisis of legitimation suspended the possibility of "objective knowledge" whereby truth is grounded on the direct correspondence of thought and reality, and instead, in some instances, posited reality as irremediably discursive. From this skeptical position postmodern antifoundationalist theories—among them Foucauldian critique, Derridean deconstruction, Deleuze and Gauttari's radical perspectivism, and Rorty's neo-pragmatism—argue for the necessary end of epistemology. This argument is based on the traditional understanding of epistemology as a normative activity which evaluates discourses by their relation to an (unattainable) transhistorical Truth rather than their production out of a particular set of historical conditions (Callinicos, 171).

To the extent that the Foucauldian concept of power/knowledge is bound to a rejection of epistemology, it shares an antifoundationalist stance. Antifoundationalism understands culture as merely finite, reality as a function of interpretation, and the criteria for evaluating interpretations as always grounded in historical points of reference. The claims of theory to explain correspondences are bracketed off and replaced by practices which can be evaluated only in terms of their historically specific usefulness. For Foucault, for example, one discourse has more value than another not because of its epistemological truth but because of the role knowledges play in constituting practices (Poster, 85).

However, a critique of metaphysics need not entail the end of epistemology, the reduction of reality to discourse, or the pragmatic claim that the materiality of knowledges can only be thought in particular, local, descriptive terms. Although postmodern critiques of foundationalism have asserted that guarantees for any direct relation between truth-claims and reality are unattainable, the problem of the relationship between knowledge and what comes to count as "the truth" remains. The work of Foucault, Laclau and Mouffe, Kristeva, Althusser, and others intervenes in reality because it makes truth-claims. If a discourse cannot claim legitimacy by appeal to a transhistorical authority or a privileged discourse, its claim to truth can be established, nonetheless, in relation to other discourses which also make claims about the real. The authority of any theoretical discourse under the constraints of the postmodern condition can be understood, then, not as metaphysical but as political.[29] From this perspective, theories claim their truth on the basis of their explanatory power, that is, their effect on and intervention in the ideological construction of reality.

The criteria for evaluating the explanatory power of any theory can be imma-nent—that is its success in solving or explaining the problems it sets itself. Such a concept of explanation is heuristic rather than deductive. Immanent criteria include the implicit aims in any theory. These criteria for evaluation are, however, never *completely* immanent because discourses circulate in a contestatory relation to each other, each setting its claims—the questions it poses and the answers they allow—against those of others. As Tony Bennett has indicated, what matters for marxism as a party to such struggles is not that it should be able to secure its discursive construction of the real and its framing of other texts and discourses within that real *absolutely*. Rather, it is a matter of securing such constructions and framings *politically* in the sense of making them count above contending ones in terms of their ability to organize the consciousness and practice of historical agents (66).

In keeping with antifoundationalism, then, postmodern marxism argues that every theoretical framework is partisan—founded on an implicit set of social-political aims. It also understands that partisanship as epistemological in the sense I have outlined above, and claims priority for the effectivity of its own theory and aims: the equal distribution of social resources and the end of exploitation and oppression. It is in terms of the contribution made toward these aims that marxism judges the effectivity of any theory. And it is this shared objective that has historically constituted marxism's and feminism's fertile theoretical common ground.

The marxist problematic has two objectives: to produce an interested revolu-tionary knowledge of overdetermined and contradictorily changing global social arrangements, and to change the exploitative and oppressive structure of those arrangements. The second object is partly accomplished by the achievement of the first. In other words, marxist theory's particular truth-claim and its objectives are mutually determining (Resnick and Wolff, 66). Theories cannot be separated from the struggle that constitutes the contradictory overdeterminations of social practices. Like all theories, marxism is produced out of these social contradic-tions, but unlike many, it takes as its object the reproduction and transformation of these same relations. Consequently, marxism's theoretical and political inter-ests are inseparable. It is this inseparability that constitutes praxis.

The materialist premise which underlies Althusser's understanding of the mate-riality of ideology is the causal primacy of human praxis in the (re)production of human life. In reading Marx through Mao Tse Tung's propositions on contradiction, Althusser offers a conception of this causal primacy which critiques the Hegelian notion of contradiction—traces of which are inscribed in other postmodern materialist theories of discourse, including those of Foucault and Kristeva. The theory of causality that underlies Althusser's reading of Marx—and the distinguishing feature of its theoretical (political) force—is the notion of the complex whole in dominance. Implicit in this concept is a critique of origins. Althusser argues that it is impossible to delve down to the birth of a simple universal—for example, "production"—"since 'when we talk of production we always mean production at a determinate stage in social development of the production of individuals living in *society*,' that is, in a structured social whole" (*For Marx*, 195). According to Marx, every simple category—"production," "the individual,"—or we might add—"woman," "discourse," "difference"—not only presupposes the existence of the structured whole of society but is also the product of this complex process.

That this structured whole is not a totality in the Hegelian sense of an original unity is born out in the concept of contradiction that informs its systemic complexity.[30] Althusser argues that marxism—at least the marxism of Marx's later work—refuses the Hegelian presupposition and in its place establishes a quite different theoretical starting point:

> Instead of the ideological myth of a philosophy of origins and its organic concepts, Marxism establishes in principle the recognition of the giveness of the complex structure of any concrete 'object,' a structure which governs both the development of the object and the development of the theoretical practice which produces the knowledge of it. There is no longer any original essence, only an ever-present-givenness, however far knowledge delves into its past. (Ibid., 198–99)

Althusser rethinks the uneven distribution of wealth and assets under capitalism as the basis for the general contradiction between the forces and relations of production in terms of this logic of the complex whole in dominance. In formulating contradiction as essentially overdetermined, Althusser establishes it as neither univocal—a category that has a fixed role and meaning—nor equivocal—subject to pure chance or contingency (ibid., 209). Rather, contradiction is always *overdetermined*. This concept of overdetermination, appropriated from Freud, makes it possible to think of the mutations and variations in a social formation not as the products of a structured unity, nor as accidental, but as the concrete restructurations inscribed in the essence and the play of each category, each contradiction, and each articulation of the complex structure in dominance (ibid., 210). The restructuration of contradictions occurs through the dual processes of displacement and condensation. In periods of stability, the essential contradictions of the social formation are neutralized by their displacement; in a revolutionary situation, they may fuse into a ruptural unity (ibid., 250). In this sense the uneven development of contradictions occurs in the internal workings of contradiction within each social formation as well as across and between social formations.

Althusser's formulation of the social around the key concepts of overdetermination and contradiction is a decisive break from theoretical humanism and economism within the marxist tradition. However, while his alternative notion of the social as a complex whole in dominance problematizes the traditional marxist theory of the social as base and superstructure, vestiges of economic determinism survive in Althusser's formulation of the relations among the various practices that make up the social (Resnick and Wolff, 68–69). Clearly, the concept of overdetermination is aimed against economic determinist theories of the social. But conceptualizing capitalism in terms of practices and giving the economic a *last instance* determining force cuts off the radical potential of Althusser's conception of the social as an overdetermined mode of production. As Laclau and Mouffe, among others, have recognized, this residual economism in Althusser excludes nonclass struggles from the social arena and suggests a model of subject formation—interpellation—that cannot account for change.[31]

Going beyond Althusser, but still making use of the powerful problematic of the social as a mode of production, would entail abandoning entirely the base-superstructure model. This would mean conceptualizing the social as an ensemble of productive spheres that are "articulated" or related "such that their identity is modified as a result of the articulatory practice" (Laclau and Mouffe, 105). In this way the concept of articulation that Laclau and Mouffe employ exclusively in reference to relations between the elements and moments of a discursive formation could apply to relations among ideological, economic, and political spheres of production, thus broadening the logic of overdetermination to social relations at all levels of analysis. Such a "global" theory of the social allows ideology to be conceptualized as a productive material practice in an overdetermined relation to economic and political practices, and not, as both Laclau and Mouffe and Foucault understand ideology, as superstructure.[32] This means that the economic is not the sole productive force or the base upon which the superstructure is erected; rather, political, ideological, and economic spheres of production mutually determine each other and are systemically implicated in maintaining particular social relations at various levels.

In a global theory of the social all three practices, including the ideological, are conceptualized as interdetermined *productive* spheres whose synchronic and diachronic interrelations can be accounted for simultaneously on multiple levels of abstraction: mode of production, social formation, and conjunctural moment. Analysis that proceeds at the level of mode of production identifies an articulated combination of relations and forces of production. Every mode of production consists of two aspects that structure its relations of production: the production of things and the production of life.[33] Analysis at the level of social formation treats specific combinations of distinct modes or relations of production. For example, explorations of the persistence of the patriarchal family-household during the early phases of industrialization in Europe or of the emergence of new forms of imperialism in the west during the transition to monopoly capitalism would proceed at this level. Conjunctural analysis investigates the concrete institutional mechanisms brought to bear on the forces and relations of production at a particular historical moment in a particular social formation.[34] A global mode of reading proceeds at all three levels.

In a global analytic contradictions are not seen as symmetrically distributed from economic to other sorts of production, but as developing at each level with its own specificity and periodization.[35] Thus, instead of a homogenous, totalizing understanding of contradictions, we have one marked by dissimilar histories, heterogenous economic and political interests, and contrary political and ideological struggles which merge or condense. These conjunctures are the articulated result of contradictions and the accompanying struggles and oppositions which are necessary for and yet potentially destructive of capitalism and patriarchy.

A global social analytic of this sort is quite distinct from a unitary body of theory which hierarchizes in the name of some fixed true knowledge. This is the "regime of truth" Foucault posits his genealogy against, and it includes quite explicitly the claims made for marxism as a science. In advocating a post-Althusserian social analytic, I am not disagreeing with Foucault's critique of efforts (including Althusser's) to establish the scientificity of marxism. But I am suggesting a break from the terms of Foucault's opposition between science and antiscience. As Foucault constructs it, this opposition equates subjugated knowledges with the critical work of releasing them and considers both to be local and discontinuous discourses. In valorizing locality and discontinuity against totalizing narratives, however, Foucault closes out *any* systemic explanation, including postmodern marxist arguments for causality that also renounce any objective claims to scientific truth.

One of the crucial features of a global social analytic for materialist feminism is that it allows us to see workplace and home, suburb and ghetto, colony and metropolis as specific and interrelated sites of exploitation. A global social theory premised on the notion that each productive sphere at any moment is determined by and determining of other spheres also makes visible how the division of labor and the distribution of extracted surplus are related to patterns of production and consumption which are affected by and in turn shape political and ideological structures. Such a social logic can make use of work already done by socialist feminists on the ways women's exploitation as producers in both unpaid domestic labor and in the marketplace is secured by and helps enable their production as feminine subjects through institutions and practices like marriage, advertising, popular romance, and their accompanying (hetero)sexual paradigms, all of which collaborate to impede women's withdrawal from the relations that exploit them. As the work of Maria Mies indicates, a global social logic makes possible differentiation of the category "woman" in the capitalist world system by making sense of the ways capitalist imperialism binds the very different patriarchal oppression of "first-" and "third-"world women in exploitative relations of consumption and production. A global social analytic also makes it possible to understand how the creation of new markets and consumer practices links patterns of consumption and production symbiotically and depends on targeting, albeit differently and in distinct social formations, women, racial minorities and "third-world" populations as the primary sites for expanding capital. Finally, conceptualizing the social in terms of a systemic logic rather than a local or contingent one implies that transformative change cannot happen within a single institution or social formation. To the contrary, it suggests that regional critiques of power may in fact help maintain the global system by obscuring the operation of exploitation across multiple and heterogeneous social spaces.

Crucial to a global social logic is a systemic understanding of power as exploitation, a theory quite at odds with post-marxist notions of power as a diffused network of forces. Exploitation conceptualizes power as a process whereby the accumulation of surplus value in the form of social resources by one "class," *depends on the work of an exploited class.* The distinguishing feature of the logic of exploitation is that the power of the dominant group over social resources depends upon the deprivation of others. The systemic operation of exploitation extends through its overdetermined relation to political and ideological relations. This conceptual framework allows us to consider how power operates hierarchically and systematically and how patriarchal and racist oppression are deeply involved in the unequal control and distribution of social assets.[36]

A global theory of the social that posits ideology as a determined and determining sphere of production makes possible a way to understand the production of racial, gendered, and class subjectivities as mutually imbricated. Because every subject is contradictorily and differentially positioned among multiple social coordinates—of race, class, gender, sexuality, ethnicity, among others—every "individual" is unevenly sutured into a nexus of subject positions. Such an understanding of the subject as multiply and contradictorily positioned can provide the basis for reformulating political alliances and (collective) intervention. While the dominant ideology will tend to separate subjectivities produced along these coordinates in support of capitalist relations of production, the relational effects of one subject position on another can produce tensions—at the level of individual or collective interests—that are counterproductive to capitalism and therefore constitute sites of potential crisis out of which a collective oppositional standpoint might be formed (Mohan, "Modernity," 31). However, elaborating the process whereby an oppositional standpoint is ideologically produced requires a more developed materialist theory of discourse, one that draws upon and rewrites the contributions of Foucault, Laclau and Mouffe, and others for a global social analytic. Before taking up the problem of discourse and the subject in chapters 2 and 3, however, I want to situate materialist feminism in relation to other feminist discourses by way of introducing the issues at stake in the various ways the reconfiguration of feminism's subject is being addressed now.

VII

The discourses comprising feminism in the west can be distinquished in terms of how each constructs "woman": as experiencing individual; as a category of signification within a symbolic system; or as an ideologically produced subject position. Each of these can be loosely identified with a particular wing of feminism—the first with mainstream liberal Anglo-American feminism, the second two with postmodern critiques of the humanist experiential subject. Mainstream or liberal Anglo-American feminism treats woman as a "self" and language as a function of natural or transparent communication. It anchors critical undertakings in experience and posits feminism primarily as a prescription for action (Jardine, *Gynesis,* 42–43). The sites of political work that emerge from mainstream feminism include demands for access to the discourse of personhood and civil rights, the possibility of an isolated sign or image as a potential site for political action, and an agenda of reform (Kipnis, 159). Continental or postmodern feminism, in contrast, focuses on the priority of a system of signification, takes the unconscious as a privileged area of exploration, and, in some versions, contends that women have no position in the symbolic order from which to speak. It is drawn from theoretical discourses emerging primarily in France in the seventies: Derridean deconstruction, Lacanian psychoanalysis, poststructuralist semiotics, and Foucauldian critique. The political subject of postmodern feminism tends to be formulated as a space—an excess of signification, the unconscious, the body, the Other—rather than as an identity or a sex (ibid., 159–60).

In *Gynesis* Alice Jardine makes a strong argument that liberal Anglo-American feminists cannot continue to pursue interrogation of what constitutes (sexual) difference from within the epistemological legacy of empiricism without risking the denial of difference altogether (46). She contends that postmodern reunderstandings of the subject can be politically empowering for feminists in that they provide a way to see how "the monological structures we have inherited are constantly being reimposed and rearranged and (particularly) . . . how women mime and reject those structures and even become their most adamant support systems" (48). If, as Jardine suggests, it is especially urgent today to look at "how these systems are being once again rearranged as we move toward a new economic crisis, a growth of micro-fascist movements, and a reawakening of the sacred" (49), the question of *how* we look remains. As the premise of Jardine's *Gynesis* implies, postmodern theory has helped locate the feminine as the paradigmatic signifier of postmodernity, trope for that which exceeds or supplements the Same, the marginal space in which otherness is inscribed. One effect has been that postmodern feminism has reaped a certain authority in the updated humanities. Laura Kipnis has argued that this tenuous legitimacy should be seen as the result of the historical conditions which made possible the emergence of postmodern feminism's objects of inquiry, events which cannot be separated from the determinants of late capital: the decline of the great imperial powers of modernity; the shift of production to the "third world"; the reordering of the western nuclear family; and the recruitment of western women into the professions. However, the mode in which continental and especially French postmodern discourses are being appropriated and touted in the U.S. academy—that is, primarily as literary/textual theory—tends to give "otherness" an ontological status, to confine the potentially quite disturbing knowledges of postmodernism to the region of culture, the aesthetic, or the symbolic, and in this way close off questions about the historical situatedness of these theories themselves (162). Gayatri Spivak has insisted that if feminist appropriations of postmodern discourses are to make use of its formulations of a new subject, they cannot remain blind to the geopolitical implications of their ways of reading and their first-world status ("Feminism and Critical Theory"). Breaking out of the potential paralysis of an aestheticized and anesthetizing textual practice need not, and in fact cannot, mean a retreat from theory. But it does require a mode of reading that can explain the relation between theory and history, between the renewed fascination with a feminized symbolic Other in the postmodern west and the neo-imperialist economic and political "underdevelopment" it depends upon.

If the process of rethinking "woman" as symbolic construct entails opening up the question of difference *within* the subject, including the ways feminist discourses have supported the very colonizing structures that oppress other peoples— women among them—we need a way of understanding difference as more than just the feminine, *jouissance*, or a marginal cultural space. While U.S. feminist theory has increasingly turned to postmodern concepts of the subject in order to rethink the category "woman," attempts to do so often poise "woman" indeterminately in the play of *differance*.[37] These analyses either ignore or anxiously point to the problematic gap between "woman" as "writing" and "women" as historical subjects, or more firmly locate "woman" in a "new" historical context by using an eclectic array of postmodern discourses to describe woman's place in a particular social formation.[38]

In advocating that feminists take seriously the texts of postmodernity, Alice Jardine addresses concerns over the disparity between the "woman in effect" (or the feminine as *written* body) and woman as speaking subject (or the feminine as written *body*). She contends that men and women exist within a symbolic system determined by "artistic and theoretical, economic and power, class and sexual systems at any given moment," all of which must be thought together if *women* hope to invent new configurations in which to act as subjects (*Gynesis*, 48). However, recognizing the importance of the symbolic construction of subjectivities in relation to other systems does not substitute for *explanation* of that intersystemic dynamic.

In couching her argument for postmodernity in terms of "gynesis," Jardine sabotages some of feminism's central concerns over difference and ends up endorsing what several of her critics see as a postfeminist position. "Gynesis" is Jardine's term for the feminine metaphor which circulates in the rhetoric of French postmodern theory as the term of difference, the Other invaginated within the symbolic order of the Same. As Toril Moi points out in her assessment of Jardine's argument, however, this equation of the Other with the feminine denies feminism's specificity as well as the specificity of other social movements organized around the social construction of difference. Treating otherness as ontological masks the concrete material grounds for oppression and ignores the difference between speaking of the feminine and speaking as a feminist (Moi, "Feminism, Postmodernism," 12). Jardine's concept of gynesis is important, nonetheless, if only because it marks out the limits of feminism's engagement with postmodernity.

One of these limits is the "other" embedded in Jardine's overview of western feminist discourses—that is, those (materialist) articulations of feminism and postmodernism emerging out of Britain, primarily, during the early seventies.[39] Her discussion of postmodern discourses on woman fixes the center of postmodernity in France, and even more narrowly, within the discourse of the aesthetic, of philosophy and psychoanalysis. In so doing it suppresses both the struggle over the *uses* of postmodern theory and postmodern *materialist* feminism. As Toril Moi's assessment of recent feminist criticism in the U.S. implies, one of the distinguishing features of materialist feminism is that it draws upon postmodern knowledges without surrendering the agonistic stance characteristic of the political discourses of modernity. Laclau and Mouffe's radical democracy resonates for materialist feminism for precisely this reason, even as it raises questions about the social analytic in which this rethinking of value from an antifoundationalist position occurs. As Moi suggests, materialist feminism shares much of postmodern feminism's concern with difference, subjectivity, and textuality, but it emphasizes their materiality and historical specificity. At the same time, as a political movement that struggles against patriarchal oppression, materialist feminism affirms the existence of social hierarchies as well as the necessity of rationalities and limits for political action.[40]

Unlike Moi, I do not think that materialist feminist theory should *include* a postmodern feminism that resists taking sides (Moi, "Feminism, Postmodernisms," 19). But I would argue that we need an analytic that can extend postmodern critiques of western epistemologies and of the centered subject without forfeiting a commitment to the possibility of transformative social change. It is in part because a post-Althusserian social analytic allows for the elaboration of this sort of *resistance* postmodernism, that I think it deserves further attention and development from materialist feminists now.

Emerging out of early second-wave feminist critiques within marxism, materialist feminism sees women as oppressively positioned within capitalism and patriarchy. Its history tells of the very difficult struggle to formulate conceptual schemas that satisfactorily explain the interrelation between these two systems. In an effort to retrieve patriarchy from exclusive relegation to the ideological where it had been consigned by marxists, but at the same time not reduce its operations to the economic division of labor along sex lines, marxist feminists during the seventies worked through what came to be known as the dual systems debates. Unable to satisfactorily generalize about the complex interrelations of support and opposition that constitute the interdetermination of capitalism and patriarchy, many of them finally declared that systemic theorizing had reached an impasse.[41] I think this rejection of systemic analysis needs to be re-evaluated now, particularly in light of the growing appeal of ludic postmodernism's regional analysis.

Much current scholarship in an increasingly loosely defined materialist feminism indicates a propensity toward this sort of local analysis. As localizing struggles extend to many cultural registers and become perhaps one of the most widely deployed mechanisms of crisis management, what was once materialist feminism's greatest strength—its focus on gender—has become its greatest liability. In order not to merely invoke the legitimizing clichés of a new leftist discourse, materialist feminism needs to attend to the theoretical issues at stake in the reformulation of feminism's "new" historical subject. We need to advance a problematic in which the articulations of race, class, gender, and sexuality can be understood in their historical specificity without abandoning analyses that situate them in terms of the social totalities that continue to regulate our lives. A global reading strategy can provide this without re-enacting the totalizing strategies of a master narrative.

So long as patriarchal and capitalist arrangements maintain a system of social relations wherein constructions of the feminine are imbricated in broad-ranging systems of exploitation and oppression, feminism as a standpoint for inaugurating a critique of those relations is still necessary. In trying to destabilize these systems, however, feminism is just one oppositional discourse. It has to develop strategies to follow through all the lines of force that radiate from the construction of "woman" to other social categories and vice versa. In doing so feminism works toward change wrought through overdetermination, change which is the effect of a collective, not just a feminist, subject.

Whether feminism can help forge such a collective subject hangs heavily on the mode of reading and writing social relations it promotes. For the social analytic which informs any theory affects its explanatory power, the extent to which the levels of analysis it provides and the subjectivities it enables intervene in and transform the production of the real in the present. Implicit in this suggestion is an argument that theory is inescapable in the sense that every discourse assumes a frame of intelligibility which contributes to the construction of what counts as "the way things are." It is in this productive capacity that theories matter. The crucial issue for a feminism that accepts the inescapable politics of theory as a material practice is not *whether* to engage with the discourses of materialism and postmodernism—an issue already decided by history—but *how* and *to what end*.

Knowledge

material in its effects?

2

The Materiality of Discourse:
Feminism and Post-marxism

Materialist feminism contributes to critiques of western epistemology that call into question the universality of liberal humanist knowledges, make visible their mechanisms of exclusion, and insist that knowledge is historical. Drawing from the insights of Marx, materialist feminism argues that material life in the form of human activity sets limits to human understanding: what we do affects what we can know. But it has also attended to more recent developments in marxist theory which stress the materiality of knowledges: how what we know also shapes what we do. Materialist feminists have given special attention to the ways in which subjectivity is constructed out of the available knowledges in a culture as they circulate in discourses and institutional practices. This concern with subjectivity has deflected back on feminism's own subject, raising questions about how to understand the relationship between the subjects feminist discourse speaks for and constructs and the kinds of change it aims to enact. In addressing these issues, materialist feminists have argued that it is through contestation among discourses and not by sheer self-assertion that social forms and institutions are shaped and emancipatory knowledges produced.

What exactly the claim that subjectivities are discursively constructed means, however, depends to a great degree upon the notion of materiality and the theory of discourse one refers to. The theories of discourse that generally inform materialist feminist work are feminist articulations of marxist and post-marxist theories. The social analytics in which these theories are framed profoundly affect what counts as materiality, discourse, subjectivity, as well as the extent to which these concepts can be useful to feminism's political objectives. My argument that feminism's aims can best be served by embracing a global social analytic implies that we need a way of thinking about the relationship between language and subjectivity that can explain their connection to other aspects of material life. Post-Althusserian theories of ideology offer this sort of conceptual framework.

There are, however, other materialist theories of discourse which do not understand its materiality as ideology or frame it within a global social logic.

In order to situate my argument for a postmodern marxist understanding of discourse as ideology within the debates over what counts as the materiality of discourse now, I want to look in some detail at three post-marxist theories—the work of Foucault, Kristeva, and Laclau and Mouffe. Each professes to be a materialist theory of discourse, and each has some relationship to feminist concerns. Yet their notions of materiality are considerably different, at times antithetical to each other. Some features of their concepts of materiality are compelling and useful ways of thinking for feminists to appropriate, rework, or embellish; others fly in the face of the political desires that inform feminism's interest in a discursively constructed subject. One of the aims of my reading is to sort out these features of their work.

It may seem that this long excursus into post-marxist theory veers from "specifically feminist" concerns. Objections to the absence of a "specifically feminist" content in these theories can be best answered, I think, by pointing to the debates over feminism's specificity now as the grounds for feminist knowledge are wrenched away from their location in reified notions of woman's experience or female identity. The effort to establish feminism's authority in the postmodern moment has made even more palpable feminism's own discursivity and historicity, its often troubled and yet necessary intersection with a host of other discourses and theoretical paradigms. It is in an attempt to open up the issue of how this intersection takes place and how it comes to bear on the specificity of feminism's (new) subject that I present the following critiques of post-marxist theory. If materialist feminists are to take full advantage of advances in contemporary theories of subjectivity and of language without lapsing into eclecticism or merely skirting the material issues at stake in the practice of appropriation, we will have to attend in a sustained way to the theoretical discourses we build our standpoint from.

It is my hope that the "excesses" of these detours through various postmodern materialist theories of discourse will fortify the critical encounter between feminism, postmodernism, and historical materialism. Ultimately, as I see it, elaborating the terms of this engagement strengthens the authority upon which feminism's fate as a political project under late capitalism will have to depend. This authority lies not in some ground prior to feminism's way of making sense of the world, but in its emancipatory reach, its disruptive work as a counterhegemonic discourse, and its contribution to the formation of a collective oppositional subject.

I

In his social and political conception of the subject-in-language, Foucault makes available a historically-specific mode of reading the relationship between subjectivity and the symbolic order. Because Foucault frames the discursive

construction of the subject in terms of the operation of power through strategies
of exclusion and regulation, his work has appealed to an intellectual liberal/left
caught up in the postmodern maelstrom of indeterminacies. Foucault's work has
been particularly interesting for feminists because of its overtly political inflection
of postmodernism. That this interest in Foucault has been a *critical* one is
evidenced by feminist readings of his obfuscation of the politics of sexuality
(Martin, "Feminism"; Walkowitz) and his insufficient attention to the sex-gender
system (Armstrong; Coward; de Lauretis, *Technologies*). Despite the explosion
of feminist appropriations of Foucault in the past decade, however, a fully
elaborated materialist feminist critique of his theory of discourse has yet to be
done.[1] That this burgeoning interest in Foucault is occurring in the throes of
stepped-up efforts to tame feminism as a political movement and a critical
discourse in the academy makes sustained feminist critiques of Foucault even
more urgent.

While some feminist attention to Foucault no doubt has been inspired by the
desire for "radical professional" credentializing, despite, or perhaps even through
these mixed motives, Foucault's project *has* opened up productive avenues for
developing materialist feminist theory. In fact, the emergence of materialist
feminism in the U.S. as a distinct theoretical discourse is to a great extent
the effect of feminist appropriation of Foucauldian concepts. Like Kristeva,
Habermas, Irigaray, Althusser, and others, Foucault addresses the relation between the political and the symbolic in a manner that seems to mediate between
formalist, poststructuralist theories of language and marxism's historicized but
monolithic accounts of the subject. Feminist readings of Foucault tend to celebrate
these features of his work as a promising alternative to theoretical "master
discourses" (Diamond and Quinby; Sawicki). In this respect, feminist appropriations of Foucault intersect with New Left critiques of totalizing narratives and
concerns over the inadequacy of atomized and homogenous notions of agency.
But invariably feminist praise for Foucault, like much post-marxism, equates a
totalizing discourse with an economistic marxism unable to address issues of
sexuality, subjectivity, and power (Diamond and Quinby; Martin, "Feminism").
From this position, Foucault's concept of discourse is seen as a way to conceive of
the links between subjectivity and sexuality at their "most material and concrete"
(Martin, "Feminism," 5). Of course, in equating marxist systemic analysis with
totalizing theory, these arguments uncritically accept and promote a reading
of marxism that suppresses the differences within marxism, including post-
Althusserian and antifoundationalist advances in marxist theory which have addressed this very issue. But they also tend to obscure exactly what counts as
the "most material and concrete" links between subjectivity and discourse in
Foucault.

In opening up the subject to the social and to discourse, Foucault's work offers
a powerful theoretical framework for analyzing historically-specific relations
between mechanisms of subjection and the symbolic order. Foucault contends

that western historiography has denied discourse and in so doing has refused to recognize that in discourse something is formed, "that, *along with* all that a society may produce ('along with,' that is to say in a determinate relationship to all that) there is the formation and transformation of 'things said' " ("Politics and the Study of Discourse," 18, emphasis mine). In stressing that in language "something is formed," Foucault acknowledges the materiality of discourse and defines it as "practice." In his critique of the History of Ideas, Foucault refigures the relationship between ideas and their "context" in terms of practices. The Foucauldian historian deals with "discursive practices in the specific relations that link them to other practices" ("Politics and the Study of Discourse," 19). As a practice, discourse is more than things said; it is the very form of action inhabited by thought "insofar as action implies the play of true and false, the acceptance or refusal of rules, the relation of oneself to others" ("Preface to History of Sexuality, vol. 2," 335). Discursive practices include external rules which provide the enabling conditions and institutional constraints on a series of statements as well as rules internal to a discourse which make possible what can be said.

Tracing Foucault's explanation of discursive practice in the texts of the seventies exposes a "gap" in his elaboration of the concept, however, in the relationship between discursive and nondiscursive practices, between discourse and "everything else"—the broadly determinate relationship hinted at in the phrase "along with" in the above quotation. Reading this gap not merely as a formal slippage of signifiers or as a problem of logical coherence, but rather, as Dominique Lecourt suggests, as a political choice, indicates the ideological limits of the terrain on which the concept of discursive practice is thought (213).

As developed in *The Archaeology of Knowledge*, Foucault's theory of discourse begins with the concept of the discursive event, a category that allows him to locate knowledge, the object of historical inquiry, in a finite, social space and to determine the connections between statements without locating them in an originating consciousness. Discursive practices do not refer back to a unified subject but to "the various statuses, the various sites, the various positions that he [*sic*] can occupy or be given when making a discourse" (*AK*, 55). The constitutive precondition for a discursive event is that it must have a material existence. This materiality consists of the relations or supports through which discourses are constituted and which are embodied in institutions. The concept of discursive practice implies that discourse cannot be conceptualized outside of this institutional system of material relations that structure and constitute it (Lecourt, 196).

Over a range of texts Foucault refers to the necessary relationship between discursive and nondiscursive practices:

> Discourse would appear in a describable relationship with the ensemble of other practices . . . instead of having to deal with a history of ideas which would be referred . . . to extrinsic conditions, one would be

dealing with a history of discursive practices in the specific relations that link them to other practices. ("Politics and the Study of Discourse," 19)

Clearly, the notion of materiality that Foucault is working with here is more than a space external to discourse. Rather, materiality is intrinsic to discursive practices themselves as they are linked to other practices. But how does Foucault conceptualize this link? What exactly *is* the material relationship between discursive and the nondiscursive practices?

As several of Foucault's critics have pointed out, the most that can be said about this relationship is that the discursive and the nondiscursive are in correspondence (Dews, "The *Nouvelle Philosophie*"). The material relations between practices are presented in terms of "a tacitly accepted, ever present, never theorized distinction between 'discursive practices' and 'non-discursive practices' " throughout the Foucauldian project (Lecourt, 198). Foucault's notion of "regulation" implies that discursive and nondiscursive practices are related at least in part through the forces that structure them. But the social logic in which they are framed only *indicates* those forces; it does not explain how discursive and nondiscursive practices are materially related. For example, in discussing the process whereby "the bourgeoisie" came to have a sexuality, Foucault argues that affirmation of the body constitutes one of the primordial forms of class consciousness. And for this reason the bourgeoisie was long reluctant to acknowledge that the classes it was exploiting had a body and a sex. In order for the working classes to be granted a sex, "conflicts were necessary . . . economic emergencies had to arise (the development of heavy industry with the need for a stable and competent labor force . . .) and lastly a whole technology of control" (*HS*, 126). Setting aside the question of how Foucault understands "class" here, what constitutes the materiality of the links between the "necessary conflicts," "economic emergencies," and the new technologies (discourses) of subjection? Foucault only suggests that they are linked. His social logic of contingency forestalls any explanation of the material and seemingly intersystemic relations that these discursive and nondiscursive processes span.[2]

The materiality of Foucault's concept of practice, then, is based on a very broad notion of materialism—the acknowledgement of the existence of a "reality" outside of thought and discourse. But, as I have indicated, Foucault does not explain the link between this "reality" and discourse. Instead, description of the deployment of discourses in their *particular* material/institutional contexts substitutes for a more general explanation. As Terry Eagleton has argued, viewing discourses in *particular* material contexts, however, is quite different from viewing them in a material context (85), especially when this "view" eclipses any sort of causal explanation of the relationship between language and all the rest.

This unexplained materiality also lies behind the transparent discourse of inquiry in Foucault's early histories.[3] While Foucault rejects the *empiricist* separation between language and its objects, his work is *empirical* in that he does not account for the theoretical frame of reference that constructs the meaning of the details he reads. Especially in his early work, the archaeological metaphors Foucault employs to describe his historiography emphasize the physical collecting or tracing of facts rather than the interpretive activity of history as a reading of these facts. This pragmatic conception of materiality obscures the materiality of his own antifoundationalist position as itself a truth-claim intervening in the knowledges and social arrangements of its own historical moment. And it also limits his analytic to empirical description of the circulation of discourses through institutions.

Even though he reads so empirically, some of Foucault's critics have argued that in his work the *real* seems always subsumed under the *word* (Aronowitz, *Crisis in Historical Materialism,* 318). The slipperiness of his notion of discursive practice and the absence of any theory of causality mean that at times *either* discursive *or* nondiscursive practice is presented as the determining material force. In "The Order of Discourse," for example, Foucault asserts that "if a discourse may sometimes have some power, nevertheless it is from [institutions] alone that it gets it" (52). And yet, at the same time, he gives discourse rather than institutions the determining force when he asserts that

> in every society the production of discourse is at once controlled, selected, organized and redistributed by a certain number of procedures whose role is to *ward off its powers and dangers, to gain mastery over its chance events, to evade its ponderous, formidable materiality.* (52, emphasis mine)

The "powers and dangers" of discourse, its "formidable materiality" loom up against the procedures aimed at mastering it, as if discourse had some intrinsic power of its own, prior to its organization and control. Clearly discourse is a material force here that is shaped by other social forces, but what exactly constitutes the connection between these forces remains hazy.

Although Foucault's notion of discursive practice situates discourse in a social field, because that social field is conceptualized in terms of a logic in which one force merely asserts its difference from another, the relation between social conflict and the discourses that construct meaning can only be vaguely formulated as local tensions within and between discursive practices. We see this effect in the concept of "discursive formation" which is presented as a localized "space of multiple dissensions; a set of different oppositions whose levels and roles must be described" (*AK,* 155). Sealed within discourse itself as "the simultaneous affirmation and negation of a single proposition," differences are closed off from any nondiscursive materiality (ibid., 156). The implications of this notion of difference are dramatically evident in Foucault's description of historical material-ism as simply a new practice within the discursive formation of nineteenth-century political economy. This reading "ignores" the distinct epistemologies and political interests of marxism and bourgeois political economy (ibid., 188). By conceptualizing the struggle over meaning here as mere discursive difference, Foucault occludes the ways these vying claims on the truth have a bearing on and are in turn affected by political struggles and exploitative social arrangements.

To the extent that it functions as the "common immanent cause" of both discursive and non-discursive practices, power/knowledge in Foucault's later work fills the space left by causality in his theory of materiality. Foucault proposes that in discourse power and knowledge are joined together "in a complex and unstable process whereby discourse can be both an instrument and an effect of power" (*HS*, 101). This "strategical model" of the "tactical polyvalence of discourse" explains the connection between the discursive and the nondiscursive in terms of power relations that are always diffuse. Discourse can be both an instrument and an effect of power, a hindrance, a point of resistance, and a starting point for an oppositional strategy (*HS*, 102). Since the relationship between power and discourse is always contingent and therefore strategic, opposition can only be random, at best a counterdiscourse formulated with respect to the prevailing rules, an inversion or "opacity" within a given social system.

Foucault argues that at the end of the eighteenth century there was a shift in the system of methods by which power operated and was guaranteed—from the rule of law to techniques of normalization (ibid., 126). At times he acknowledges that this restructuring of power was linked to the development of capitalism, and at times he refers it to a "class opposition." But the terms of this development and the nature of the opposition are not explained. Moreover, the discursive system itself is not presented as the product of vying interests, but as existing before, in spite of, or parallel to social struggle. Such an understanding of the production of knowledge locates oppositional discourses and the subjects they construct in an ambiguously oblique position—outside? beside?—their culture.[4] Because power along with its complement, resistance, is everywhere, the distinctive political force of some discourses over others cannot be explained. So, not only does Foucault's conception of discourse foreclose ways of explaining the relations between discursive and nondiscursive practices, his theory of power also precludes understanding relations among discourses hierarchically. Consequently, it is impossible to imagine how discursively constructed subjects could effect radical social change.[5] Without a framework that addresses the hierarchical relations among discourses, the continual references to "struggle" and "battle" that so pervade his analysis of power/knowledge seem rather hollow allusions to a nebulous universalized "will to power" as the basis for social change.

The shift in Foucault's work from the archaeologist's implicit claim to speak from outside any horizon of intelligibility to a genealogy that professes only to be a practice in and for the present allows him to acknowledge the necessity for truth-claims—albeit provisional and local ones. But positing truth-claims within a localized "practice" does not dispel the problem of causality at which the anitfoundationalist critique of rationalism is aimed. Although Foucault's concept of power/knowledge relinquishes a foundationalist explanation of any causal connections between knowledge and nondiscursive "realities," causality in fact re-enters his concept of discursive practice by way of a neo-Nietzschean conception of the materiality of the body.

The importance Foucault gives to the body is particularly appealing to feminists struggling to devise a materialist understanding of subjectivities. But as a complement to his notion of discursive practice, the Foucauldian body poses several problems that *materialist* feminism needs to be on guard against. As the taproot of genealogy, the ultimate micro-instance, the body for Foucault is the fundamental materiality on which history has been inscribed (Smart, 75).[6] Especially in his work after *The Archaeology* the body becomes increasingly important for Foucault as "the inscribed surface of events, the locus of a dissociated self . . . a volume in perpetual disintegration" ("NGH," 148). Genealogy attaches itself to the body "because the body maintains, in life and death, through its strength or weakness, the sanction of every truth and error, as it sustains, in an inverse manner, the origin—descent" (ibid., 147). Of course, Foucault's intervention into traditional historicism is premised on a critique of origins. He contends that "nothing in man [*sic*]—not even his body—is sufficiently stable to serve as the basis for self-recognition or for understanding other men" (ibid., 153). However, the "truth" of genealogy does come to be anchored in the body, ambiguously figured as subject and object of discursive and nondiscursive practices.

As discursive object, the body is "molded by a great many distinct regimes . . . broken down by the rhythms of work, rest, and holidays; it is poisoned by food or values, through eating habits or moral laws"; but at the same time it has a sort of prediscursive force in that it "constructs resistances" and so takes on a peculiar agency of its own (ibid., 153). It is this doubleness in Foucault's conception of the body that is particularly worthy of attention, for it points to some of the potentially dangerous political implications of his social analytic.[7] The body's peculiar status as agent and object is implicit in Foucault's now infamous utopian vision at the end of *History of Sexuality,* vol. 1. Here he sums up his critique of the deployment of sexuality as the great disciplinary technology to emerge in the nineteenth century by pointing to the means by which this pervasive sexualization might be resisted. He argues that the "grips of power" embedded in the various technologies of sexuality can be countered with "the claims of bodies, pleasures and knowledges" (*HS,* 157). "The rallying point for the counter attack against the deployment of sexuality," he contends, "ought not to be sexual desire, but bodies and pleasures" (ibid.).

What does it mean for the body to be the "rallying point" of resistance to the apparatuses of power which simultaneously inscribe themselves on it? For one thing, it means that the body is located both *inside* and *outside* the social deployment of power. This contradictory conception plays itself out in Foucault's references to the body as a force of production. In describing the technology of the body, Foucault asserts that

> it is precisely as a force of production that the body is invested with relations of power and domination; but its constitution as labour power is possible only if it is caught up in a system of subjection . . . the body becomes a useful force only if it is both a productive and a subjected body. (*Discipline and Punish,* 26)

Several questions arise from this formulation: What does it mean for the body to be a force of production? In what sense are the body's subjection and production reciprocal relations? What is the materiality of the productive, subjected body?

Because the Foucauldian analytic disallows intersystemic theorizing, reciprocal relations between apparatuses of production and subjection are never explained. One result is that Foucault's concept of "production" as it spans these various domains remains muddled. Throughout *Discipline and Punish,* Foucault posits disciplinary regimes of *subjection* as mechanisms for producing individuals. At the same time, he contends that "discipline is the unitary technique by which the body is reduced as a 'political' force at the least cost and maximized as a useful force" (221). This statement implies not only a distinction between productive and political forces, but also the possibility that the body might be a political force prior to its productive capacity. At times Foucault's analysis of a particular historical moment links the "apparatus of production" with the development of "disciplinary methods" (219). But because he cannot offer a coherent explanation of the relations between social apparatuses, the semi-autonomous relations between practices of subjection which inscribe the body and their function in economic and political production also remain unexplained.

As a result, the body takes on a certain idealistic—even mythic—dimension as extra-discursive site of truth and resistance. Appropriations of the Foucauldian concept of the body often tend to ascribe oppositional agency either to the body itself (as nondiscursive excess or extra-discursive materiality) or to the discourses that inscribe it.[8] As materialist feminist debates on the social constructedness of the body have long made emphatic, theories that aim to combat oppression, domination, and exploitation, can only situate the body outside the social at great risk to any program for change, because doing so means that the agency for opposition or resistance also remains *outside* the social.

The following comment of Donna Landry's, posed as part of her critique of the conceptualization of motherhood in French feminist thought, indicates the ways this Foucauldian body threads its way through materialist feminist work and underscores the need for a more rigorous understanding of the body's materiality:

> surely motherhood is a cultural and ideological phenomenon, unlike the "womb" and "clitoris," material sites of reproduction and women's sexual pleasure respectively, the social control of which constitutes a cross cultural basis of women's oppression. (127)

In distinguishing "womb" and "clitoris" from "motherhood," Landry rehearses the problematic relationship between the body and discourse in Foucault. For the "womb" and the "clitoris" are also inescapably cultural and ideological phenomena. Like "motherhood" they never assert their meaningfulness in and of themselves. Often—although not necessarily—functioning as a way of making sense of the female body, "motherhood" defines a particular set of social arrangements, and in this regard it is as much a material site of (re)production as "womb" and "clitoris." All of these signifiers only become meaningful within the available frames of intelligibility in any culture at any particular historical moment. Whether "womb" signifies hysterical excess or productive incubator of the race, whether "clitoris" signifies unproductive sexual pleasure (that which must be removed, controlled, or censored) or feminine *jouissance* (subversive erotic power), the materiality of "womb," "clitoris," *and* "motherhood," like the materiality of the body in general, is inextricably bound to the discourses by which they are understood. As the above discussion of the problem of discursive practice in Foucault indicates, however, a rigorous materialist theory of the body cannot stop with the assertion that the body is always discursively constructed. It also needs to explain how the discursive construction of the body is related to nondiscursive practices in ways that vary widely from one social formation to another.

II

Like Foucault's discursive practice, Kristeva's theory of signification emerges out of the configuration of theoretical discourses attending the crises of the subject, of marxism, and of the state in France during the late sixties and early seventies. As part of the general critique of economistic marxism's exclusion of questions of subjectivity and language from politics or its relegation of them to a secondary place, Kristeva advanced poststructuralist inquiry into the problem of the subject's construction within and through discourse (Rose, 149). Focusing on language as the starting point for a new kind of thought about politics and the subject, the *Tel Quel* group, of which Kristeva was a member, served as the gravitational center of French poststructuralism in the late sixties, basing its work on an understanding of history as text and of writing as production (Moi, *Kristeva,* 4). Implicit in the projects emerging from *Tel Quel* was a vision of the social as a signifying space. Among them, Kristeva took to its limits the intersection between semiotics and psychoanalysis, "an engagement that seemed to stall at the concepts of interpellation and the subject's position in language which had been brought in to buttress Althusser's theory of ideology and the state" (Rose, 143).

Reading Kristeva and Foucault together illustrates significant intersections in their work with the new political consensus coalescing in France in the wake of the events of 1968. As Peter Dews has argued, among the major doctrines of this new consensus were the contention that marxism is responsible for the Gulag, that reason is inherently totalitarian, and that seizure of state power is dangerous and vain:

> The underlying principle is a reversal from the anti-humanist structuralism of the sixties to various forms of romanticism and individualism in which "science" and any totalizing movement of reflection are denounced in the name of the spontaneous, the immediate and the particular. (129)

This reversal crystallized in the evolution of the journal *Tel Quel*: from rapprochement with the P.C.F. and the strong influence of Althusser in the sixties, followed by a long detour through Maoism which translated into the abandonment of historical materialism in the seventies, to a realignment with political pluralism, enthusiasm over democracy in the United States, and the discovery of Christianity and literature as the true bastions against totalitarianism and "the political view of the world" (ibid., 130). The history of *Tel Quel* is an extreme version of the general reactionary movement among the New Philosophers. But the use of Foucauldian theories of power by both groups to argue for a kind of "pointillist conception of pluralist resistance . . . or to reject discourse entirely in favor of religious and Free World defenses of individual rights" (Jones, 91) indicates an alignment between *Tel Quel*'s veer toward conservatism and a general ideological resurgence of the right in the west.[9]

Materialist feminists—among them Nancy Fraser, Ann Rosalind Jones, Donna Landry, and Gayatri Spivak—have critiqued Kristeva's work for its ahistorical conception of the sign, its dismissal of the political, and its essentialist notion of the body. Reading Kristeva's claims for a materialist understanding of language (especially in her early texts) beside and against Foucault's materialist theory of discourse builds upon and extends this work. Kristeva's rewriting of several key marxist concepts—among them, materiality, contradiction, and practice—illustrates a trajectory to her thinking that is distinct from Foucault's. And yet, the post-marxist stance both adopt indicates a certain similarity between them. Teasing out this similarity underscores the ways both have participated in a general containment of the crisis of western subjectivities by helping to produce a subject of knowledge which is "new"—that is, re-formed and updated—but nonetheless supportive of the hegemonic interests of multinational capitalism.

It is important to acknowledge that Kristeva's work does intervene in several of the problematics she works within, however. Her theory of language critiques traditional and Saussurean linguistics which do not allow for a discourse of desire. Shifting the object of inquiry for linguistics and semiotics away from *langue* as a structured system and toward the speaking subject, Kristeva posits language as both structured and heterogenous. Her work also critiques Lacan's schema for psychic divisions.[10] In emphasizing the heterogeneity underscoring the subject's entry into language, Kristeva displaces Lacan's distinction between the Symbolic and the Imaginary with a dialectical relation between the semiotic and the symbolic, a relation which Kristeva calls the signifying process (Moi, *Sexual/Textual Politics,* 161). For Kristeva, the semiotic is linked to pre-Oedipal primary processes, anal and oral pulsions. These are gathered up in the "chora," a concept she borrows from Plato's *Timaeus.* The "chora" signifies "a mobile and extremely provisional articulation" constituted by movements "receding and underlying figuration and thus specularization, and . . . analogous only to vocal or kinetic rhythm."[11] The subject's entry into the symbolic order takes place through a splitting of this semiotic chora. It is this disruption/rejection which serves as the basis for difference, whose roots are lodged in the ceaseless heterogeneity of the chora itself (44). Once the subject enters the symbolic order the chora is repressed, but not absolutely, for it erupts as a pulsional pressure on symbolic language in the form of contradictions, meaninglessness, disruptions, silences (25–30; Moi, *Sexual/Textual Politics,* 162).

In opening up the subject-in-language to difference, Kristeva's theory of signification also sets out to remedy shortcomings in the ways marxism, particularly the marxism inflected by phenomenology, was trying to address the problem of subjectivity. The materialist understanding of Hegel, Kristeva contends, "was accomplished at the cost of a blindness to the Hegelian dialectic's potential . . . for dissolving the subject" (114). Kristeva returns to Hegel by way of a critique of his formulation of negativity in *The Phenomenology of Spirit.* She confronts his presentation of the negative here as a space that is Other than Understanding, as freedom from thought, and argues that because Hegel was unable to situate negativity within a concrete signifying practice, he ends up superseding negativity "under the unity of the Understanding and of reason" (114). As a result, Hegelian negativity remains an opaque force in an idealist totality. Kristeva's project is to shift Hegel's concept of negativity onto materialist grounds and in so doing open the unitary subject of judgment and understanding to heterogeneity and struggle. The aim here is to use a theory of the unconscious in order to present the subject as "an impossible unity," not as a negation *within* judgement, but as that which produces the signifying function "prior to the constitution of the symbolic function" (118, 122). For Kristeva, negativity derives from the conflictual state which constitutes the heterogeneity of the semiotic. Reading Hegel through Freud, she posits this negativity as "instinctual (social and material)" (118). The question is, does her reading of Hegel through Freud explain the relationship implied by the parentheses in the above quotation, that is, between the "instinctual" and the "(social and material)"?

In arguing for the materiality of negativity in signification, Kristeva equates the social with the symbolic and the material with the presymbolic. This understanding of materiality as "the before logic; before language, before being and consciousness" closes off the oppositional potential of Kristeva's critique of Hegelian idealism by situating her theory of negativity on similar idealist ground (*Desire*, 188). In "The Novel as Polylogue" Kristeva argues that there is no such thing as a materialist logic or materialist linguistics "because logic and linguistics have been based on a repudiation of heterogeneity in the signifier and conformity to the subject as transcendental ego" (ibid., 183). While Kristeva's critique of the transcendental ego opens the subject up to difference, she restricts the social operation of difference to the realm of signification. She also limits her own materialist logic by conceptualizing the materiality of signification as the effect of heterogeneous forces rooted in presymbolic corporeal drives that inject difference into signification.

In that it locates *social* difference exclusively within the symbolic order, Kristeva's theory is similar to deconstruction, a similarity which signals their common genealogy in the anti-Hegelian position of *Tel Quel*. Unlike Derrida, however, Kristeva posits heterogeneity as an instinctual material force which erupts into the symbolic and interrupts the play of signification. In this respect, Kristeva introduces into the logic of signification heterogeneities that *différance* effaces (143–45). As she understands Derrida's concept of *différance,* this formulation of the infinite delay of the heterogenous element in the symbolic "brushes aside the drive 'residues' " that are not included in that concept of the sign (143). She insists, however, that they do return, "heterogenous, to . . . make language a practice of the subject in process/on trial" (143–44).

Kristeva's critique of *différance* resituates heterogeneity within the dialectical logic of contradiction. However, her materialist premise ultimately subverts this logic. By positing the heterogenous forces of contradiction as presymbolic, Kristeva substitutes a presocial ontology for deconstruction's social semiology. Kristeva recognizes that deconstruction's critique of structuralism neutralizes a productive and materialist notion of negativity. But rather than opening up deconstruction's limited focus on the regional/textual aspects of the economy of the sign to the historical conditions which produce the textual marks of alienation, her critique pushes in the opposite direction, desocializing even further the operations of difference within signification. By positing originary difference in a presymbolic, instinctual space, Kristeva grounds her theory of signification in an ahistorical, mythic notion of materiality and forecloses the possibility of making any connection between a non-unitary subject and "the ferment of the dialectic—the *struggle, contradiction* and *practice*" taking place in other spheres of production (138).

It may be argued that Kristeva's theory of the semiotic complicates the reading I've just offered. It seems to me, however, that the ambiguous status of the semiotic in Kristeva's theory of the signifying process indicates a symptomatic contradiction in her notion of materiality. At some points Kristeva argues that the semiotic precedes what she calls the "thetic" ground of historical meaning— the syntactic divisions and linearization of signification. At other points, however, she presents the semiotic as an eruption of the drives in the thetic, as the chora tears open and remodels the symbolic order. Thus, the semiotic is both precondition and transgression of the symbolic/thetic (63). It is simultaneously "already put in place by a biological setup and is always already social and therefore historical" (68). Here the distinctions in which the division between the semiotic and the symbolic have been inscribed break down, distinctions which underscore Kristeva's concept of materiality: between the instinctual and the linguistic, the prelogical and the social, the biological and the historical. Kristeva posits "materiality" as alternately presymbolic and social/symbolic but without explaining the material relation between the two domains. Her concept of materiality is in this sense caught between a reductive materialism—in which the material is matter—and a historical materialism—in which materiality is socially produced. As I will explain, this contradiction is not a matter of a slip in purely cognitive logic, but a historically and ideologically produced "crisis" in her text.

Kristeva contends that the drives or "shocks from energy discharges" provide the primary matter for difference and in turn generate thetic heterogeneity: "The body, as if to prevent its own destruction, *reinscribes [re-marque]* rejection and, through a leap, *represents* it *in absentia* as a sign" (171). Here the multiplication of matter in the form of energy charges is offered as the ground for a *materialist* theory of the subject. As a result, the terms of the "ferment of the dialectic"— material *contradiction* and *struggle*—which supposedly constitute the dynamics of this process, no longer refer the historical construction of difference to disparities in social production. Instead, the dynamics of difference are yoked to universal life and death drives (170). In such an economy, the presocial body takes on all of the powers of agency Kristeva's critique of the unitary subject was aimed at dismantling. The "heterogeneous" element that is the condition for signification is primarily a corporeal excitation, "that part of the objective material outer world which cannot be grasped by the various symbolizing structures the subject already has at his [*sic*] disposal" (182). For Kristeva, then, the material is matter that exceeds the symbolic function, both the matter of the body and the matter of the objective world. Moreover, an instinctual drive rejection becomes the motor of history. Because this concept of materiality is articulated within an ahistorical theory of the subject, it replicates the very same sort of contemplative materialism Marx faults Feuerbach for. This is a materialism which abstracts the essence of the human individual from the ensemble of social relations.[12] While Kristeva critiques Marx's transformation of the unitary subject of Feuerbach's naturalist metaphysics, in rethinking the subject by way of a reductive materialism, her theory posits a newly atomized subjectivity, one whose heterogeneity is the effect of pulsions from a presymbolic, corporeal space cut off from the social workings of difference.

As many of Kristeva's critics have indicated, corporealizing the transgressive force of signification closes off any possible treatment of the relation between the symbolic features of subjection and other social practices. It reduces the social to an interplay between individual drives and symbolic functions.[13] This prioritizing of the body as "material" origin links Kristeva's theory of signification to Foucault's genealogy in which the "sheer materiality of the body" serves as "history's ground zero" (Starn, 2). Without an explanatory frame for connecting the materiality of the extra–symbolic/discursive to the symbolic/discursive, it is but a short leap from Foucault's socialized body to Kristeva's corporeal excess. As in Foucault's concept of discursive practice, there is no way to understand how symbolic coherence is jeopardized by contests among signs or discourses or to determine what exactly the material relation might be between this symbolic heterogeneity and other social practices. For these reasons, despite its suggestiveness as a critique of the unitary subject of western rationalism, Kristeva's conception of heterogeneity *within* signification, her notions of the materiality of the disruptive "Other," of contradiction and heterogeneity, are inimical to a feminist agenda committed to emancipatory social change.[14]

It has been argued that Kristeva's work shifted after the late seventies as she moved from linguistic and semiotic analyses of the subject to psychoanalytic examinations of femininity and motherhood. This "shift" is less noteworthy, however, if her work is considered in terms of the psychoanalytic problematic she consistently works out of.[15] The bourgeois family romance on which psychoanalysis depends underlies Kristeva's early materialist theory of discourse. The dehistoricized subject of psychoanalysis also buttresses the highly individualistic and "apolitical" conception of dissidence and worth in her later promotions of an ethic of love (Rose, 151). Implicit in these continual returns to psychoanalysis is an identitarian mode of thought which allows her, despite her critical appropriation of Lacan, to link the Other to a presocial origin—the feminine (m)other and the opaque body.

It is consistent with this encapsulation of difference in an individualized and ahistorical body that the aesthetic becomes for Kristeva the privileged site of textual practice, indeed "the only means of transgressing the thetic" (69). Interestingly, this (re)installation of the aesthetic as *the* site of transgression re-enacts the recuperative gestures of the late nineteenth-century avant-garde Kristeva celebrates as exemplary instances of textual practice. In a moment that borders on unconscious self-recognition, her description of the cultural function of these texts reads like a summary of her own work. At the end of the nineteenth century, she argues, the gap between social practice and its representation widened and deepened. Working-class dissatisfactions erupted in a series of revolutions, but the most powerful representations of this dissent (those of Comte, Renan, Marx) were pushed to the margins because the ideological systems of capitalism more often than not worked either to suppress revolt or to consolidate it back into the center, the field of the coherent subject and of the state. As Kristeva describes this historical moment, the avant-garde are the premier target and effect of this broad-reaching process of crisis containment:

> When objective conditions were not such that this state of tension could be resolved through revolution, rejection became symbolized in the avant-garde texts of the nineteenth century where the repressed truth of a shattered subject was then confined. (211)

Although these avant-garde texts offered themselves as a compensation to bourgeois society and its technocratic ideology, the social struggles exploding the coherence of the self toward heterogeneity remained hidden in them. This was in part the effect of their representational systems which brought the alienation of this historical moment back within subjective experience. The occultism of the symbolists and surrealists defended a certain "truth" about the subject that the dominant ideology could no longer sustain. Even while it exhibited the symptoms of social crisis, the avant-garde text of the nineteenth century renounced any part of the contemporary social process. As a result, the avant-garde text served dominant ideology by providing it with something to replace what it lacked, but without directly calling into question the role of signification and the subject in its system of reproduction (212).

Like the nineteenth-century avant-garde texts she valorizes, Kristeva's narratives offer themselves as a supplement to a now late-capitalist society and its technocratic ideology. They, too—to paraphrase her own analysis of the nineteenth-century avant-garde—critique the humanist subject within a representational system that insures that the historical moment of struggle exploding the subject toward heterogeneity remains hidden. The ideological management of this explosion is inscribed in the textuality of Kristeva's theory of discourse—in the gaps in her concept of materiality, in her ambiguously biological and social semiotic, and in the terms of her reading of Hegel through Freud. This supplementary character of her theory is especially evident in the essay "Women's Time." Here Kristeva treats "the problematic of women in Europe within an inquiry on time," culminating in a utopian vision of the "demassification of the problematic of difference" (52). For Kristeva, the explosion of heterogeneity across the conceptual frameworks of western thought, particularly the separation of identity from persons and conflict from rival groups comprises the revolutionary potential of the postmodern moment. What "woman" means in the aftermath of this revolution depends very much on the discourse that supports it. Significantly, Kristeva contends that the only discourse other than religion that can buttress such a project is the discourse of aesthetics.

> The role of aesthetic practices must be not only to counterbalance the storage and uniformity of information by present-day mass media, data

bank systems, and, in particular modern communication technology, but also to demystify the symbolic bond itself . . . the community of language as a universal and unifying tool. (52–53)

As in the texts of the symbolists and surrealists she reads, art's demystifying function is insulated within the domain of the symbolic, cordoned off from any material relation to the historical forces which have produced the information explosion of the late-capitalist technocracy it is meant to "counterbalance." Hidden within these narratives of pulsions and heterogeneities are the struggles over the history of signs and resources. Out of them emerges an updated and much more fragmented feminine subject, but one that finally doesn't relate the disruptive force of difference in language to social struggle. It is, however, a subject more adequate to the uneven developments of capitalist production in the age of information, embracing both a residual *singularity* and a postmodern *multiplicity* (53).

Like Foucault's, Kristeva's formulation of the marginal forces of subversion has a romantic, even mythic, dimension, and it is this dimension which binds their projects to some of the more conservative strands of modernism. For both, literary texts have a special place in the cultural margin, a signal that their aesthetics are in many ways still captive to the romantic agon. As Ann Rosalind Jones has argued, for Kristeva the solution to all lack is individual—the solitary poet, the postfeminist losing her energies in language play, and, most recently, the analysand in long hours of private care. Similarly, Foucault's later work endorses an ethics and an aesthetics of self-fashioning as the paradigm for social practice.[16] This trust in an individualistic avant-garde rather than anything that could call itself a revolutionary collectivity can be seen as part of a general intellectual backlash in the west. These features of the new philosophy in France have their ideological counterparts in the New Right in the U.S. and the U.K. The turn to private relationships, local interventions, and traditional authorities to replace endangered philosophical traditions has its parallel in the clamor for a return to "family" and a politics of self-help in other cultural registers.[17]

The conservative ideological landscape these strands of their work help to define is certainly related to the ways in which Foucault and Kristeva ground difference in a space outside the symbolic. But their work also shares another "otherness"—the political alternative they often pit their arguments against. In "Psychoanalysis and the Polis" Kristeva contends that her argument for psychoanalysis should displace the "epistemological attitude" of political interpretation. For Kristeva, the ultimate consequence of political criticism "consists simply in the desire *to give meaning*. . . . political interpretation is thus the apogee of the obsessive quest for A Meaning" (78). As she sees it, this quest has produced two powerfully disruptive results: fascism and Stalinism (78). Kristeva recognizes that the giving of meaning is "not innocent," but she cannot see that it is precisely for this reason that meaning is inexorably political. That meaning-making entails variously interested claims to truth is enacted in the very terms of Kristeva's essay. Throughout the piece, Kristeva's argument for psychoanalysis is set against—at the same time as it constructs—its discursive "other": the discourses of the "political," in particular marxism.

This is a marxism which Kristeva tellingly presents as both marginal and "deafly dominant" (77). The emergence of the discourses of postmodernism in the U.S. academy, including their so-called "political" versions and critiques, helped foment the crisis in the humanities that prompted the conference on the "Politics of Interpretation" where Kristeva first read this essay. Although much more marginalized than dominant in the humanities, the discourse of marxism—"exercis[ing] a fascination that we have not seen in Europe since the Russian *Prolekult* of the 1930s"—quickly becomes the main target of the essay's polemic, symptom of a lingering *dis-ease* to which psychoanalysis will provide "an antidote" (78).

In Kristeva's essay that "antidote" takes the form of the desiring subject whose discourse of delirium marks the place reserved for the maternal and the feminine and which appears in the symbolic as the *unnameable* "origin" (82–84). This "other" constitutes "A Meaning" as solid in its claims to truth as the political discourses Kristeva contests. Located in an "elsewhere" "resistent to meaning," like Lacan's Real and Foucault's "unthought," Kristeva's abject mother obscures the ways meaning is constructed through contesting and interested differences (84). Furthermore, this "antidote" helps keep invisible the "dis-ease" over contesting claims on social reality that psychoanalysis is mustered to heal. Although Kristeva sets psychoanalysis against "political" discourses, the very way she presents it as the "one theoretical breakthrough (that) seems consistently to *mobilize* resistances, rejections, and deafness" collapses the opposition between political and nonpolitical knowledges (77). Surely this "mobilizing" is political! The debate here is not, therefore, over political discourse vs. nonpolitical (ethical) discourses on the social, although Kristeva and Foucault both construe it in these terms, but over contesting versions of knowledge and the social and their (political) consequences.

To the extent that both Kristeva and Foucault tend to set up political discourse as discrete and totalizing, they bracket off questions about the "other" within their own theories, questions about the power/knowledge relations their own discourses are implicated in. Locating alterity within the symbolic field as historically and discursively produced would entail seeing the other not as a force outside culture and signification (drives or instincts, unnameable opacities, or unspeakable elsewheres) but as a position or way of making sense which circulates within an overdetermined symbolic order. What is intelligible or unintelligible in any historical moment—including constructions of the body, of the "feminine," or of the "irrational"—is so from a given historical position within a symbolic system which is part of an ensemble of mutually determining social practices. From this vantage point, alterity is to be found in the cracks and gaps of the dominant discourses as well as in the contest between and among discourses. This way of understanding differences has profound implications for rethinking the subject of feminism. Not the least among them is the recognition that it is not enough to claim that feminism's subject is discursively constructed rather than forged out of experiences common to all women. The political effectivity of this claim rests to a great degree on how discourse itself is understood.

III

The implications of the analytics which frame Kristeva's and Foucault's conceptions of discourse can be seen most readily in the arguments for a new ethics that constitute the utopian moments in each of their work. For both Kristeva and Foucault, *ethics* is set against *politics* as the preferred category through which to construct an understanding of social relations. Like the "political," "ethics" signifies within a discursive field. That politics and ethics are being set against one another now points to a contest between discourses which have historically privileged either of these two categories. While both Foucault and Kristeva, as well as their commentators, often collapse the opposition between these two terms or use them interchangeably,[18] I am interested in looking at the ways the opposition between politics and ethics in some places in their texts strains against the claims made for ethics at other points. Making visible some of the assumptions and consequences of these tensions indicates quite tellingly the convergence of Kristeva's conservative social logic with the seemingly more progressive analytic of Foucault.

Ethics has a long and complex genealogy, threading its way through many contesting problematics. Postmodern marxists like Fredric Jameson have argued that in its narrowest sense ethical thought projects as permanent features of human "experience" what are in reality the historical and institutional specifics of a determinate type of group solidarity or class cohesion (Jameson, *Political Unconscious,* 59). In our time, notions of identity tend to stand in for older themes of moral sensibility so that the prevailing forms of ethical criticism are couched in theoretical frameworks which endorse the individual as the source of meaning. While ethics has tended to take this form in its dominant mode, it has also been articulated within postmodern analytics that critique the centered subject of liberal humanism, including those of Foucault and Kristeva as well as some versions of resistance postmodernism that address the opposition between ethics and politics by rewriting "ethics" as social practice.[19]

The issue is not whether "ethics" has an intrinsic reactionary or conservative value. In fact, as Nietzsche's analysis of the genealogy of morals has taught us, it is just this binary opposition between good and evil that constitutes the informing ideology of ethics. To suggest that the ethical binary itself is "bad" merely draws Nietzsche's critique back onto itself. As Jameson has suggested, this paradox is avoided only if the ethical binary between good and evil is grasped as a form of social praxis, that is, as a symbolic resolution to a concrete historical situation (*Political Unconscious,* 117). To my mind the proliferation of discourses on ethics now functions in this way, as a symbolic resolution of the crisis of the subject, one of many cultural efforts to quell anxieties over the shaken foundations of western philosophy.

Feminists have produced an extensive and diverse body of work on ethics which spans a range of these contesting discourses. Much of this work has critiqued as male-biased and masculinist those systems of "objective" thought that have made women and women's values invisible in a humanism authorized in the name of "man." Many of these arguments that set out to reclaim ethics for women or from a woman's standpoint are couched in terms of "women's experience" or of gender understood as biological sex difference. They also tend to accept the traditional formulation of ethics as concern over what constitutes the good life, and then go on to insist that questions of right and wrong conduct should include the woman's voice. Some recent feminist work on ethics, however, has begun to offer a more sweeping critique of the hierarchical assumptions in the category "moral theory."[20]

Like feminist critiques of humanist ethics, postmodern discourses have dismantled a conception of ethics based on *a priori* categories of "goodness" and "man," but in many cases without a commitment to any alternative normative standards. On the contrary, these discourses often take the form of neo-Nietzschean inquiries into "morality" which question *any* possibility of thinking value in normative or hierarchical terms. Instead, they posit value as always contingent, and ethics as its "practical" enactment. Given the claims made in the name of "ethics" among the far right "Moral" Majority, and the resurgence of concern with ethics in the liberal center, one cannot help but wonder to what extent this appeal to a practical "ethics" is being resorted to as a way to fend off the more dangerous political potential of postmodernism's critique of the humanist subject.[21] Is practical ethics indicative of a general effort to "heal" the crisis of the subject by resecuring the individual "newly," within more porous, atomized social relations? How empowering is such a conception of value for a feminism struggling to articulate the many different ways women are socially positioned without abandoning the normative concepts that enable us to convey the widespread, persistent, violent operations of misogyny across a range of interconnected social relations? How are we to evaluate formulations of a "new" ethics in the name of feminism?

When international feminism is upheld as "an ethical project more harmonious than any on the current scene," I think we should be suspicious (Siebers, 219). The conjunction of feminism and harmony here signals that some of feminism's most trenchant critiques are being tempered in the name of a new ethics. Kristeva's work, in particular, has been pointed to as an instance of "a new ethicity [*sic*] being mapped out at the crossroads of a certain modernity and a certain feminism" (Jardine, "Opaque Texts," 98).[22] Why should "ethicity" be the term for the intersection of feminism and modernity now? What does this configuration help guarantee, and at what cost? In other words, given that feminism is a political movement, what are the politics of this new ethicity?

Both Kristeva and Foucault offer ethics as an alternative to the "totalizing" discourse of the political. We have seen Kristeva's construction of this opposition in "Psychoanalysis and the Polis." In an interview on politics and ethics, Foucault makes much the same argument when he asserts, "what interests me is much more morals than politics, or, in any case, politics as an ethics" ("Politics," 375). Later he adds,

> I believe precisely that the forms of totalization offered by politics are always, in fact, very limited. I am attempting, to the contrary, apart from any totalization—which would be at once *abstract* and *limiting*— to *open up* problems that approach politics from behind. (375–76)

In keeping with his work on discourse, Foucault's attention to ethics aims to broaden the field of the political. The question is how and to what effect this broad approach to politics proceeds. Like Kristeva in her latest work on psychoanalysis and love, Foucault in an interview just before his death argues that morality is a matter of interpersonal relations:

> in the work of reciprocal elucidation, the rights of each person are in some sense immanent in the discussion. They depend only on the dialog situation. . . . Questions and answers depend on a game—a game that is at once pleasant and difficult—in which each of the two partners takes pains to use only the rights given him by the other and by the accepted form of dialog. The polemicist, on the other hand, proceeds encased in privileges that he possesses in advance and will never agree to question. ("Polemics, Politics, and Problematizations," 381–82)

In making the authority for discourse ideally immanent in the exchange, in rights each partner gives the other, his model of interpersonal dialogue reinstalls the hegemonic contractual and democratic subject. It also mystifies the social dimension of discursive "rights" even in the terms Foucault grants elsewhere. What is obscured in this dialogic model is that exchanges often occur in situations where the rules are already set to one member's advantage and the other's detriment. It is certainly possible—even imperative—to consider the questions and answers that circulate in culture as more than either a free dialogue or an authoritarian imposition. Invariably in this circulation there are high-stakes and risks, and more often than not the odds are stacked unevenly from the start. If this is acknowledged, polemics can be understood not as an authoritarian truth posed against an innocent interpersonal dialogue, but as a discourse that can interrupt the "game" of dialogue by naming the systematic distribution of odds, and in that naming begin to rearrange the rules of play.

Foucault's formulation of practical ethics is of course bound up with his antifoundationalist critique of dialectics which in turn underpins his theory of power. His antifoundationalist dismissal of intersystemic connections ("I think we have to get rid of this idea of an analytical or necessary link between ethics and other social and economic or political structures") and truth-claims (setting aside the truth-claims of local discursive and ethical practices, of course) almost necessitates that the authority of ethics comes to rest on a (familiarly modernist) aesthetic ground—the *art* of choosing or inventing oneself, turning one's body into a work of art ("Genealogy of Ethics," 236). In this respect, what Foucault calls "ethics" is much like nineteenth-century dandyism: "the kind of relationship you ought to have with yourself" (ibid., 238). Although he acknowledges that this relationship is not isolated as such, he nonetheless frames it in terms that harken back to the version of individualism formulated by the modernist avant-garde:

> But couldn't everyone's life become a work of art? Why should the lamp or the house be an art object, but not our life? . . . From the idea that the self is not given to us, I think that there is only one practical consequence: we have to create ourselves as a work of art. (Ibid., 236–37)

That Foucault's notion of social value emerges finally in an argument for the art of self-fashioning certainly raises questions about the recurring motif of social struggle and conflict in his work.

While the aim of their conceptions of ethical practice is not the same, Foucault's concern with the freedom to invent a self and Kristeva's attention to the pleasureful lifting of prohibitions in an analytic-dialogue of love both pose "art"—not social change—as the practical goal of ethics. Ethics fills in for the (absent) telos in Foucault and "solves" the problem of agency with the promotion of an updated individualized aestheticism.[23] This "new" ethics is less a code of conduct than a strategical indeterminacy that allows uncertainty, the position of being "else-where," a focus on the limits of language, and its unspeakable grounding in the unsignifiable (Jardine, "Opaque Texts" 111). It is here in a mythical aestheticized freedom that the ethics of Kristeva and Foucault converge. Mary Lydon's proposal that Foucault's analytic allows consideration of an ethic of resistance for women from a ground "elsewhere," outside any frame of intelligibility, suggests how the appropriation of this notion of ethics for a theory of oppositional power ends up subverting any sort of social oppositionality altogether. Much like the counterdiscourses of modernism or the postmodern valorization of indeterminacy, "resistance" from this sort of "elsewhere" can breed only a disengaged quietism.

IV

Laclau and Mouffe share with Foucault a post-marxist argument for a social logic of contingency. Like Foucault, they embrace ethical knowledge as distinct from Enlightenment versions of reason and the sciences. In this sense, ethics has little to do with abstract universalism; rather, it is those knowledges dependent on the *ethos*, the cultural and historical conditions current in a community (Mouffe, "Radical Democracy," 36). While Foucault's post-marxism, as we have seen, leads him to bind his ethics to a practice of self-fashioning which ultimately has a lot in common with Kristeva's seemingly more conservative ethic of love, Laclau and Mouffe situate the multiple forms of rationality signified by their notion of ethics within "a new form of individuality that could be truly plural and democratic" (ibid., 44). As they acknowledge toward the end of *Hegemony and Socialist Strategy*, the ethical principle—in the sense of a set of informing values—which defines this new form of individuality is the principle of liberalism "which defends the liberty of the individual to fulfill his or her own human capacities" (184). They argue that this principle is more than ever valid today, but that it requires *another* conception of the individual, "an individual that is no longer constructed out of the matrix of possessive individualism" (184). Their alternative is the matrix of postmodern liberalism, whose materiality lies in what Laclau and Mouffe define as hegemony.

As I indicated in chapter 1, this matrix has many of the limitations of bourgeois liberalism and ludic postmodernism. The primacy they grant to the political sphere is very much in keeping with a liberal analytic. Its postmodernization—that is, its formulation as a plural, polysemic space—does nothing to change the fact that the priority they give to the political arena obscures the question of "rights for what?" The polemical force of this question insists that notions of liberty and freedom, the social movements they organize, and their incipient norms and values are never isolated in the political sphere. They spill into other social arrangements, regardless of how provisionally, affecting the allocation of resources, the division of labor, narrative closure and the constitution of cultural difference.

The consequences of Laclau and Mouffe's postmodern pluralist ethic are played out in their reformulation of the social as not only an open but an exclusively discursive space. Before launching my critical reading of their concept of discourse, I want to affirm, however, that in critiquing the class subject of marxism and formulating in its stead a much more heterogeneous subject of social change, they develop several very useful concepts. One of these is the concept of discursive articulation. Reworked within a global analytic, this concept offers suggestive avenues for understanding more fully the discursive processes by which subjectivities are formed and makes available a much more detailed conceptual vocabulary for formulating the construction of difference within and across subjectivities. However, for all of its suggestiveness, their theory of discourse also has several problems.

First of all, as I have explained in chapter 1, their social logic of contingency, like the Foucauldian analytic upon which it draws, brackets off the materiality of discourse from any systemic relation to other practices. Unlike Foucault, however, who is ambivalent about the relationship between the discursive and the nondiscursive, for Laclau and Mouffe, there is only discourse. The indeterminacy of the social on which their analytic is founded—that is, the premise that "there is no single underlying principle fixing—and hence constituting—the whole field of differences" (111), is presented as an effect of *différance,* the slippage of signifiers inherent to the symbolic order. But they do contend that the social construction of identities forces limits upon this open and polysemic field. Necessity enters through the back door as "the partial limitation of the field of contingency" (111), and discourse is the means by which this partial limitation is exercised. Discourse arrests the flow of differences that comprise the social space. The points at which it is arrested—the privileged signifiers that fix the signifying chain—constitute "meaning." The oppositional logics of the necessary and the contingent are thus reworked as complementary. But what for Laclau and Mouffe constitutes the materiality of discourse?

They do acknowledge that a contingent field of differences in some way deforms every identity and prevents it from becoming fully sutured or sewn into the signifying chain of discourse (110–111). And they contend that the same holds true for the larger social space. No discursive totality is absolutely self-contained: "there will always be an outside which distorts it and prevents it from fully constituting itself" ("Post-Marxism," 89). This "outside" might seem to offer a way out of the problem of the unexplained material relation between the discursive and the nondiscursive in Foucault. However, Laclau and Mouffe locate this disruptive contingency exclusively within the "field of discursivity" which they define, circular fashion, as "the impossibility of any given discourse to implement a final suture" (111). In keeping with their concept of overdetermination, the complementary relationship between the necessary and the contingent exists exclusively within the symbolic field. The overdetermined dimension of subjectivity is its "intertextuality;" the excess that "overflows" every social identity is discursive (113). As Nicos Mouzelis has argued in his critique of *Hegemony and Socialist Strategy,* Laclau and Mouffe never spell out the conditions of existence of the discursive field, how discourse is limited "by the more permanent institutional structures of capitalism" or whatever (114). This is because for Laclau and Mouffe the "surplus" inherent in every discursive situation is grounded in a formalist understanding of signification. As a result, the radical potential of their materialism is subverted as it joins with a number of contemporary currents of thought from Derrida to Haraway which posit the indeterminacy of meaning as the basis for the social. The difficulty here is not their insistence on the impossibility of ultimately arresting meaning, but *how* both the provisional fixing and the surplus of meaning are explained.

Laclau and Mouffe's theory of discourse begins with Foucault's definition of the discursive formation in *The Archaeology of Knowledge* as "regularity in dispersion" (105). They proceed to explain this regularity in terms of Benveniste's critique of Saussure's theory of the sign and its implications for value. Beneveniste finds traces of an incipient positivism in Saussure's assertion that the relativity of values is grounded in the arbitrariness of the relation between signified and signifier. He claims that this understanding of value rests on the assumption of a real object to which the sign refers. Benveniste argues instead that the relation between sound and idea is not at all arbitrary. If one considers the sign itself the carrier of value, the relativity of value is not a function of the arbitrary nature of *the sign per se* but of the systemic relation of signs to each other. It is this *formal* differential system which constitutes the *necessity* of their relation (Benveniste, 47–48). On the basis of this formalist understanding of signification, Laclau and Mouffe conclude that "necessity derives . . . not from an underlying intelligible principle but from the regularity of a system of structural positions" typified in the system of signification (106).

That "society never manages to be identical to itself" is ultimately for Laclau and Mouffe the result of formal properties of the sign (111). This is also the position Ernesto Laclau takes in his brief essay on "Psychoanalysis and Marxism." Here Laclau contends that the "destruction" of the history of marxism can be brought about "as the result of the generalization of the logic of the signifier to the ensemble of [marxism's] theoretical categories" so that "these categories are neither removed nor reabsorbed by a higher rationality but *shown* in their contingency and historicity" (333). According to Laclau, this "destruction" is the effect of

> the generalization of any the phenomenon of "unequal and combined development" of the imperialist age into any social identity which, as in the Heideggerian image of the broken hammer, transforms the *dislocation* into a horizon from which all identity may be thought and constituted (these two terms being exactly synonymous). (333)

Although he posits the links between the contingency of identity and the logic of the signifier as the effect of a certain historical arrangement—the postmodern/ imperialist moment—by the end of the statement, under the telling force of the Heideggerian hammer, signification itself is the shaping horizon of history. Thus the logic of the signifier becomes a transhistorical given upon which the hegemonic subject, the history of marxism, and the formulation of a post-marxist radical democracy all meet.

In *Hegemony and Socialist Strategy* the logic of signification which Laclau's essay brings to bear on marxism by way of psychoanalysis joins with Derrida's critique of the structures of signification. In basing their argument for the openness of the social on an unquestioned appropriation of Derrida's concept of *différance,* Laclau and Mouffe affirm and reinforce deconstruction's assertion that the indeterminacy of signification is a formal property of the *logos.* Congealed in Derrida's concept of *différance* is a critique of the centered structures of western metaphysics that reunderstands this center not as a fixed locus but as a function by which coherent meaning is secured (112).[24] However, as Barbara Foley has indicated in her critique of the political uses of deconstruction, Derridean deconstruction "extracts binary oppositions from their historical moment, formalizes, hypostasizes contradiction, and elevates undecidability to the status of historical subject" (128). In this regard it is distinct from the marxian reading practice of defetishization which takes to task not the existence of opposed categories *qua* categories but rather their historically specific contents.[25]

Like Derrida, Laclau and Mouffe assert that "the ambiguous character of the signifier, its non-fixity to any signified, can only exist insofar as there is a proliferation of signifieds" (111). This polysemy, they contend, "*establishes* the overdetermined, symbolic dimension to every social identity" (111, emphasis mine). Thus the "excess" of signification, the "contingencies" which continually irrupt into the necessity of suture, reside within the formal properties of discourse. This reading of discursive "excess" echoes those features of the deconstructionist problematic that make it *in itself* inimical to a materialist theory of discourse and to any viable mode of political practice.

In her incisive argument for the materiality of *différance,* Rajeswari Mohan suggests, however, that Derrida's concept of *différance* can be understood as an effect of late capitalist ideology and at the same time appropriated for a materialist theory of discourse ("Modernity," 110–136). Reading Marx's labor theory of value through his theory of ideology, Mohan demonstrates that *différance* can be understood as a late capitalist refiguration of value. Her argument is premised on Marx's insight that the value which accrues from the appropriation of labor power under capitalism assumes various forms. The alienation of labor which underlies value formation under capitalism is not just an economic process but informs its ideological productions as well. Sheered away from its intimate connection to labor, value is mystified or appears as a property of its reified forms. As an instance of ideological production under late capitalism, *différance,* which posits the weave of differences in language as a function of signification, displaces the mediatory workings of value and purges it of its historical implications in labor. A materialist theory of *différance,* however, reinvests value with its historical character. This argument presupposes that value functions as objectified labor in the dual registers of commodity and language. As in the commodity, value takes on alienated forms in signification under capital. Fetishizing the separation of signifier from signified as the property of signification is one instance. Mohan argues that *différance* can be seen from this vantage point as the linguistic mark of capital's super-alienation which becomes operative in exacerbated and pervasive forms as a consequence of historical shifts in productive relations under late capitalism. As more and more aspects of social life are commodified, as sites of production shift to "invisible" centers, and the labor force becomes minutely diversified, labor has become increasingly alienated. As a result, ideological processes—signification and subjectivities—gain an appearance of autonomy: the referent recedes and signifiers seem only to refer to each other.

However, in that it makes visible the instability of the processes of signification, deconstruction *can* help open the space of critique, displaying the operation of historical crises at the level of textuality. As Mohan makes clear, the slippage of signifiers foregrounded by the concept of *différance* can be read as the visible mark of the historicity of the sign. This entails understanding the indeterminacy of meaning not as an ontological given of language but as a localized instance of the contradictions of capitalism enacted in the contesting claims on the sign (136).[26]

Laclau and Mouffe collaborate with deconstruction's mystification of the operations of late capital at the level of the sign by taking what they claim is the ultimate precariousness of all difference as the basis for their formula for antagonism. Their emphasis on antagonism wrenches power away from its connection to labor and binds it to a notion of social struggle as the exclusive effect of signification. As they see it, the slippage of the signifier is equivalent to antagonism (128). Explaining antagonism as an effect of the instability of signification mystifies the relationship between signification and the commodity, between alienation at the level of cultural meaning and at the level of economic and political relations. It reifies in the processes of signification the highly mediated relation between discursive and nondiscursive practices, in other words, what is at stake in the history of struggles waged over words.

This ahistorical reading of the economy of the sign is central to their concept of hegemony. Founded on the formalist logic of signification, hegemony for Laclau and Mouffe consists of the components of a field of articulatory practices. Articulatory practices establish a relation among free-floating discursive elements such that their identity is modified as a result of the articulation. Discourse is the structured totality resulting from the articulation of discursive elements. Any discourse is constituted as an attempt to dominate the field of the social through the articulation or partial fixation of privileged discursive points (what they call nodal points) that secure the meaning of a signifying chain. The enabling condition for the articulation of these points, and thus for the formation of hegemony, is the "excess" of signification. But because they rely on a notion of *différance* that locates this excess within the formal contingencies of discourse—the forms of "symbolization, metaphorization, paradox which deform and question the literal character of every necessity" (114)—its material relation to political and economic arrangements remains unexplored. As I will elaborate in chapter 3, the concept of hegemony which Laclau and Mouffe appropriate from Gramsci can be thought otherwise, within a global social logic. Here it functions as a useful concept for detailing how under capitalism the suturing of subjects to the social real through the articulation of discourses mediates in the sphere of ideology alienated forms of labor and value which inform social struggle. Formulated in terms of this logic, their ideas on the discursive articulation of difference can be quite usefully appropriated for the development of a materialist feminist standpoint.

V

Reading critically the claims to a materialist theory of discourse in Kristeva, Foucault, and Laclau and Mouffe is an important step in formulating a materialist feminist theory of discourse. Certainly these post-marxist theories span a range of explicit feminist interests: no overtly feminist interest in Foucault; a rescinded allegiance to feminism in Kristeva; and an explicit inclusion of feminism by Laclau and Mouffe in the series of social movements comprising the hegemonic discourses of radical democracy. But the lessons they offer materialist feminism lie as much in their gaps and faults as in any professed alliance.

Materialist theories of discourse like Kristeva's that equate the material with matter or with energy emanating from a corporeal space naturalize the forces of social and discursive change and so push the ground for difference as well as its potentially disruptive power beyond any sort of determining social register. For feminism this notion of "materialism" conserves rather than dismantles a metaphysics that locks "woman" and feminine excess into the maternal body. Feminist appropriations of the work of Laclau and Mouffe are few to date.[27] But their articulation of a liberal "ethic" within a postmodern social logic and theory of the subject is an important caveat to materialist feminists aiming to address similar issues—the inadequacy of marxism's class subject, the problem of difference within the subject, or the relationship of feminism to other emancipatory social movements. Materialist theories of discourse like those of Laclau and Mouffe or Foucault that dismiss or cannot explain the relationship between the discursive and the nondiscursive impede our understanding of the ways the production of subjectivities in one local site, the U.S. academy, for example, depends on economic and political arrangements in other sites. In failing to explain the material connection between the discursive and the nondiscursive, Foucault and Laclau and Mouffe help mystify the relationship between capital's insidious and pervasive operations and an increasingly fetishized notion of language. Like Kristeva's seemingly more conservative version of materiality as an ahistorical, asocial space, Foucault's conception of discursive practice and Laclau and Mouffe's notion of hegemony block ways of understanding the relationship between the discursive and the nondiscursive production of value.

Reading Foucault in relation to Kristeva is also strategically useful for materialist feminists because doing so highlights some of the more conservative features of Foucault's work. And it is a Foucauldian notion of discourse that materialist feminist studies have most enthusiastically embraced. For that reason I want to attend in more detail to some of the dynamics of this appropriation. Feminist interest in Foucault's ideas on discourse has been tempered primarily by forceful critiques of his blindness to gender. But feminists have for the most part not acknowledged that admitting into Foucault's analytic the category "gender" as a hierarchical system within which subjectivities are produced requires rethinking the entire Foucauldian project: the conception of the social and of the materiality of discourse it depends on, the historical and "ethical" subject it promotes. Perhaps more importantly, they have not seen the relation between Foucault's insistence on local analysis and the absence of any discussion of imperialism in his narratives of the nineteenth century. Certainly they have rarely confronted the bearing this "oversight" might have on theorizing the feminine subject from within a Foucauldian framework.

Gayatri Spivak's critique of Foucault's blindness to imperialism makes visible the historicity of Foucault's work and offers an admonition to western feminists. As Spivak sees it, this "oversight" is not merely an omission. It has its own positive effects on the (re)production of western subjectivities. Within the ensemble of postmodern knowledges, it serves as a "radiating point, animating an effectively heliocentric discourse, [that] fills the empty place of the agent with the historical sun of theory, the Subject of Europe" ("Can the Subaltern Speak?" 274). Spivak's critique of the shape this sovereign subject takes in Foucauldian and other post-marxist liberatory narratives indicates a striking similarity between the claims of these narratives and those of feminist discourses on the left: both are quick to valorize the oppressed subject and both are committed to establishing conditions where the oppressed would be able to speak (ibid., 274).

Western academic feminists looking for ways to address the differential construction of woman need to approach this project not by trying to give voice to the experience of the other but by occupying more fully our own uneven positions within the late capitalist social arrangements out of which this occidental subject is being reconstructed. This "occupation" can only happen by devising ways to read the analytics we employ and which write us so as to make visible their function in perpetuating the divisions of labor and productions of value on which our privileged positions as western academic intellectuals depend. One step in this process should be to take seriously Spivak's argument that the antitheoretical appeal to concrete experience and the recourse to an ethics of the self in Foucault's micro-analytic is a contemporary version of the positivism that serves as the ideological foundation for neo-colonialism. Implicit in this charge is the very powerful assertion that theories of discourse and their social logics have, quite literally, global political and economic effects. A feminism that aims to understand the discursive construction of "woman" across multiple modalities of difference—race, class, gender, sexuality—requires a problematic that *can explain* the connection between discursive constructions of difference and the exploitative social arrangements that shape them. Claiming a standpoint that aims to disrupt the complicity of western knowledges in the reproduction of exploitation means that we have to confront the very material effects of the theoretical discourses we work through.

Women have served all these
centuries as looking-glasses
possessing the magic & delicious
power of reflecting the figure of
man at twice its natural
size. Virginia Wolff —

Theory as expression of individual's subjectivity

3

Feminist Standpoint, Discourse, and Authority: From Women's Lives to Ideology Critique

I

Feminist standpoint theory occupies a significant place among materialist critiques of western epistemology. Socialist feminists initially developed the notion of standpoint from the insights of Marx, Engels, Lukacs, and others in order to formulate a more coherent explanation of feminism's authority, who it speaks for, and the forces of oppression and exploitation it contests. Standpoint refers to a "position" in society which is shaped by and in turn helps shape ways of knowing, structures of power, and resource distribution. Feminist standpoint theorists have posited feminism as this sort of position, a way of conceptualizing reality from the vantage point of women's lives: their activities, interests, and values. Most significantly, in attending to the complex material forces that structure the relations between social positioning and ways of knowing, feminist standpoint theories have challenged the assumption that simply to be a woman guarantees a clear understanding of the world. Instead they argue that the feminist standpoint is a position that is socially produced and so not necessarily immediately available to all women. For feminist standpoint theory, then, both the representation of a feminist perspective and its "truth" are reached through philosophical and political struggle (Jaggar, 383–84).[1]

Written into feminist standpoint theory, however, are several knotty problems. One of them is how to understand the relationship between standpoint as a critical discourse and the referent "women's lives." At the same time standpoint theorists insist that the feminist standpoint is a socially constructed way of making sense of the world, they also pose "women's lives" as an empirical point of reference prior to feminism.[2] However, the relationship between the discursive materiality of feminism and the empirical materiality of women's lives invariably isn't explained. Another related problem feminist standpoint theorists have more recently confronted is how to formulate the relationship between the interests that shape feminism's admittedly partial position and those interests that traverse a no longer monolithic view of "woman." In other words, how can feminism assert both its specificity and the intersections of its own political aims with other emancipatory standpoints?

While the appeal to women's lives as the ground for authority in feminist standpoint theory is often claimed in the knowledge of feminist critiques of empiricism and of the experiential subject, the epistemological difference between women's lives and women's experiences as the foundation for knowledge is not always clear. Moreover, many of the same problems that the critique of women's experience as the ground for feminist knowledge has posed are resurrected in standpoint theory's appeal to women's lives. As feminists working in many quarters have by now recognized, basing feminist knowledge in any transparent appeal to women's experience tends to homogenize "woman" as a universal and obvious category. It also tends to lock into the structures of feminist epistemology a binary opposition between male and female which naturalizes gender and erases the other social categories across which "woman" is defined. Appeals to experience in feminist work invariably tend to draw the theorist back to biological women and obscure the distinction between feminist and women-centered work (Grant, 111).[3]

These problems appear most emphatically in feminist standpoint theory when women's lives are defined primarily in relation to men. Sandra Harding, for instance, argues that in order to count as a standpoint and not just a claim about listening to women narrate their experiences, feminist theory must insist on women's lives as the place where feminist research should begin. In her early work she takes men and women to be fundamentally (and presumably in some ways obviously) distinct genders (*The Science Question*). Harding later stresses that the concept of gender does not in itself reveal how the social distinctions between the sexes are mediated in historically specific ways by a symbolic order of gender, race, and class difference. In her current work Harding acknowledges that standpoint theory contains within its logic an essentializing tendency—that is, its positionality is defined in terms of reified differences between groups. And she concedes that this focus is at the expense of clearly addressing how differences traverse identities (*Whose Science*, 177). But she also contends that the logic of standpoint contains the resources to combat this tendency (ibid., 178).

Exactly what these resources are isn't entirely clear, however. In part they are embedded in the discourses Harding cites that deconstruct the objectivity of Science and feminism's unitary subject, discourses that hint women need not be the unique generators of feminist knowledge and that promise to align feminism with other liberatory projects. For all of the rhetorical power of these assertions, however, Harding's elaboration of standpoint theory marks the ways in which a theory of standpoint rooted in a notion of "position" as the objective condition of *people's lives* strains against postmodern formulations of "position" as *discursive*. The question is whether postmodern knowledges, which have been so important in the development of western feminism's challenge to the humanist subject and rational-empiricist foundations for knowledge, have also made appeals to the objective condition of women's lives untenable as the ground for feminist theory.

Postmodern theories of the subject-in-language have provided feminist standpoint theory with useful frameworks for conceptualizing "woman" as differentially and discursively constructed. One effect has been heightened attention to discursive positionality with minimal analysis of the relationship between the discursive and the nondiscursive in explaining "women's lives." We see this played out in feminist standpoint theories like Harding's, which admire the potential of postmodern formulations of the subject's positionality and at times equate "subject positions" and "woman's lives," even as they hint that the relationship between the lived world of women and their narratives of it are not coterminous ("Subjectivity"). If the subject is theorized as an ensemble of discursive positions, are women's lives both discursive and nondiscursive, and if so, how are we to understand their relation?

It is important to remember, as Harding points out, that the usefulness of postmodern theories of the subject to feminism has been compounded by their historical intersection with critiques from within feminism of feminism's exclusive focus on gender. Theorists like Norma Alarcón, Cheyla Sandoval, Chandra Mohanty, Cherrie Moraga, Gayatri Spivak, and others have emphasized that the insistent primary focus on gender in Anglo-American feminist theory reinscribes the subject of western feminism in the racist imperialism and empiricism upon which Eurocentric epistemology depends. As Norma Alarcón has argued,

> with gender as the central concept in feminist thinking, epistemology is flattened out in such a way that we lose sight of the complex and multiple ways in which the subject and object of possible experience are constituted. The flattening effect is multiplied when one considers that gender is often solely related to white men. There's no inquiry into the knowing subject beyond the fact of being a "woman." But what is a "woman" or a "man" for that matter? (361)

Alarcón implies in this essay that in their refusal of binary or dualistic thinking the critical voices of "women of color" who claim a "multiple self" speak as much out of the postmodern crisis of subjectivity as the discourses of Derrida, Foucault, or Lyotard. She emphasizes that an epistemological shift away from the class-based ethnocentrism of the Anglo-American subject of consciousness will have to take into account "that we are culturally constituted in and through language in complex ways" (364). And she suggests that addressing this complexity will require attention to the historically-specific social arrangements difference organizes.

Postmodern feminists have, of course, also affirmed the inadequacy of the subject-in-difference to a humanist notion of experience as the ground for knowledge, and they have at times acknowledged that postmodern feminist attention to difference issues from a critique within feminism. In the words of Naomi Schor, "no proper name, masculine or feminine, can be attached to this critique as its legitimating source; it arises from the plurivocal discourses of black, Chicana, lesbian, first and third world feminist thinkers and activists" ("The Essentialism Which Is Not One," 42). How these plurivocal discourses, the voices of dissent within feminist theory, are being understood is a crucial feature of the rewriting of feminism's theoretical subject now. The "difference" of these voices of dissent is not explained by Schor, but instead is just described as plurivocal discourses. As a result, the materiality of their critiques is mystified. In contrast, Cherríe Moraga's bald statement that "in this country lesbianism is a poverty—as is being brown, as is being a woman, as is being just plain poor" (29) links the difference of being lesbian, Chicana, poor—and its potential critical force—to a hierarchical economy of signification inextricably imbricated in the political economy of wealth. The critical power of difference for feminism, Moraga suggests, is the effect of much more than plurivocal discourses.

In that it stresses the social constructedness of "speaking from," standpoint theory's claim to ground its knowledges in research on women's lives is distinct from analyses that profess to speak from women's experience. But substituting women's lives for the empirical given of "women's experience" doesn't in itself explain the material relation between lives and ways of making sense. Echoing Alarcón, Mary Hawkesworth has argued that this is because the feminist standpoint "fails to grasp the manifold ways in which all human experiences . . . are mediated by theoretical presuppositions embedded in language and culture" (544). Hawkesworth's suggestion doesn't solve the problems raised by Harding's standpoint logic in which the subject of feminism both *is* and *is not* discursive. Nor does it address the question of the materiality of discourse raised by Schor's and Moraga's statements. But her proposal that a serious response to the postmodern critique of empiricism would shift the grounds for feminist epistemology's claims to truth from women's experience to a feminist perspective does imply that a radical paradigm shift might be necessary in order to rewrite the ambiguous materiality of feminism's subject as standpoint theory currently posits it.

Hawkesworth's call for understanding knowledge as cognitive practice poses some problems of its own, however. She argues that knowing is involved in a social process "replete with rules of compliance, norms of assessment, and standards of excellence that are humanly created" (549), a formulation that critiques the empiricist notion of knowledge as unmediated access to the world. The alternative she proposes—understanding knowledge as a cognitive practice— treats cognition as a social event. But her notion of the social event confines knowledge practices to a very restricted, empiricist rationality. And her pragmatic view of social practice forfeits standpoint theory's systemic concept of social relations which has been an important feature of its materialist problematic. In her proposal, the materiality of the "theoretical presuppositions" we take up— that is, how they are invested in an array of political and economic interests, and how they come to shape social arrangements and social hierarchies—is never addressed.

In this respect, Hawkesworth's neo-pragmatist revision of standpoint theory is similar to Sandra Harding's suggestions for feminist epistemology. Both confront the incoherence in standpoint epistemology's privileging and universalizing of woman's position. Both argue for replacing feminism's desire to unify around women's common experiences with a political solidarity based on goals shared with other groups struggling against western hegemony. And both attach these arguments to a rejection of systemic analysis. Like Hawkesworth's call for a practice of cognition, Harding's contention that feminism needs to embrace the instability of theoretical categories is problematic, because in celebrating instability it forestalls *explanation* of the structures of power to which knowledges are connected and their overdetermined relation to other social practices. Harding suggests that "the distinctive characteristics of women's activities" are also to be found in the "labor and social experience of other subjugated groups" ("Instability," 659), but the relationship of this activity to women's discursive positioning or to a subject of feminist knowledge in which race, class, and sexuality cannot be separated is not worked through. Harding contends that white, western, bourgeois feminists should "attend to the need for a more theoretical and political struggle against our own racism, classism, and cultural centrism." But it is "history" rather than our analytic efforts "that will resolve or dissolve this problem" of how cultural differences prevent our federating around shared goals (ibid., 660). What is the relationship between "history" and "our analytic efforts," our ways of making sense? Harding never says. This unexplained relation between history and theory, like the space between women's lives (labor, activity) and the feminist standpoint that will make sense of them, points to the need for further work.

Donna Haraway's now widely read "Manifesto for Cyborgs" radically rewrites any stable notion of identity on which standpoint theory's appeal to women's lives depends even as it draws upon similar explanatory frameworks. This essay is important to standpoint theory for Haraway's use of a systemic analysis to detail the objective conditions that shape women's alienated labor, and for her formulation of the cyborg as emblem for a new feminist subject. Haraway acknowledges at the start that a transparent identity as women has become historically unavailable for western feminists. Her proposal for an "ironic political myth faithful to feminism, socialism, materialism" (65) outlines an alternative politics rooted in the changes that have transformed an industrial society to a polymorphous information system. And it is out of this history that she offers the figure of the cyborg as the new self feminists must code (82).

Drawn from the economic and technological forces which have produced an "informatics of domination," the cyborg is an imaginative resource for rethinking the dualisms and accompanying organic, totalizing visions on which western knowledges have been based. As an alternative to the natural female identity implicit in feminist appeals to "woman," the cyborg underscores Haraway's argument that "woman" is no longer adequate as a category on which to ground feminist rhetoric, now that being female has been shown to be a "highly complex category constructed in contested scientific discourses and other social practices" (72). With its double face of technocratic domination and counteridentity resistance, the cyborg challenges all that the goddess signified as emblem of feminine/feminist authority and displaces this talisman of a powerful, transcendent, female self with a metaphor for the post-gender, postmodern, pulverized subject of late capitalism and the resistant regenerative dynamics of oppositional affinity.

Haraway's manifesto is framed in a dazzling catalogue of the multiform and globally expansive features of the technological revolution of late capitalism. She brilliantly details their effects on the mobility of capital, divisions of labor, and women's historical locations in advanced industrial societies. For all the subtlety and scope of her accounting, however, there is a tension in this essay between two ways of formulating what amounts to the feminist standpoint, a tension that has much to do with the problematic relationship between—to use Sandra Harding's phrase—history and "our analytic efforts." At times the feminist standpoint is represented by the anti-myth of the cyborg; at other times it is figured by the distinctly different logic of women in the integrated circuit. The effect is that the manifesto's political narrative offers two conflicting conceptions of the authority for feminist resistance. In one instance that authority derives from group affinity; in the other it depends upon a particular way of making sense of the world. Each of these logics is encoded in the conflicting conceptions of subjectivity the cyborg embraces: a personal/group identity and a disassembled/reassembled postmodern collective.

For Haraway "women of color" constitute the prototypical instance of both—"a potent subjectivity synthesized from fusions of outsider identities" (93). Although her analysis makes visible the racism on which the cyborgean "preferred labor force" for science-based industrial societies depends, the analogy between cyborg and "women of color" does not explain the relationship between identity—even group identities—founded on appeals to an empirical marker of group affiliation and identity as discursive positioning. Moreover, as at least one of her critics has pointed out, the fetishization of skin in Haraway's "women of color" metaphor can be read as yet another romantic attribution by white feminists to minority women of *the* authentic oppositional politics (Scott, "Commentary," 217).

In conceptualizing "women of color" as a conflation of outsider identities, Haraway equates ways of knowing with (group) identity or alliance and so underscores one of the essay's two logics for standpoint. At other points in the essay, however, she presents feminist knowledge as the effect of either "elementary units of socialist feminist analysis" (91) or a "powerful infidel heteroglossia"

(101). The "elements of socialist feminist analysis" appear in the form of Haraway's history of women in the integrated circuit. The feminist subject in this narrative does not rest upon a reified group identity. Rather, it speaks a discourse that explains relations between economic, political, and cultural domains and presents the social as "a historical system depending upon structured relations among people" (85). This feminist knowledge locates women historically in advanced industrial societies from a standpoint which resists a totalizing vision and yet does not forfeit a systemic one.

But this formulation is at odds with Haraway's presentation of feminist knowledge in the essay's closing metaphor: the image of women speaking in tongues. Certainly, the metaphor of a powerful infidel heteroglossia subverts feminism's one-time "dream of a common language" and exposes the totalizing mythology that supported this desire for sameness. But this celebration of difference as multiplicity *within* signification is suspiciously like those postmodern discourses whose promotions of heteroglossia, local strategy, play, and pleasure celebrate difference for its own sake and at the expense of unhinging it from its overdetermined structuration in systems of exclusion and exploitation. That is, difference here is divorced from a social logic in which social activity operates systemically. In this logic systems of signification, power, resource allocation, and divisions of labor overlap and affect one another in such a way that differences are structured hierarchically.

The emphasis on knowledge as local and indeterminate which is finally endorsed in Haraway, Harding, and Hawkesworth situates the feminist standpoint in a logic which to varying degrees disclaims that social arrangements are systemically interrelated. In contrast, Dorothy Smith's contributions to feminist standpoint theory conceptualize modes of knowing within a much more emphatically systemic analytic.[4] Smith's critique of the patriarchal power relations inscribed in the social sciences foregrounds the ways in which the disciplining of knowledge operates much like the logic of the commodity. She makes visible the ways disciplines produce both economic and ideological value by occluding the dependence of their dominant conceptual modes and their administering subjects on the work of invisible subservient groups—women, blacks, working-class people. These are the workers who feed and care for administrators and clean their work places even as their "experiences" are excluded from the ruling regimes of truth their labor supports ("Women's Perspective").[5] At some points in her analysis Smith problematizes the notion of experience as the self-evident ground for knowledge. But more often than not she relies upon an empiricist division between the subject and object of knowledge. Even though she appropriates Foucault's conception of discourse, frequently she refers to women's "direct experience" as the basis for feminist knowledge ("Femininity"). Smith says that she retreats from the radical critique of the subject-object division on which Foucault's theory of discourse is premised in order to resist what she reads as his overtextualizing of social relations. But her alternative analysis tends to jockey between the objective conditions of women's lives and the discursive construction of the feminine rather than explaining more fully the material relationship between them.

In her critical overview of the uses of poststructuralism for feminist politics, Linda Alcoff implicitly advances Smith's provisional and contradictory appropriation of the Foucauldian concept of discourse ("Cultural Feminism"). Alcoff's notion of gendered identity as positionality, like Smith's and Harding's concepts of the feminist standpoint, sees women's lives as a necessary point of departure for a feminist epistemology, but she understands that referent in terms of a discursively positioned rather than an experiential subject. In an effort to hold on to the "agency" which she sees post modern theories of the subject dispelling, however, Alcoff calls for an uneasy—and ultimately incompatible—amalgam of postmodern and humanist subjectivities: a subject who can "choose" the discursive positions she occupies:

> the concept of positionality allows for a determinate though fluid identity of woman that does not fall into essentialism . . . being a "woman" is to take up a position within a moving historical context and to be able to *choose* what we make of this position and how we alter this context. (435, emphasis mine)

Like identity and experience, the notion of "choice," so embedded historically in the humanist ideology of the "free" individual, cannot simply be invoked within a postmodern theoretical framework. Along with other categories linked to the free individual, it has to be rewritten so as to map out more coherently the mechanisms—both discursive and nondiscursive—that affect the historical availability of particular positions to some subjects and not others as well as movements across and between them.

One of the primary theoretical questions these various versions of the feminist standpoint leave open is how to understand the relationship between "women's lives"—as at least in part discursively constructed—and the subject of feminism. That is, how can the grounds for feminist knowledge be formulated congruently with new notions of the subject-in-language so as to maintain both some oppositional power and specificity for feminism as a political practice? Alternative ways to address these impasses in feminist standpoint theory are suggested, I think, by considering discourse as ideology.

II

Some of the most useful advances in theorizing the materiality of language and its function in the formation of the subject have arisen out of elaborations of Louis Althusser's work on ideology.[6] Foregrounding the material and productive role of ideology in social arrangements, Althusser's theory of ideology stimulated developments in postmodern marxist and feminist formulations of the discursive construction of the subject. As is now commonly acknowledged, Althusser's theory of ideology has also been widely critiqued and for several important reasons. His understanding of ideology's role in social reproduction has been seen as overly functionalist, and his concept of interpellation has made theorizing subversive agency difficult. These problems have been compounded by questions from feminist quarters about the adequacy of Althusserian marxism's homogenous class subject for emancipatory movements that are not organized primarily around class.

There are, however, some important features of a post-Althusserian theory of ideology which have been useful to materialist feminist efforts to rethink what is meant by "standpoint." Chief among them is the way this theory understands the materiality of language. As the medium of social action and the mechanism through which subjects are constructed, ideology produces what can be seen, heard, spoken, thought, believed, valued—in other words, what counts as socially made "reality." Ideology is overdetermined in the sense that in any particular historical formation it is both shaped by and in turn helps delimit the contradictory development and displacement of economic and political forces. To say that ideology is a material force in that it (re)produces what counts as reality suggests that other material forces, both economic and political, are not merely reflected in ideology but that they, too, are at least in part shaped by ideology. Such an understanding of the materiality of ideology reformulates the empiricist notion of materiality based in an objective reality outside discourse by including the discursive within the materiality out of which the social is produced. As Althusser has argued, "the raw material which is the object of knowledge is distinct from the real object in that the raw material is ever already elaborated and transformed by the imposition of the complex structure which defines it as an object of knowledge" (*Reading Capital*, 43). This notion of the materiality of knowledge rests on a distinction between the Real object (or the actual world) and the object of knowledge. The Real object is a material force, but it is unavailable except through the modes of intelligibility or discourses which comprise the object of knowledge. From the vantage point of ideology, the material can be understood as that which intervenes in production of the social real by being *made* intelligible.[7] At the same time, the discourses that constitute the *material* structures through which ideology works are shaped by the *material* relations which comprise economic and political practices. This means that "reality," whether in the form of "women's lives" or the feminist standpoint, is always social. It is an ideological construct whose parameters are unevenly and contradictorily shaped in specific historical moments by divisions of labor and relations between state and civil society.

In developing theories of ideology beyond the limits of Althusser's problematic, neo-marxists, and feminists among them, have recognized the usefulness of Gramsci's concept of hegemony for conceptualizing the discursive face of power. Gramsci's theory of hegemony seems to avoid many of the impasses in Althusser's notion of ideology while still maintaining the distinguishing global social logic in which it is formulated.[8] According to Gramsci, hegemony is the process whereby a ruling group comes to dominate by establishing the cultural common sense, that is, those values and beliefs that go without saying. Significantly, as Laclau and Mouffe recognize, the concept of hegemony also suggests that cultural power is not simply exercised from the top down, but instead is negotiated and contested through a process of discursive articulation. The concept of "articulation" is a crucial feature of hegemony because it makes possible a critical theory of ideology and of feminist standpoint as critique as well as explaining more specifically the dynamics of discursive positionality.[9]

Ideology for Gramsci is a productive and material force inscribed in multiple political and cultural apparatuses including, most notably, intellectual and moral discourses. Gramsci emphasizes, however, that the coherent ideological discourse which hegemonic arrangements create is forged out of ideological struggle. The objective of ideological struggle is not to reject the entire ideological formation but to reconfigure it, to sift through its elements and see which ones can serve to maintain the interests of a new ruling group (Mouffe, *Gramsci,* 192). The universal appeal which unifies any hegemonic bloc therefore includes ideological elements from varying discourses, but its cultural power stems from an articulating principle which is always shaped by, at the same time it helps shape, the contradictory social arrangements it serves to maintain. The values and norms a hegemonic formation enforces are the result of the way in which elements from various contesting discourses are drawn into a coherent frame of intelligibility. The struggle to reconfigure a hegemonic ideology or the prevailing regimes of truth is, then, both a process of contesting the articulating principle within a hegemonic formation and a process of disarticulating discourses from one frame of intelligibility in order to rearticulate them in another. Any articulation, however, will always be an ensemble whose particular contents can never be determined in advance, but are specific to the forces at work in the struggle for hegemony in any historical moment (Gramsci, 333).

The theory of ideology implicit in the concept of hegemony is "critical" in the sense that ideology is no longer thought to be a monolithic determining force, but rather an articulated ensemble of contesting discourses which produce what comes to count as "the way it is." This conception of ideology is related to Althusser's distinction between Ideology and ideologies. In any historical moment there are only ideologies; but their circulation is bound to the (re)production of "reality" through the process of hegemonic articulation. The dominating ideology never dominates without contradiction. Therefore it cannot exhaust all social experience. It potentially contains space for alternative discourses which are not yet articulated as a social institution or even project.[10] As a result of the articulatedness of the hegemonic ideology, there will never exist any hegemonic discourse without slips or cracks in its coherence. And it is the potentially subversive force of these slips that constitutes the epistemological basis or the authority of ideology critique.

In order to explain the relationship between the discursive materiality of women's lives and feminism as a counterhegemonic discourse, we need to understand more specifically how articulation occurs. Michel Pecheux's elaboration of a post-Althusserian materialist theory of discourse is helpful here. Pecheux attends to the textuality of ideology and draws connections between signification and discourse in ways that make his work particularly useful to feminist efforts to address the historical and discursive construction of "woman." Like Althusser, Pecheux argues that marxism's authority rests upon its break from the epistemology of the subject on which other bourgeois knowledges are founded. According to Pecheux, marxism is a science in that it is a discourse *without a subject.* Instead, he contends, it is a discourse that *works on* the category of the subject. Giving marxism the status of a discourse without a subject has the effect of situating it on the same foundationalist grounds *outside ideology* as empiricist science. Pecheux's notion of marxism's scientificity as well as his reductive understanding of class, like Althusser's theory from which they derive, have been critiqued for the impediments they pose to theorizing the discursive production of a counterhegemonic feminist subject. But his analysis of the textuality of ideology can be reworked within a theory of hegemony which is useful for feminism as an emancipatory project.

Developing Althusser's notion of meaning as the effect of the struggle over words, Pecheux contends that it is through the discourses in which words are used that subjects take up positions. These positions are antagonistic as a result of struggles which traverse discourses but which also extend outside them. This means that what is at stake in the struggle over meaning is not just words or discourses, but a whole set of social arrangements. But because meaning in most discursive formations is presented as transparent, the complex of discursive formations that make up the hegemonic and the social organization they secure is concealed (Pecheux, *Language,* 113).

Pecheux devises the concept of the *interdiscourse* to explain the textuality of hegemony. It is a very useful concept because it allows us to conceptualize in much more specific terms the discursive processes by means of which subjects are produced and the common sense maintained. As Pecheux formulates it, the interdiscourse consists of two features: the *preconstructed* and *articulation*. The preconstructed is the feature of any discursive formation that produces the effect of an "always already there," conveying the sense of what everyone already knows. Articulation is both the means by which the subject is constituted in the dominant discourse and the discursive mechanism that determines the domination of the dominant form. It operates through a process Pecheux calls the *transverse discourse* which establishes relations of part to whole, cause to effect. The *intradiscourse* is the set of co-references that secure the thread of discourse as the discourse of a subject; it is the set of linear connections between what I am saying now and what I said before and after (ibid., 116). The intradiscourse thus crosses and connects together preconstructed discursive elements. It appears as intradiscursive reminders—"as I have said"—that provide subjective coherence and universalizing gestures—"as everyone knows," or "as everyone can see" (ibid., 121). The articulation or sustaining effect of discourse is the result of the linearization of the transverse discourse in the axis of the intradiscourse, or the operation of discourse with respect to itself. The discursive process is thus a system of relationships of substitution and paraphrase which operate between discursive elements or signifiers in a given discursive formation (ibid., 113). The values which form the backbone of a hegemonic formation are the product of the interdiscourse. To the extent that it exercises a limit on the formation of subjectivities and the social real, the interdiscourse functions as the homogenizing force of ideology.

As the articulating principle, the preconstructed has a key role in helping to delay and impede the process of rearticulating existing discursive structures. Even under the guise of reform, it works to maintain traditional paradigms by means of a symbolic order of differences onto which discourses are articulated. The naturalizing effect of the preconstructed reifies these differences and so helps to perpetuate categories of alterity as universal givens. The preconstructed thus becomes a useful concept for examining at the level of discourse the complex interrelations between and among the various nodal points along which alterity is constructed. As the discursive space where the "always already there" secures a hierarchical social arrangement through an "obvious" system of oppositions, the preconstructed serves as an anchor in the symbolic order for the articulation of subjectivities across race, class, gender, and other salient differences. While specific articulations of these differences will vary within each historical formation, depending on the particular discourses comprising the interdiscourse, the reification of the hierarchical structuring of difference in the preconstructed constitutes a mechanism by which hegemony operates across social formations. Because the preconstructed is a crucial ideological regulator, it is a powerful site for critical intervention. Once the textual ambiguities concealed by its naturalizing operation are explained—not as a property of language but as the displacement and condensation of the contradictions of patriarchal and capitalist social arrangements—the transformative potential of working on the construction of the subject in the interdiscourse can be unleashed.

Women's lives are shaped by ideology in the sense that their lived experience is never served up raw but is always made sense of from a host of vantage points, including those of the woman experiencing the events and those of the feminist critic, scholar, or theorist who appeals to women's lives as the basis for her knowledge. Woman's lives are only intelligible at all as a function of the ways of making sense of the world available in any historical moment. Understood as always ideologically constructed, women's lives can be read in terms of woman's contradictory position under capitalist and patriarchal arrangements where the symbolic economy of an opposition between man and woman comprises only one of the preconstructed anchors and articulating principles of the prevailing truths. The hierarchy often only thinly concealed within this opposition underwrites the ideological construction of the feminine as excess or lack, and is materialized from and in a corresponding unequal division of labor and allocation of social resources. The concept of the interdiscourse allows us to consider at the level of textuality the discursive mechanisms whereby "women's lives" are constructed across a range of articulated discourses, the effect of a series of subject positions sutured into or against the interdiscourse in any historical formation.

Understanding "women's lives" from *this* vantage point makes it possible to consider how the patriarchal gender system is imbricated with other nodal points on which difference is articulated so that the categories of gender and sex have not always been congruently integrated in the interdiscourse of patriarchal ideologies. As the discourses of imperialism demonstrate, the patriarchal gender system can be disarticulated from sex differences and rearticulated onto racial or national difference in order to legitimize imperial interests. The construction of the colonial male in terms of feminine sexual excess is only one example that what counts as the "feminine" subject is not always merely a matter of empirical sex difference. However, while the ideological boundaries of the feminine are not limited by an essential female body, the construction of woman's reproductive capacity and sexuality as property to which masculine subjects can lay claim *has* been the cornerstone of a patriarchal social order whose genealogy precedes imperialist conquest and the emergence of sexuality as a discourse. The particular articulations of this reproductive/alienated female body and the interests they serve are, nonetheless, historically variable.

III

The concept of the interdiscourse makes available a way to advance contemporary materialist feminist work on the representation of woman which takes as its starting point a systemic theory of the social. Crucial to this project are debates on how to read the figuration of the feminine as "excess" in the symbolic economy of western patriarchal culture. Materialist feminists have read critically postmodernism's focus on femininity as the supplementary figure that exceeds the bounds of the symbolic order, threatening from within the stability of its economy. Theorists as loosely aligned as Teresa de Lauretis, Alice Jardine, Mary Poovey, and Gayatri Spivak have pointed to the double-edged political/ ideological effects for feminism of deconstruction's equation of the feminine with *différance*, charging that reading the feminine as a trope for excess reifies and reinforces the patriarchal symbolic system.[11] Displacing the question of the feminine onto an ahistorical, purely textual figure has the effect of rendering invisible the nexus of hierarchies that the modalities of difference are entangled in and the exploitative social relations they serve in any historical moment. To the extent that it strips the textual construction of feminine excess of its historicity, deconstruction helps to undermine feminist claims upon this excess as the textual mark of patriarchy, and in this way it reinforces broader ideological efforts both inside the academy and elsewhere to neutralize feminism as a political movement. Materialist feminists have also addressed the ways feminist theory—particularly French feminist treatments of feminine excess—has contributed to this conservative hegemonic reconfiguration. As distinct as they are, the theories of Kristeva, Irigaray, and Cixous share a common argument for the feminine as that which disrupts the (male) symbolic order. But by equating this symbolic excess with a feminine body prior to the word, their demystification of the patriarchal symbolic order reconfigures the feminine in terms of the very equations (Masculine-logos = Culture :: Feminine-excess = Nature) they set out to dismantle.[12]

Despite their strong objections to postmodern textualizations of the feminine, however, materialist feminist appropriations of postmodern theories of subjectivity have often led to impasses on exactly how to account for woman's eccentric position in the symbolic order in relation to feminist political opposition. A critical reading of Teresa de Lauretis' work offers a useful instance of how these problems are being addressed by a feminist whose work is increasingly being positioned at the "cutting edge" of feminist theory in the U.S., and opens a space to consider how they might be reframed in terms of the problematic I have presented above. From her earliest book, *Alice Doesn't* (1984), de Lauretis is indebted to Foucault whose work she credits with shifting the theoretical discourses of film theory away from reading cinema as art or a self-contained semiotic system to analysis of the ideological effects of cinema on its spectators (86). Her reading of Foucault offers a strong critique of his blindness to patriarchy and sexual differentiation, cautioning feminists on the implications of these "oversights" for theorizing an oppositional concept of power and resistance (ibid., 94). However, her turn to Kristeva's formulation of feminine negativity as a more productive explanation of "a radical and irreducible difference" avoids the problems of Foucault's "paradoxical conservatism" (ibid.) only by taking up a discourse that reifies sexual difference and reverses the patriarchal hierarchy by treating its feminine term as the figure for "that which is not represented . . . that which is left out of namings and ideologies" (ibid., 95). This critical conjuncture situates de Lauretis' early work precisely within the interdiscursive space where Foucault's and Kristeva's analytics overlap, a space which, as I have indicated in the previous chapter, serves to re-form the western hegemonic subject on the Same (preconstructed) terrain. As my argument there implies, moving from Foucault's formulation of resistance in terms of bodies and pleasures to Kristeva's feminine negativity as symbolic excess does not reframe the question of feminine resistance/excess in historical materialist terms but rather locates this excess, as well as the grounds for resistance it offers, outside a historical symbolic economy altogether. The tension within de Lauretis' work on the feminine subject, then, is less the effect of the contradictions between her appropriation of a Foucauldian and a French feminist analytic than it is the result of the ways both subvert her professed commitment to historicizing the discursive construction of the subject by locating feminine resistance in an indeterminate space.

The terms of this elusiveness shift somewhat from essay to essay across her work, but its general contours are indicative of the ideological crisis western feminism is struggling to negotiate in rethinking "woman" and the relationship of feminism's critical stance to the symbolic order. In the introductory essay to her second book, *Technologies of Gender* (1987), she addresses the disruption of feminism's singular subject, "woman," by way of a critique of how feminist thinking is bound within the frame of a universal sex opposition "which makes it very difficult to articulate the differences of Woman from women, that is to say the differences among women, or perhaps more exactly, the differences *within* women" (1–2). However, her argument that Foucault's notion of "technologies" can be used to think through the relationship between sex and gender ultimately abandons the effort to "articulate the differences of Woman from woman" and focuses exclusively on gender as the primary category of difference. By the end of this essay it is precisely "the movement in and out of gender as ideological representation" which comes to constitute the subject of feminism (ibid., 26).

Not only does gender become the prime category of feminist theory at this point in de Lauretis' work, defining both its subject and object, but gender itself as a category of analysis is bound to a (preconstructed) assumption of sexual difference. Thus she can assert at one point that femininity is not any more or less outside discourse than anything else; it has to be understood "not as a biological difference that lies before or beyond signification, or as a culturally constructed object of masculine desire, but as a semiotic difference—a different production of reference and meaning" (ibid., 48). But she can also argue at another point in the same essay that the problem with Foucault—and with the larger culture in general—is not that sexuality is not gendered ("as having a male form and a female form") but that it is exclusively male (ibid., 37). This charge is drawn from Luce Irigaray's contention that all western discourses on sexuality are male-centered, a critique inscribed in Irigaray's neologism—"hommosexuality"—which emphasizes the male (*homme*)-centeredness even of homo-sexuality. De Lauretis contends that feminine otherness or "excess" is not grounded in biological difference, but is rather "a space-off, the elsewhere of hegemonic discourses" (ibid., 26, 36). But the assumption that gender is based on "a male form and a female form" undermines this argument, even in the very suggestive analysis of lesbian representation in her later work.

In the essay "Sexual Indifference and Lesbian Representation" (1988), de Lauretis contends that within the dominant conceptual frame of heterosexual patriarchal sexual desire women are assumed to desire "the same" as men. As a result, female desire for the self-same cannot be recognized. The woman whose object of desire is another woman is figured within the symbolic economy of *hommo*sexual desire as the mannish lesbian. De Lauretis argues that representations of the lesbian as sexual subject are still caught in this paradox of socio-sexual (in)difference, unable to think *hommo*-sexuality and homosexuality at once separately and together. The female homosexual subject is *hommo*sexualized as butch and the excessive sexuality of her female "object" choice is altogether occluded.

Certainly this critique is an important intervention in the symbolic economy of heterosexuality. It points to the boundaries of intelligibility—the preconstructed nodal points—which define both the unthought of the discourse of (hetero)sexuality and the conditions of possibility for lesbian representation. Furthermore, in this essay, more than in her earlier work, de Lauretis deals with intersections between sexuality and other modalities of difference, most notably in her allusions to the metaphor of "passing" as it intersects the boundaries of racial and sexual positionality in texts by Audre Lorde, Jewel Gomez, and Cherrie Moraga. And her analysis of the relationship between a heterosexual frame of intelligibility and representations of lesbian desire that exceed that frame do explore the shifting historical shapes representations of feminine "excess" assume. Nonetheless, her overall argument that lesbian representations are caught in the paradox of socio-sexual (in)difference assumes that sexual difference is based on a transhistorical binary relation. This assumption wrenches the contradictions which the discourse of sexuality manages from their historical and material forms into the realm of an *a priori* sexual difference. Despite her invocation of Foucauldian technologies, the effect is to reinforce a reified femininity and sexuality. The equation of gender with sexual difference circumscribes her own problematic in such a way that her insights into the heterosexual assumption on which the discourse of sexuality is premised cannot extend to a reading of the multiple modalities of difference the discourse of (*hommo*)sexuality has historically helped suture. Thus the slip from treating gender as discourse to reading it as originary sexual difference helps guarantee the ideological boundaries around "woman" as an obvious and universal category. The significance of these limits is most telling in her essay "The Essence of the Triangle" (1989).

Here de Lauretis proposes that feminist theory should follow the lead of the Milan Bookstore Collective and consider taking the risk of essentialism, a risk which entails assuming "the notion of an originary or primary character of sexual difference" (17). She claims that this argument is less a biological or metaphysical view of woman's difference "(from man)" than a "historical materialist analysis of the 'state of emergency' in which we live as feminists, and as such is more a difference of symbolization, a different production of reference and meaning out of a particular embodied knowledge" (ibid., 27). This particular "embodied knowledge" marks for de Lauretis an "epistemological rupture in the continuum of Western thought" (27), a rupture whose theoretical strength rests upon its "radical and uncompromisingly separatist stance" (27). In examining the barrage of objections the Milan Bookstore Collective's work has received, de Lauretis details the ways in which the embodied knowledge they call for is code for a lesbian desire and identity that have remained "the great unsaid" of the Italian feminist movement. For de Lauretis the panicked response to the Milan Bookstore's separatist argument is an index of the heterosexual fundamentalism that continues to structure feminist thinking not only in Italy but also in North America. The Italian example thus becomes a vehicle for de Lauretis' charge that what motivates the construction of a fantom form of essentialism on the part of Anglo-American feminists "may be less the risk of essentialism itself than the future risk which that entails: the risk of challenging directly the social symbolic institution of heterosexuality" (32).

Before pursuing the implications of this argument, it is important to note that de Lauretis claims the Italian feminist call for essentialism is historically enabled by a social formation (Italy) where race or color have not been an issue. This is a most revealing comment on the standpoint from which she writes here. The claim is, first of all, a "misrepresentation" not only of the Italian social formation but of the essay's "other" audience: Anglo-American feminists debating the merits of essentialism. For the latter, race—as well as class—differences are very much an issue. Moreover, such a claim can only be made for western feminism—of any national stripe—if the operation of patriarchy in the west is shorn from its implication in capital's global interests and viewed in the most local and reified of terms. And it is exactly this which de Lauretis does, basing her model of feminist practice on "the conceptual and discursive space of a female genealogy" which "can effectively mediate woman's relation to the symbolic, allowing her self-definition as female being or female-gendered speaking subject" (ibid., 15).

For de Lauretis and the Milan Bookstore Collective, taking the risk of essentialism means overturning the presupposition of an originary Man and the prescription to think sexual difference as a derivative of this "monstrous universal." Instead feminist theory can begin with "an absolute dual," a conceptualization of "being man" and "being woman" as originary forms of being. This originary duality allows women to reclaim their difference in the form of "the symbolic mother," a notion of women's knowledges and existence as subjects "not altogether separate from male society yet autonomous from male definition and dominance" (25). De Lauretis uses this example of Italian feminist theory to enjoin Anglo-American feminists to re-examine the ways their criticisms of essentialism mask a hesitation to challenge the institution of heterosexuality. However, the terms of the critique of heterosexuality she outlines here, hinged to her endorsement of the notion of the symbolic mother and an originary sexual duality, retain a homogenized notion of woman which obfuscates patriarchy's historical and material conditions of possibility and the complex ways women are differentiated within them.

This position on essentialism is substantially elaborated and somewhat modified, however, in her essay "Eccentric Subjects: Feminist Theory and Historical

Consciousness" (1990). Here she addresses the problem of consciousness as an organizing concept for feminist thought, examining how it has been shaped by various phases of feminist thinking on "woman" since the seventies. In its initial phase, feminist theory posed woman as paradoxically both captive and absent in discourse. It is only in the latest stage of feminist thought—what de Lauretis calls its "post-colonial mode"—that woman has been thought in terms of a subject multiply positioned across variable axes of difference, redefinitions of theory and of identity (Eccentric Subjects, 116). In making her argument for how this phase of feminist theory might be enhanced, de Lauretis places herself squarely within the discourses of materialist feminism, tracing the salient issues in feminist theorizing about consciousness and identity through the work of De Beauvoir, MacKinnon, Hartsock, Delphy, and Wittig. But for her it is the critiques of feminism from writings of women of color and lesbians in the eighties that mark the turn in materialist feminism—and, although she doesn't acknowledge it, in her own work—away from a discourse that was "anchored in the single axis of gender as sexual difference . . . and that was finding itself stalemated once again in the paradox of woman" (ibid., 131).

De Lauretis details the effects this disengendering of feminism has had on the gradual drafting of a new feminist notion of identity. This new subject of feminist consciousness is "unlike the one that was initially defined by the opposition of woman to man on the axis of gender and purely constituted by the oppression, repression, or negation of its sexual difference" (ibid., 137). It is not unified but rather multiply organized across positions on several axes; it is capable of agency or "self-determined dis-location" (ibid.). In all of these respects this new subject provides the basis for de Lauretis' contribution to feminist standpoint theory, her rewriting of feminist consciousness as the eccentric subject.

In contrast to her earlier arguments for an essentialism founded in the symbolic mother, here de Lauretis takes her concept of standpoint from the materialist feminist premise that women's shared interests are based on "their specific condition of exploitation and domination, gender oppression, [which] affords them a standpoint, a position of knowledge and struggle" (ibid., 139). The process of claiming this standpoint, of coming to consciousness in a political movement, is for her what feminism is all about. Drawing upon the work of Catherine MacKinnon in particular, de Lauretis argues that feminism distinguishes itself from historical materialism by attending to experience. In doing so it brings about a new understanding of the political domain—redefining oppression as a political and subjective category "distinct from the economic, objective category of exploitation" (ibid., 140). I agree with de Lauretis that feminist theory broadens historical materialism's understanding of oppression by extending it to issues of subjectivity, the private and the personal. But I would argue that feminism's aims are best served if we do not treat subjectivity or "experience" as distinct from economic and political spheres. In severing subjectivity from other domains of social and material production the enormous critical potential of the feminist *important*

standpoint and of feminism's aims as an emancipatory social movement are undermined.

In keeping with her earlier work on feminine excess, de Lauretis uses the example of the lesbian to re-write the subject of experience as the "eccentric subject" of a feminist standpoint. But here she much more deliberately aligns the lesbian as resistant and critical subject with an array of other critical positions including Anzaldúa's "new mestiza" and Smith's "home girls." Encoded in her understanding of the lesbian as eccentric subject is an enormously important shift in her thinking on gender. Drawing upon the work of Monique Wittig, she argues, and this time with no ambiguity, that the power differential between men and women is not the effect of biological fact, but of the institution of heterosexuality (ibid., 128). Shifting the focus from the difference between men and women to this most taken-for-granted of institutions *is* a radical dislocation for feminist theory. And it is this critical position "conceptually apprehended outside or in excess of the sociocultural apparatus of heterosexuality through a process of 'unusual knowing' or a 'cognitive practice' " (ibid., 139) that she posits as an exemplary instance of the feminist standpoint.

Despite the ways in which her shift away from gender to the institution of heterosexuality re-directs the object of feminist critique toward the hegemonic arrangements which organize gender, there are several problems with this formulation of the feminist standpoint. For one, the enormous potential of making visible the "unsaid" of heterosexuality is compromised by unhinging that institution from its relation to economic and political forces. This dislocation is primarily the effect of the concept of oppression de Lauretis adopts from MacKinnon and Wittig, a theory of power that tends to separate the personal/experiential—the domain of subjectivity, of usual and unusual knowing—from other material practices. If her endorsement of Wittig's argument that "the struggle against the ideological apparatuses and socioeconomic institutions of women's oppression consists in refusing the terms of the heterosexual contrast" (143), it is not entirely clear from this essay what those socioeconomic institutions might be, or even how heterosexuality is related to them. As a result, the materiality of heterosexuality remains elusive.

So, too, is the materiality of the feminist standpoint, signified by the lesbian as "eccentric subject." Although she contends that this lesbian is not "an individual with a sexual preference" but a "rewriting of self," a subject constituted "in a process of interpretation and struggle" (ibid., 144), the lesbian is also, as the eccentric metaphor implies, a position outside or in excess of the discursive-conceptual horizon of heterosexuality, "experientially autonomous from institutional heterosexuality" (ibid., 143). While disavowing utopian or mythic notions of "lesbian society" as a world apart, this concept of the eccentric lesbian subject as outsider to heterosexuality occludes the ways in which the critique of heterosexuality, and lesbian subjectivity as a position circumscribed by that critique, emerges from contradictions within that institution and its discourses, just as the critique of patriarchy emerged from contradictions within *its* discourses. Claiming along with Wittig that lesbians are "not women," because to be lesbian is to reject or exceed the categories of a patriarchal gender system, has a certain strategic usefulness in denaturalizing the signifier "woman." But it also implies, as de Lauretis' earlier work does, that feminism's eccentric subject issues from autonomous spaces-off, that it is possible to *escape* the center, the institution of heterosexuality with its preconstructed gender system and hierarchies of race and class difference, merely by dislocating oneself.

The dream of escape here is bound up with the conception of "agency" (as opposed to choice) that underlies this "dis-placed point of articulation." De Lauretis does not explain how this agency works, except to indicate that it is not a *choice* since "one could not live there in the first place" (ibid., 138). How we think of this dislocation, this leaving-home of our feminist standpoint, is very much bound up with how we understand the materiality of consciousness, of subjectivity, and discourse. However, the use of metaphors of deterritorialization and dislocation often occlude the material conditions which have helped produce this "new" notion of agency. For de Lauretis, feminist theory's dislocation and reckoning with the materiality of its own standpoint as critical consciousness only came into its own in "a postcolonial mode." But post-coloniality here is simply a metaphor for a Foucauldian social analytic—an understanding of the social field as "a tangle of distinct and variable relations of power and points of resistance" (ibid., 131). In part because she works out of this (Foucauldian) social logic, de Lauretis cannot connect the discourses of postmodernity—of fragmented and multiply positioned subjects—with the workings of multinational capitalism. But it is exactly this connection that Gayatri Spivak has so forcefully asserted in her essay "Can the Subaltern Speak?" when she argues that the position of deterritorialized minority is available for the poststructuralist critic to choose precisely because the global encroachment of multinational capitalism makes unconstrained mobility possible. As Spivak's argument implies, formulating the subject of feminist critique as "eccentric" dislocation compromises our understanding of the historicity of subjectivities and of feminist critique, how their multiplicity and contradictoriness are forged out of struggles which are affected by the overdetermined entanglements of discursive and nondiscursive social arrangements.

Implicit in my argument with de Lauretis' notion of excess is a concept of alterity as ideology. Understood as ideology, alterity is integral to the historicity of the limits of acceptability in culture, a historicity which materialist feminism acknowledges as its own horizon. As ideology, alterity is not a reified Other outside discourse. Rather, the category of "other" is immanent in the texts of culture. It delimits the dominant discourses by marking out the negative pole of preconstructed categories, and by defining through the interdiscourse the boundaries of intelligibility. Otherness is not, then, ever wholly "eccentric" because it is always housed within the discourses that make up "the way things are." No more than feminists are born feminist, lesbians and "people of color" learn their "unusual ways of knowing" in and through the prevailing ways of making sense. Inhabiting the gaps in the coherence of the social imaginary, these critical positions disclose the arbitrariness and historicity of its boundaries. The "unthinkable" possibility of alter-native ways of making sense and the social arrangements they speak from is not absent from the hegemonic texts of culture, but merely suppressed or "underground" in them. Understood discursively, alterity does appear in the form of textual gaps and narrative *aporias* "holes" in the interdiscourse. But if we take these textual excesses to be gestures toward an eccentric or alter-narrative, it is important how we understand the materiality of this eccentricity, for this will have a bearing on our formulations of the feminist standpoint as the ground for critique. Positing the materiality of alterity as just a textual gap or narrative space-off not only situates other ways of knowing outside the hegemonic culture, it also confines them to the domain of culture. If this "alter" is understood as the textual mark of social contradiction, however, its materiality and the critical standpoint it enables can be tied to broad-ranging social arrangements. Read as symptoms of dis-ease in the coherence of the social imaginary, narrative gaps and spaces-off can be seen as potential sites for the irruption of oppositional alter-na(rra)tives aimed at nothing less than the transformation of the real.

IV

In order to foreground the systemic relations linking gender and sexuality to other modalities of difference, the powerful critique of heterosexual coherence Teresa de Lauretis offers would need to be disarticulated from the Foucauldian social logic that informs even her latest work and reformulated within a systemic analytic. To illustrate how this rearticulation might proceed, I want to turn to the specific instance of "woman's" inscription in hegemonic western culture in the nineteenth century. Foucault argues that during the nineteenth century sexuality in western culture became an "especially dense transfer point for the relations of power" (*HS*, 103). However, Foucault's analytic will not allow him to explain *why* sexuality came to be "endowed with the greatest instrumentality: useful for the greatest number of maneuvers and capable of serving as a point of support, as a linchpin for the most varied strategies" (ibid., 103). If his insights into the crucial function of sexuality in the formation of new social arrangements are articulated within a systemic theory of the social and of discourse as ideology, however, the role of sexuality in producing women's lives can be seen in relation to the overdetermined pressures brought to bear on the division of the social into separate spheres and the increasing demands for new markets during the transition to monopoly capitalism.[13]

In Foucault's narrative, relations of sex gave rise in every society to a deployment of alliance—a system of kinship ties. As economic processes and political structures could no longer rely on the family alliance as "an adequate instrument or sufficient support," a new apparatus—that of sexuality—was superimposed on this previous one (ibid., 106). The deployment of alliance has as one of its chief objectives "to reproduce the interplay of relations and maintain the law that governs them," while the deployment of sexuality "engenders a continual extension of areas and forms of control" (ibid.). Foucault never specifies what this governing law is that the system of alliance maintains, but we can write at least one of its tenets as the patriarchal institution of heterosexuality. Although alliance and sexuality are distinct apparatuses, each with its own particularities, historically they are interdependent. The anchor for this interdependence is the preconstructed axis which articulates sexuality to kinship alliances in "engendering" areas of control: in Wittig's terms, heterosexual coherence and its complementary patriarchal gender hierarchy.

Thinking of heterosexuality as one of the nodal points in the interdiscourse of capitalist-patriarchal gender ideology allows us to address the ways "the regulatory fiction of heterosexual coherence" is written into the cultural common sense as a way of making sense of sex difference.[14] Heterosexuality depends upon the assumption that sex differences are binary opposites and the simultaneous equation of this binary sex difference with gender. The naturalizing function of this equation contributes to the expressive model of the individual in that the opposition of the sexes is taken to be substantive, preceding social and historical bodies as an essence which the core of the self manifests. In disguising itself as a law of nature, this "fiction" regulates the sexual field it purports to describe (Butler, "Gender Trouble," 336). The fiction of heterosexual coherence is one of the most firmly entrenched and invisible anchors for the ideology of individualism. In naturalizing the organizing principles of identity it shores up the "tyranny of the proper" on which individualism relies and whose broad reaching effects in the west reinforce an international division of labor (Spivak, "Scattered Speculations," 86).

The heterosexual and patriarchal "family cell" on which the system of alliances depends provides sexuality with permanent support. It is the site where systems of sexuality, gender, and alliance are articulated. As Foucault puts it, "the family is the interchange of sexuality and alliance: it conveys the law . . . and it conveys the economy of pleasure . . . in the regime of alliance" (HS, 108). The four specific mechanisms of knowledge and power centering in sex which Foucault targets—the hysteriazation of women's bodies, the pedagogization of children's sex, the socialization of the couple as reproductive unit, and the psychiatrization of "perverse" pleasure—all reinforce a naturalized equation of sexuality and reproduction which assumes a heterosexual patriarchal gender system. The heterosexual paradigm embedded in the articulating discourses of the regimes of alliance and sexuality serves to guarantee that the deployment of sexuality, in itself potentially disruptive of the family alliance, is brought within the range of interests served by the family at the same time that alliance is being re-formed.

Including Foucault's insights into the function of sexuality within a systematic mode of analysis means that this contradictory feature of the discourse of sexuality can be explained in terms of its impact on the re-formation of the social imaginary and its overdetermined relation to political and economic practices. The ideological force that the discourse of sexuality exercises in disciplining subjects is specific to the crises posed by the transition to monopoly capitalism—and again, in a different figuration, in the transition to late capitalism. Feminist historians have addressed the ways the deployment of alliance in the form of the ideology of separate spheres binds the bourgeois family to a capitalist economy not only through the role it plays in the transmission or circulation of wealth, but also in the extraction of surplus value from women's productive labor in the home. Sexuality, in contrast, is linked to the re-formation of these arrangements. It affects the "free" market economy which is now dependent on a much more diffuse marketplace and consumer culture and operates via "various subtle relays," chief among them the body that produces and consumes (*HS*, 106). And it affects the political sphere as discourses of sexuality articulated within the legal apparatus provide new mechanisms for colonizing a host of practices in previously "private" spaces—the bedroom, schoolroom, examining room, library.

That the first body to be invested by the deployment of sexuality, the first to be sexualized and consumerized, was the "idle" woman was clearly no accident, although Foucault never addresses why this may have been the case (ibid., 121). Ambiguously positioned within bourgeois individualism, always threatening to rend the fabric of the social imaginary, the bourgeois feminine subject was the keystone of the familial alliance on which capital's free market depended, the significant "other" inscribed within the logic of the patronymic. Because she served to organize hierarchically class and racial subject positions, the bourgeois feminine subject helped preserve the symbolic order on which a broad range of social relations depended. The deployment of sexuality exacerbated the potential threat "she" already posed. Sexualizing the middle-class woman challenged the arrangement of separate spheres and everything that went with it: the sexual division of labor, the control of reproduction, the regulation of imperial subjects, the equation of bourgeois femininity with moral influence. At the same time, the maintenance of a preconstructed heterosexual interdiscourse worked to guarantee the re-production of a patriarchal gender system which supported a re-formed (sexualized) feminine subject.

In late nineteenth-century western societies, this shift in the ideology of feminine alterity was itself overdetermined, effected by changes in economic and political arenas—in the distribution of wealth, markets, and capital investment, in imperial policy and relations between state and civil society. The recruitment of middle-class women into the marketplace and the intervention of the state into previously inviolable areas like the family—an intervention reinforced by collective, including feminist, demands for representation—all brought pressure to bear on liberalism's sovereign individual. At the same time that they were the product of these shifts, the discourses of sexuality helped produce new subjectivities more adequate to these new social arrangements. Reading the sexualization of bourgeois feminine excess in terms of this reconfiguration addresses the articulation of sexuality and femininity as an overdetermined site through which a systemic ensemble of relations is ideologically managed.

Because the discourses of sexuality in the nineteenth century have had a pivotal role in the systemic rearticulation of the feminine as "excessive," they offer a useful instance for inaugurating feminist critique. The aim of this critique is not to recover the actualities of nineteenth-century life but to offer a way of reading those discourses which continue to exert ideological force in the present. The deployment of sexuality in the late nineteenth century imbricated preconstructed equations between sex and gender, femininity and morality in a far-reaching state-directed racism and class politics. While the particular ideological force sexology and eugenics had at the turn of the century has shifted, many of the preconstructed assumptions embedded in these discourses continue to shape social reality in the west.[15]

Reading sexuality under capitalism as an ensemble of discourses whose hegemonic articulation relies upon a preconstructed patriarchal and heterosexual organization has several implications. One of them is the claim that totalities like patriarchy and heterosexuality continue to organize people's lives in systematic and oppressive ways. Implicit in this assertion is the argument advanced by recent feminist work, like that of Sylvia Walby, which contends that the re-configuration of relations of production under late capitalism, for all of its atomizing effects on social arrangements, has not eroded these systems of domination so much as it has re-scripted them. We see this modification in new household arrangements among the middle class, for instance. As gender hierarchies become less rigid in middle-class households, many women spend fewer hours of their day as housewives and are given more permission to leave their husbands, re-marry, or have children without marrying. In comparison with men of a generation ago, many middle-class husbands and fathers are given less permission to take up the traditional position of master of the house and are encouraged to be more "involved" fathers. But even though patriarchal divisions of labor and controls over reproduction are being more flexibly managed in the domestic sphere, this does not mean that patriarchy is disappearing. Household labor and childcare are still devalued; although women spend less time as housewives, they still perform many more hours of housework and child care than men and earn lower wages in a sex segregated market (Folbre and Hartman 93). As the recruitment of more and more middle-class women into the labor market re-formulates the ideology of separate spheres and the boundaries between public and private become more porous, one effect has been the production of new frontiers for capitalist and patriarchal colonization. Electronic media and the advertising industry are prime technologies for disciplining the unconscious and the body through the sexual saturation of the subject. In the informatics of domination which increasingly define our everyday lives, patriarchy is alive and well and continues to rely upon a preconstructed heterosexual norm.

Although in postmodern culture the arbitrariness of this norm is at times made visible, the field of this visibility is limited, and more often than not fertile ground for discourses of pleasure, stimulation, or style rather than critique. In some registers of the culture (in avant-garde art, advertising, film and video, for instance) formerly "dangerous" or "perverse" sexualities have been re-scripted as "hot" or "chic" (witness Calvin Klein's ads, or Madonna's *Truth or Dare.*) However, representations of lesbian and gay subjectivities that are not encoded as excessive (abnormal, deviant, problem-fraught) often tend to validate (homo)-sexuality merely as matter of lifestyle. This representation of (homo)sexuality as style also appears in postmodern gay and lesbian theory where critiques of heterosexuality are increasingly formulated in terms of *différance* and couched within a critical framework that understands sexuality as performance or pleasure. The relationship between the stylization of sexuality in mainstream culture and in postmodern lesbian and gay theory is an important and relatively unexamined area of cultural politics for a materialist feminist ideology critique to pursue. Among the many issues which this line of inquiry would need to address are the enabling global historical conditions for the proliferation of sexualities under late capitalism and their bearing on the re-scripting of patriarchy; the problem of how to assess the critical difference of a range of eccentric sexualities, and the anti-hegemonic uses and limits of postmodern lesbian and gay theory.

V

Theorizing discourse as ideology implies that the feminist standpoint is a critical discursive practice, an act of reading which intervenes in and rearranges the construction of meanings and the social arrangements they support. I have resisted an equation of the feminist standpoint with a marginalized identity ("woman of color" or lesbian) in order to stress this point. Feminist work in general has emphasized that reading is a social act. Drawing upon a theory of discourse as ideology, materialist feminists have extended the concept of "reading" to include all of those meaning-making practices which enable one to act and which shape how one makes her way through the world.[16] In doing so, materialist feminists have challenged empiricist conceptions of reading (whether formalist or phenomenological) as a process of decoding. The increasing appeal of postmodern neo-formalist hermeneutics and the residual empiricism within new historicist versions of cultural studies have made it quite clear, however, that a feminist standpoint aimed at radical social transformation needs a more developed (materialist) explanation of the relationship between reading in this sense and feminism as a critical practice.

Materialist feminism's reading practice is critique. Critique has historical affinities with consciousness-raising as a feminist critical practice. As opposed to the empiricist notion of the subject as experiencing self which served as the frame of intelligibility for much feminist consciousness-raising, critique understands consciousness as ideologically produced. This framework breaks out of the empiricist dilemma of the self's mediated relationship to the world by opening consciousness up to discourse and history. Critique is bound to crisis and to ideology in a definitive way. In that the dominant ideology continually works to seal over the cracks in the social imaginary generated by the contradictions of patriarchal and capitalist social arrangements, it is continually engaged in crisis management. As an ideological practice, critique issues from these cracks, historicizes them, and claims them as the basis for alternative narratives. Critique "works on" the subject-form of discourse by continually historicizing the contradictions in which it is inscribed.[17]

Once ideology is understood as always an uneven and contested ensemble of discourses, the space from which critique issues need not be situated outside ideology—in science or in a discourse without a subject, as Althusser and Pecheux would have it. Instead, the alternative narrative of critique can be thought of as a counterhegemonic discourse, the enabling conditions for which are the contradictions produced by exploitative and oppressive social relations under patriarchal capitalism. These contradictions which inform the "lived reality" of an alienated existence are embedded in the various and contesting ways of making sense available in any historical moment. They leave their mark in the form of textual in-coherences in the narratives of the dominant culture.[18] These textual crises—gaps, contradictions, *aporias*—indicate the failure of the hegemonic discourses to successfully seal over or manage the contradictions displaced in the texts of culture. But they also serve as the inaugural space for critique. Feminism's history as a critique of patriarchy can be understood in these terms, as arising out of the contradiction between the democratic political promise of individualism and equality in modern societies and women's subordination in many arenas of social life.

One of the distinguishing features of critique as a counterhegemonic discourse, then, is that it not only arises out of crisis, it also causes crises in the narrativity of ideology. It does this first through an immanent reading which points to the self-contradictory moments in a text's logic. These aporias are exposed not in terms of an appeal to "objective" logic or to the logic of signification, but in terms of the historical contradictions they speak to. De-fetishizing textual crises by reading them as ideological displacements of contradictory historical forces is the second phase of critique. De-fetishizing occurs, moreover, with reference to an alternative way of making sense implicit in these textual crises. The third step of critique is the supersession of the text's problematic by this alternative narrative. It is in this sense that critique foments and makes use of ideological crisis for social transformation. Critique does not aim to heal over the crises it takes up; instead it tries to demonstrate that internal contradictions in a text are the product of and in turn help promote crises in the larger social formation, contradictions which cannot be satisfied by the system as it is at present (Benhabib, 109). As Seyla Benhabib has argued, critique is "crisis diagnosis" which enables future social change.

Recent work in marxist hermeneutics has developed a theory of symptomatic reading which advances this model of critique by way of postmodern theories of representation. As a critical practice, symptomatic reading has an enormous potential for feminism in that it develops at the very specific level of the discursive articulation of particular texts of culture, and by way of a systemic mode of analysis, a theory of subjectivity as ideological/discursive positionality. Symptomatic reading politicizes the Freudian concept of "symptom." It applies Freud's theory of the dream-work (as the process of translation from an unconscious to a conscious logic) to a materialist understanding of representation as ideology. Hegemonic ideology performs the work of displacement, condensation, and substitution in the discursive articulation of meaning. In the process, the political unconscious—the historical forces mystified by the naturalizing impulse of the social imaginary—are obscured. However, as in the dream-work, they are not concealed for good. They make their reappearance in the form of "symptoms," lapses in the coherence of the hegemonic culture, indexes of the insistence of another logic in everyday life.

Feminist work on symptomatic reading has tended to remain within the ahistorical boundaries of the psychoanalytic problematic. Luce Irigaray's reading of Freud, for example, in *Speculum* uses a Freudian symptomatic reading against Freud's own texts, locating in his representation of sexuality the "symptom" of a crisis point in western metaphysics which, once probed, exposes the "sexual indifference"—the problematic of (male) sameness—which guarantees coherence and closure in the narratives of western culture. In that Irigaray reads the textual symptom in Freud as politically interested—Freud is "a card carrying member of an 'ideology' that he never questions" (28)—she challenges neo-formalist concepts of textual crisis.[19] Like de Lauretis' reading of the gaps and spaces-off in narrative, Irigaray's reading of the symptom traces it to the hidden assumptions of an overarching patriarchy. As a result, her reading closes off the possibility of historicizing the textual symptom in terms that are at once more specific and inclusive.

By opening the symptom and the text up to history and systemic analysis, the work developed out of a materialist appropriation of Freud's symptomatic reading offers a promising avenue for developing the political interestedness of the symptom and its implications for understanding the feminist standpoint as a critical practice. As a strategy of ideology critique, symptomatic reading draws out the unnaturalness of the text and makes visible another logic haunting its surface. For Althusser, this "invisible" problematic can be detected in the form of "an answer which does not correspond to any question posed" (*Reading,* 27). The symptom points to this unsaid that informs any text. But unlike empiricist notions of excess, this "*non dit*" is not that which is left out or can't be conceived, but rather that which the text contains but cannot speak, certain "silences in its discourse, certain conceptual omissions and lapses in its rigor; in brief everything in it that 'sounds hollow' to an attentive ear, despite its fullness" (ibid., 30). Althusser conceptualizes these silences mainly in terms of problematics—theoretical frameworks that inform the use of words or phrases; he does not extend his theory to the more specific level of textuality or discourse. Furthermore, because he argues against Gramsci that Marxism is not an organic ideology but rather a scientific theory which breaks from ideology, he closes off the possibility of developing—within the terms he has set up—the historicity of symptomatic reading as a form of critique. If ideology is understood in terms of hegemony, however, the silences in a text may be read as the irruption of counterhegemonic discourses into the thread of narrative. As Pierre Macherey has suggested,

> what begs to be explained in the work is . . . the presence of a relation or an opposition, those disparities which point to a conflict of meaning. This conflict is not the sign of an imperfection; it reveals the inscription of an otherness in the work through which it maintains a relationship with that which it is not, that which happens at its margins. (80)

This "other" within the text is both the manifestation of the text's unconscious and the inaugural site for the work of critique. It defines the initial moment of symptomatic reading—the recognition of an area of "shadow" in or around the work. Symptoms appear as "excesses" in the narrative, disruptions in its logic or linearization which are either suppressed or "explained" (articulated onto preconstructed categories) so as to quell their disruptive force. These "shadowy" excesses which haunt the coherence of the text point to the play of history beyond the secured edges of ideological closure.

Symptomatic reading draws attention to the vexed question of the relation of the text to history. Any text is produced out of historical contradictions which are resolved in their narrativization. The specific form which a text's narrativization and naturalization of historical contradictions takes constitutes its intervention in a particular historical conjuncture. As Pecheux's theory of discourse illustrates, however, the relationship of narrative to history occurs through a complex sequence of discursive mediations. Symptomatic weaknesses in the coherence of any text are the residues of unanswered questions inscribed in the structuring of the interdiscourse, disrupting the preconstructed categories on which it depends. To read a text symptomatically is to make visible that which hegemonic ideology does not mention, those things which must not be spoken, discursive contestations which are naturalized in the interdiscourse but which still shape the text's diseased relation to itself. To read symptomatically is to reveal this historicity in the texts of culture and in so doing put on display the exploitative social arrangements that they so often manage.

VI

As a strategy for intervention in prevailing knowledges, ideology critique offers a way to rethink the feminist standpoint as a critical practice. From the outset, however, this project must confront the incompatibility of postmodern materialist theories of the subject with the group identity "woman" that has long been the basis for feminist knowledge.[20] Once subjectivity is theorized as an ensemble of discursive positions, no monolithic identity can serve as the subject of representation or liberation. It is important to remember, however, that the pressures which postmodern problematics bring to bear upon identity politics are the product of ideological interventions from a range of counterhegemonic sites within the liberal "tradition."[21] The appeal of the postmodern critique of the subject for feminism, for example, gains its force because the ideology of representation in which the subject of feminism circulates has generated refusals which suggest the limits of feminism as an identity politics (Butler, *Gender Trouble*, 4). Similar pressures from within marxism have made visible the inadequacy of its monolithic proletarian subject. The mode of politics called for by any group or organization acting in the name of the whole poses the same kinds of representational problems as liberal identity politics.[22]

Taking her cue from Foucault, Judith Butler has argued that the notion of group identity as the subject of a political movement ("women" for example as the subject of feminism) is itself the effect of a historically specific juridical version of representational politics (ibid., 2). Because juridical power inevitably produces what it aims to represent, the subject never truly "stands *before* the law," that is, before its representation *in* the law or in discourse. Confronting the implications of this knowledge means that feminists will have to continually monitor the hegemonic articulations of "woman"/"women" as the subject of feminism even as we use this group identity strategically.[23] This monitoring will require that we attend to the material conditions of exploitation and alienation in a new world order that celebrates "plurivocal discourses" (ibid., 4).[24] It will also require some skepticism in the face of formulations of feminist standpoint theory, like those of Donna Haraway or Fredric Jameson, which equate "standpoint" with the experience of (various) groups (Jameson, *"History and Class Consciousness,"* 665). Positing the "phenomenologically specific way" a group sees and knows as the basis for its standpoint, as Jameson does, begs the larger question of what constitutes both a "group" and its "seeing or knowing" and in so doing reinserts the feminist standpoint back into an empirical notion of group identity not very different from the liberal juridical one.

If it is acknowledged that the mechanisms of political and social identity are discursive and that it is an overdetermined discursive formation which sets the terms by which subjects are formed, feminists can claim that the grounds for their authority are always theoretical. Put differently, from the vantage point of ideology, women's lives are never outside theory because theories inform the discursive ways of making sense and their accompanying structures of value and belief which circulate in any culture. As such, theories are articulated in a culture's social imaginary and contested in its various counterhegemonic truth-claims. One of these counterhegemonic discourses constitutes the feminist standpoint.

Pecheux's concept of "dis-identification" is a useful way to reimagine the feminist standpoint not as the group identity of a juridical representational politics but as the collective subject of ideology critique. "Dis-identification" constitutes a relation to the hegemonic distinct from both identification and counter-identification. The former defines the good subject who "freely" consents to the hegemonic interdiscourse. The latter characterizes the "bad subject" who rebels against or counter-identifies with the position(s) offered her by the interdiscourse. However, because the bad subject is a symmetrical inversion of the good, it keeps in place through negation the framework of the hegemonic ideology. (In that they tend to merely reverse a patriarchal gender hierarchy without altering the terms of its framework, the woman-centered discourses of feminism produce a counter-identified subject.) The third positionality, that of dis-identification, consists of *working on* the subject-form (Pecheux, *Language,* 158). Dis-identification is critique, enacted in the disruption and re-arrangement of the pre-constructed categories on which the formation of subjects depends. The authority for a dis-identifying critique(al) subject need not be epistemological—grounded in science or truth, as Pecheux argues. Instead, it can be political—founded in an understanding of knowledge as ideology. A critique(al) discourse that dis-identifies with the interdiscourse of a culture does so by virtue of its own historicity and its systemic reach. This "position" is not limited to a reversal of one of the preconstructed nodal points on which the interdiscourse is based (the equation of man-woman with Same-Other, for example) but calls into question *and then historicizes* the preconstructed system across which subjectivities are constructed.

The dis-identifying subject of critique does not claim any one group identity as its ground but instead speaks from/for a counter-hegemonic collective subject. The "place" for the standpoint of critique, then, is not experience as we are used to thinking of it, but "an articulated system of positions" in the historical process and the subject produced out of that system (Althusser, "Is It Simple," 184). The collective subject of the feminist standpoint is the product of at the same time it produces a critique(al) discourse or analytic. It supersedes the individual or group identities of juridical representation by exposing the historicity of the preconstructed system of differences on which they depend. In rewriting political identity, this standpoint does not aim to eliminate differences, but rather, as Cornel West has argued, "to ensure that such differences are not employed as grounds for buttressing hierarchical social relations and symbolic orders" ("Marxist Theory," 26). Unlike the subject of a group identity who strives for the reformation of one axis of the symbolic order, the collective subject of a counter-hegemonic ideology critique emerges from a discourse which calls for a sweeping rearrangement of the social imaginary and the political and economic structures it supports. Once the feminist standpoint is formulated as this sort of dis-identifying collective subject of critique, the emphasis in its claims for authority can shift from concern over the *grounds* for knowledge—woman's lives or experience—to consideration of the *effects* of knowledges as always invested ways of making sense of the world.

But if feminism embraces this sort of collective standpoint, what constitutes its specificity? What distinguishes feminism from any other radical political agenda? The answer to both questions, I think, can be posed from the alternative notion of the subject I've outlined above. This alternative requires, however, a willingness to forfeit the sense of certainty that a politics lodged in group identity tends to guarantee. If it is understood that feminist knowledge is not *prior to* but rather produced *through* critical inquiry, feminism's specificity can be claimed as a feature of the systemic analytic that constitutes its mode of inquiry. This analytic reaches from the most local and historically specific to the most abstract level of analysis. It is this reach that makes it possible to conceptualize alterity at various levels of theoretical abstraction and across multiple modalities of difference. If the *object* of feminist inquiry is defined as the complex ensemble of social relations in which the feminine subject is reproduced, then, likewise, the collective *subject* of feminist critique can maintain some specificity—as the subject of a critique that *begins with* inquiry into and opposition to the devaluation of "woman" under patriarchy in all of the relations of production it spans. At the same time the feminist standpoint maintains the specificity of its starting point and special interest, it can also align with the subjects of other political discourses that use a systemic analysis of the social production of difference. The specificity of feminist critique, in other words, lies in its particular entry into and articulation of these various levels of analysis.[25]

This concept of the feminist standpoint as a critical discourse which draws upon postmodern and marxist analytics clearly challenges recent arguments for "taking the risk of essentialism."[26] The case has been made that the postmodern critique of identity politics is misapplied to national, ethic, racial, or sexual subjects whose historical entry into the discourses of individual identity is vastly different from that of the bourgeois western individual. That post-colonial, African-American, lesbian, and gay subjects make claims for group identity from a position rooted in cultural invisibility and political disenfranchisement is offered as an argument for the strategic value of identity politics for "subaltern" groups (JanMohamed and Lloyd, 16).

Gayatri Spivak's reading of the strategic use of essentialism underscores the political interests of the critical framework in which identity is articulated. In the breaking and relinking of the interdiscourse which Spivak calls the displacement of the function of signs or "the name of reading as active transaction between past and future" ("Subaltern Studies," 5), an "essential subaltern consciousness" rewrites the western notion of collective singular subject. Initiated from discourses whose counterhegemonic relationship to the western individual subject has been mediated through an exploitative division of labor, institutionalized political domination, and inscriptions of racial and ethnic difference, this rewriting serves not merely as emancipatory lever for the subaltern but as a reminder to the western historian that "the subaltern is necessarily the absolute limit of the place where history is narrativized into logic" ("Subaltern Studies," 16). The strategic effect of the subaltern's uptake of an essential identity is to turn western historiography back on itself and in so doing mark out the limits—the symptomatic blanks—in western knowledges. Of course, such a reading of the strategic use of identity is in its own way strategic, intervening in contemporary hegemonic claims on historiography. But it is also quite distinct from the discourse of individualism which offers self-evident persons or groups as the guarantors of access to rights and representation before the law. For here the strategic moment is defined from the vantage point of a systemic critique which reads the uptake of an essentialist consciousness symptomatically—as a troubling ideological "excess" in the hegemonic discourse. Upon this common ground of their "excessiveness," feminist and other counterhegemonic standpoints can meet.

In supporting the work of the Subaltern Studies Group, Spivak argues that the value attached to the strategic use of an essential subaltern *consciousness* is inextricably bound to the "scrupulously visible political interest" of their work ("Subaltern Studies"). This political interest places Subaltern Studies in a critical relation both with and against the great western antihumanist critical discourses. The challenge to western feminism is to negotiate its notion of standpoint with just this sort of "transactional" reading of an identity politics in "other" counterhegemonic discourses. In Spivak's argument for the strategic use of essentialism, the question of identity politics is not simply put to rest by suggesting, as Diana Fuss does, that its "permissibility" depends on the subject position from which one speaks (Fuss, 32), although that positionality *is* an important component of its political interest. As Spivak's text implicitly contends, and as she later elaborates, the strategic use of essentialism also depends upon understanding strategy as persistent critique. For Spivak this relentless critique entails a double consciousness, "an awareness of the unavoidable usefulness of something that is very dangerous" and the "acknowledgement of the dangerousness of what one must use" ("In A Word," 129). What comes to count as the political interest both of this persistent critique and of the position from which it is launched depend to a great extent on *how* that critique and that positionality are articulated.

In delineating these explanatory frameworks and mapping out what it means to be a woman in the integrated circuits of late capitalism, the work of feminists like Gayatri Spivak, Donna Haraway, Dorothy Smith, and others displays its disidentifying strength. Chandra Mohanty and Biddy Martin's reading of Minnie Bruce Pratt's essay "Identity: Skin, Blood, Heart" suggests that Pratt's narrative offers another rewriting of the feminist standpoint. In Pratt's rendering, they argue, identity and community are not the product of essential connections, neither are they the offspring of political urgency or necessity, but the effects of "a constant re-contextualization of the relationship between personal and group history and political priorities" (210). It is precisely in offering a framework for thinking this "re-contextualization" that a theory of ideology contributes to feminist praxis. In situating the historical construction of the feminine subject in a systemic analysis, it offers feminists one way to explain more fully "our" mediated and uneven historical positions. In so doing, feminism's subject is transformed from an empirical group, "women," to the collective subject of a critical discourse which pushes on the boundaries of western individualism. That the force of this critique is fed by "other" counterhegemonic discourses indicates both the historicity and the ideological limits of a feminist praxis always in the process of rearticulation.

4

New Woman, New History

The New Woman is critically important to new feminist scholars.
— Carroll Smith-Rosenberg, "The Body Politic"

. . . this new history will leave open possibilities for thinking about current feminist political strategies and the (utopian) future, for it suggests that gender must be redefined and restructured in conjunction with a vision of political and social equality that includes not only sex, but class and race.
— Joan Scott, "Gender As a Useful Category of Historical Analysis"

I am what Dora would have been if the history of women had begun.
— Helene Cixous, *The Newly Born Woman*

I

Materialist feminist work in general is distinguished by its insistence on historicizing. But what does it mean to historicize? What counts as "history"? And how do we understand history's materiality? I have been arguing in the preceding chapters that conceptualizing discourse as ideology offers feminism a systemic theory for understanding the materiality of power/knowledge relations, a framework which to my mind advances feminism's political aims. Here I want to extend this argument to the problem of history, particularly histories produced by feminists. Nowhere is the question of who feminism speaks for more crucial than in the histories we tell. But often in feminist historical work rigorous attention to the questions "*which* history?" and "history for what?" is elided by treating them as theoretical rather than properly historical concerns. However, it seems to me that it is urgent for feminists to wrestle with these theoretical questions precisely because they are *historical,* undergirding the historian's enterprise and history's function as a narrative in the culture. These issues are especially compelling in the face of feminist historians' claims to be writing "new" histories. Exactly what constitutes "the new"? In what way does it affect the feminine and feminist subjects our histories construct?

Like literature, history is one of the preeminent transmitters of hegemonic culture and tradition. The stories it tells serve to legitimate standards of value and define the boundaries of intelligibility and subjectivity. For this reason, pressures brought to bear upon the liberal subject under late capitalism have often been played out in challenges to history. Over the past thirty years, western history's staunchly empiricist logics of representation and identity have been tested by challenges circulating in the discourses of oppositional political movements and postmodern "theory."[1] From different vantage points both have questioned the epistemological assumptions on which the traditional relation between historian and fact are based: the notion that historical sources speak to or stand for actual events and the assumption that the historian's task is to gather and record the facts. The effect of this questioning has been registered in various proposals for a new history which is more aware of its status as narrative and which is at least suspicious of, if not rejecting outright, the universal and disengaged subject of empiricism.

Although these challenges to history as a record of the past have met with much resistance, the theoretical relation between historian and object of inquiry has always been somewhat blurry. Very few historians actually subscribe to a reductive realism—the idea that histories directly apprehend the past. Most admit that historians do not work with sheer accumulations of fact, but rather mobilize their sources into accounts.[2] The empiricist historian typically claims, however, that a sufficient amount of scholarly caution can bracket off personal prejudices and that stylistic variations in the presentation of historical evidence shouldn't affect the essential information in a historical account. At the same time, the still reigning historical methodology dictates that the scholar use "primary" sources because they are "closer" to the evidence. Jockeying between interpretation and data, the traditional historian's scholarship tends to get entangled in the classic contradiction of empiricism: gathering the facts from primary sources, he nonetheless produces a secondary text. The conventional strategy for managing this contradiction is to formulate the historian's interpretative role as a mediating one: shuttling between past and present he tries to uncover/construct at best a more accurate version of the past.

By questioning the empiricist separation of subject and object and its accompanying disengaged knower, as well as the notion of language as a transparent vehicle of communication, and by insisting that history is a narrative, historians like Joan Scott, Hayden White, Fredric Jameson, and Dominick La Capra have pressured the empiricist foundations of historical methodology.[3] As questions about the narrativity of history make the boundary between literary studies and history more permeable, resistance to the disruption of the power/knowledge relations this boundary secures has grown. Postmodern historiography, for example, is still considered eccentric by many historians and is read as philosophy rather than "real" history. For others, the invasion of history by theory is the result of the meddling literati who with their "superior sensibilities" pontificate in the form of searing critiques of their "dull but worthy colleagues, the historians" (Stansall, 27; Chevigny, et al., 41).

As historiographers like White have argued, how we understand this debate over history's status as science or philosophy/literature/theory is bound up in the very history of history as a cultural narrative and a discipline. Construing the contest over history as a war between "theory" and "history," however, deflects attention from what is at stake in this debate by reducing it to a competition between disciplines. Understanding these challenges to history's subject and object as a disciplinary war actually helps to maintain the interests that history "proper" has so long and so firmly secured. It is a strategy that in itself depends upon a vision of the social in which crises in the production of knowledge are understood in very local terms. As a result, the bearing these local crises have upon the formation of new subjectivities, in particular subjectivities adequate to a "*new* world order" orchestrated by U.S. capitalist hegemony, is obscured.

Feminist discourses across the disciplines have contributed to, helped articulate, and been shaped by these debates over history. I want to review feminism's engagement with the problem of history by reading texts from various sectors of contemporary feminist work: a pair of texts appearing in the *New York Times Magazine,* a set of essays on feminist historiography, and a series of critical readings of Freud's *Dora.* All are indicative of the multiple cultural spaces feminist history circulates in and all are traversed by a discourse on the "New Woman." Reading them in relation to each other situates the arguments made for a New Women's History in relation to other ideological investments in the New Woman and locates the articulation of woman's *new-ness* within a larger symbolic exchange system in western capitalism now. Taken together, they return us to the problem of the subject of feminism, and of materialist feminism in particular, by raising the question of the effectiveness of the New Woman as a signature for feminism. Re-visions of the New Woman are interesting as histories because of what they display about the dynamics of new-ness in the arguments for a new way to read history and a new feminist subject. It is this latter feature of history as narrative—that is, its bearing on the production of a feminist subject for the present—that links histories of the New Woman of the 1890s to the "newly born woman" of the late twentieth century.

Read as ideology, histories of the New Woman and New Women's histories problematize the bond between historian and archive, scholar and text. Understanding history as ideology implies that no matter how covert, the narrativity of history always issues from a set of values that support or disrupt a particular social order. As Joan Scott indicates in her vision of the new history in one of the epigraphs to this chapter, a historicism which owns its oppositional political agenda—as feminist history does—always has inscribed within it a "utopian future." It is, in other words, a reading *of* the past *from* the present *for* the future. Reading the figure of the New Woman in feminist histories as ideology entails attending to the ways the discourse of *the new* situates "woman" in the symbolic order now. Statements like Helene Cixous' "I am what Dora would have been if the history of women had begun" (*The Newly Born Woman*) and Carroll Smith-Rosenberg's "The New Woman is critically important to new feminist scholars" ("The Body Politic," 120) emphasize that the New Woman *is* being inserted into contemporary feminist discourses. The question is, then, whether the discourse of *the new* can be marshalled for feminist historicizing that advances transformative social change.

II

The project of developing a materialist feminist historiography is implicated in a nexus of debates on how to understand modernity—its periodicity, its political economy, its displacement by postmodernity. The terrain these debates traverse is complex and broad—including in its contours challenges to a host of categories seen by some to be inherent to modernity—chief among them a theory of the subject as autonomous individual. Rather than attempt to situate the claims made for feminist history within these discussions, I want to address, briefly, a related issue: one of the preeminent features of modernity—the discourse of the new— and its relationship to the construction of "woman."[4]

One of Marx's most important contributions to social history is his notion of a revolutionary connection between capitalism and modernity. In *The Communist Manifesto* he argues that capitalism's particular form of social organization marked a radical change in the history of humanity. The separation of the laborer from ownership and control over the means of production and his consequent division from both himself and a communal collective labor process under capital's specialized organization of work are linked in Marx's analysis to the continuous revolution in all of capital's sphere of production—economic, ideological, political.[5] Whereas earlier modes of production were essentially conservative, the technical basis of modern/capitalist industry is revolutionary because it never treats the existing form of any production process as the definitive one.

But Marx contends that this hunger for the new—the hallmark of capitalism— is not all bad. On the contrary, it affirms that human activity can bring about radical change. For Marx, appeals to new-ness are not essentially radical or reactionary; rather their effects depend on the forms of social production they support. Under capitalism this constant urge for new-ness is contradictory: the form it takes often closes off its richest possibilities. Driven by competition, the mechanisms and directions of social change are aimed toward the accumulation of power and wealth in the hands of a few at the expense of the many. This contradiction in capital's drive for innovation plays itself out at the level of ideology in the shape that people's desires for change take.

The conservative face of the new appears in its function as a mechanism whereby oppositional modes of thinking are sutured into the prevailing regimes of truth in order to maintain a particular symbolic order. The discourse of the new can serve to anchor emergent modes of thinking in traditional categories that help support rather than disrupt the prevailing social order. In this way, the discourse of the new operates conservatively to tame counterhegemonic ways of making sense which threaten the coherence of the social imaginary. In its conservative manifestation, the appeal to new-ness serves as the guarantor of repetition, an articulating instrument whereby the *preconstructed* categories that comprise the symbolic infrastructure of the social imaginary are sustained through moments of historical crisis by their dissimulation in the guise of the new. In this way the appeal to the new serves as an instrument of hegemony, working to reproduce the subjectivities that will be adequate to capital's extending markets and to elicit consent to the ways things are.[6]

One of the ways the discourse of the new works to maintain the symbolic order is through a strategy of transference. Under pressure from overdetermined shifts in the social formation, modes of thinking and desiring which had been thoroughly sanctioned in one ideological formation become inadequate to the reproduction of social subjects in another. As a result, their circulation in the social imaginary must be publicly inhibited and repressed. But the symbolic grid on which they depend invariably returns, displaced from one site to another. This transference allows the social order to be reproduced through times of social upheaval by being attached to "new" ideas, signs, objects, or activities that pass through the cultural censor of reformed public values. Thus, when a set of values becomes forbidden in the hegemonic culture it can continue its hold upon the social imaginary by merely acquiring a "new" life in disguise. In this way structures of oppression and domination survive under the mantle of new-ness because they are embedded in the *preconstructed categories* onto which "new" subjectivities are articulated. Deployed in this capacity, the signifier of new-ness" conceals the return of the repressed symbolic order and in the process extends the ideological reaches of capitalism's colonization without disrupting its symbolic anchors.[7]

This conservative rearticulation of the social imaginary, however, does not necessarily exhaust the disruptive force of counterhegemonic discourses. And it is because it does not that they are continually available as the site for oppositional claims on the new which bring the mechanism of repetition underlying capitalism's crisis-ridden foundations to a halt. This is the "other" or revolutionary face of the new. At the same time that appeals to the new can function within the social imaginary as the continually re-formed shelter for the structures of meaning on which the prevailing regimes of truth depend, they can also serve as the vehicle for the explosion of those categories. In other words, appeals to the new can interrupt capitalism's overriding pattern of crisis management by disrupting the symbolic infrastructure on which the formation of subjects in the prevailing social order depends. And in so doing they can offer a transformative vision of the future.

"Woman's" contradictory position under capitalism and patriarchy has served as one of the prime sites for the deployment of the discourse of the new. While the particular articulations of the New Woman have shifted from one historical moment to another, they tend to share a similar function—negotiating the dual registers of new-ness, both voicing and suppressing oppositional discourses that make visible the contradictory social relations which patriarchal ideologies manage. The figure of the New Woman first emerges in the pages of popular middle class journals and novels in Britain and the U.S. during the last two decades of the nineteenth century. As a construction of the feminine that circulated within and breached the cultural common sense, she can be read as a symptom of a more general crisis of subjectivity, an index of the disruption and recontainment of the hegemonic bourgeois ideology of the feminine. This crisis of subjectivity and the function of the New Woman within it can be understood in materialist terms as overdetermined by the general recomposition of capital in the west between 1880 and 1920. Taking the example of Britain, the expansion of capitalist investment and the opening up of new markets as well as competition from other rapidly industrializing western nations helped produce changes in imperial policy and inaugurated a reformation of industrial class categories. Adjustments in all of these areas ultimately affected and were in turn affected by alterations in the British hegemonic subject. The New Woman appears within this configuration of new subjectivities, less a direct target of repressive state intervention (as were the prostitute and the delinquent), than a site wherein was coalesced the rearticulation of middle-class femininity. The institution of compulsory state education and the consequent population of trained and literate women, the opening up of new job categories within the burgeoning finance industry, the desirability of a cheap female labor force to fill these posts, feminist organizing for women's entry into higher education and the professions and for the inclusion of women's interests in the new collective state all exerted pressure on the entire edifice of proper bourgeois femininity.[8]

The representation of the New Woman in British middle-class journals displays the ways this pressure was figured and managed. In some cases the signifier "new" merely serves to reinforce the hegemonic discourse by setting the New Woman outside women's proper place—that is, as not a woman at all. Often the New Woman is explicitly coded as transgressor through an array of signifiers for the unfeminine. In one of the series of "Character Notes" in *Cornhill* (1894), for instance, she is presented as "dark," single and uninterested in children, "crushing" to men, not pretty, simply dressed, sallow-complexioned and unblushing—all of which mark her as violating the acceptable norms of white, middle-class heterosexual femininity.[9] That she strides, is intelligent, and unfilial—keeping her mother firmly under her thumb—all mark her as emphatically masculine (Eastwood).

By the late 1890s, the New Woman began to be claimed by the hegemonic culture. Ideas of imperial destiny as well as class and racial superiority were grafted onto traditional views of refined English motherhood to produce a revised version of the New Englishwoman as citizen, involved in the public sphere through her civic-minded duty as global civilizing agent (Hammerton, 163). The key element in this project was "motherhood." Around the turn of the last century claims made for the "true" New Woman invariably construct her as a mother whose civilizing task—whether in the colonies or at home—is often filtered through the discourse of eugenics. Her mission is to maintain the values of a slightly remade middle class by monitoring a now much widened domestic sphere (Davin).

Securing "woman" as civic-minded mother neutralized the threat the scandal-ous New Woman posed to the whole edifice of bourgeois patriarchy. If woman's role as mother in civilizing the race were to be acknowledged by the state, some claimed, "we wouldn't hear any more from women holding marriage and motherhood in contempt" (Avling, 587). The re-formation of the strident, epi-cene, independent New Woman into the "true new Woman"—the imperial mother—is an index of the ways the discourse of the new worked to reform the hegemonic construction of woman by reinscribing the proper feminine subject within the preconstructed categories of a patriarchal symbolic order even as middle-class women were being recruited into new jobs and gradually granted legal rights.

Capitalism in the post-industrial west, increasingly in competition with the "third world," has had to revise, readjust, and even abandon altogether the ideology of separate spheres in order to draw more middle-class women into its labor force. Doing that without risking the patriarchal symbolic order has required delicate renegotiations of the contradictions in the prevailing ideology of the feminine. Throughout the twentieth century these renegotiations have taken the form of various versions of the New Woman. Most recently she is figured as the professional career women, often juggling work with the domestic responsibilities of "home and family." One of the functions of this figure of the new woman professional is to offer women an image of themselves which will help them perform successfully in this dual workplace. More and more in the past thirty years women in the post-industrial west are represented in the hegemonic discourse as "liberated" equals to men. But the discourse of equality and liberation often mystifies the ways in which the rearticulation of woman merely updates a precon-structed patriarchal order.

The discourse of the New Woman traverses a multiplicity of cultural spaces in post-industrial cultures—appearing in popular films, magazine articles, advertise-ments, novels. As in the late nineteenth-century debates over the New Woman, the claims made for her new-ness now are vigorously contested. Issuing from left and right, they indicate an effort to come to terms with "woman's" inscription in a set of social arrangements that can no longer be taken as obvious and are not automatically sanctioned. *Good Housekeeping*'s New Traditionalist ad campaign is one telling example of a particularly conservative recruitment of the discourse of the new to rearticulate what counts as "woman." Inaugurated in 1988 and lasting into the nineties, this series of portraits by photojournalist Mary Ellen Mark used the logo of "The New Traditionalist" to promote the magazine as optimal space for prospective advertisers. It has been received as an extremely successful project by marketing strategists and cultural critics alike, creating the sort of excitement and attention most advertisers only dream of. As Marcy Darnovsky's incisive analysis so thoroughly details, "The New Traditionalism" sent tremors across the cultural landscape.[10] The ads are all black and white photographs of women (actual—real live—women, not models) with their children in a range of settings. They appeared in newspapers, billboards, radio spots and at least one T.V. commercial. "The New Traditionalist" was alluded to in magazines like *Time* and *Mademoiselle* as an index of women's position in the nineties, and angry feminists responses were duly reported in the *Los Angeles Times* and the *Village Voice* (Darnovsky, 73). The ideological force of the ads lies in part in the unusualness of their product. As Darnovsky indicates, ads like these that sell advertising space, display more blatantly than most the invisible commodity that all ads sell—that is, an audience. In other words, what is being sold in these appeals to buy ad space in *Good Housekeeping* is much more than "space." The product here is an articulation of woman which, as Darnovsky argues, "strides into several fierce battles" including among them a fight about the meaning of feminism and gender (74). While many of the ads indicate the woman pictured also works outside the home, all of them invite their readers to equate "good housekeeping" with woman's work at a time when housekeeping as a woman's domain—and hence the survival of the magazine's market—is being challenged. And, of course, all of them invite the prospective advertiser to make sense of woman primarily as mother.

I want to look briefly at one of the earlier ads in the series, a portrait of a woman who "started a revolution with some not so revolutionary ideals" (see figure 1). In this example the equation between good woman and mother is extreme. Unlike many of the other New Traditionalists who are presented as career women *and* mothers, this one is not. The allusion to revolution in the ad's headline emphasizes the postfeminist discourse that circumscribes the New Woman here. As the small print details it, "She was searching for something to believe in—and look what she found—her husband, her children, her home, herself." The element of surprise in this statement ("Look what she found"!) depends on the invisible "other"—the discourse of feminism—on which the New Traditionalist depends. This "other" woman's search for something to believe in leads her, of course, to question woman's boundedness by motherhood, good housekeeping, marriage. That the ad's invitation to "look what she found" still makes sense despite the husband's absence from the scene indicates the viability of a residual ideology of separate spheres on which this image of woman as good housekeeper and mother depends. In appealing to the discourse of revolution, here couched in terms of new-ness, the ad uses a familiar conservative tactic—much like the right's use of "political correctness" to quell progressive change in academia—of appropriating and rewriting the signifiers of an oppositional discourse. This appeal to revolution clearly presents the ad's message as a counter to the disruptive force of feminism, that "trend" that has managed to make "some people" think that traditional values are "old fashioned." That market researchers are calling this return to home and "family" the biggest social movement since the sixties, firmly establishes the contradictory logic of the equation of new-ness with the old-fashioned here: the return to tradition is a corrective to the potentially still viable social upheaval bred in those revolutionary times.

THE NEW TRADITIONALIST.

SHE STARTED A REVOLUTION — WITH SOME NOT-SO REVOLUTIONARY IDEALS.

She was searching for something to believe in – and look what she found. Her husband, her children, her home, herself.

She's the contemporary woman who has made a new commitment to the traditional values that some people thought were "old fashioned."

She wasn't following a trend.

She made her own choices. But when she looked over the fence she found that she wasn't alone.

In fact, market researchers are calling it the biggest social movement since the sixties.

The quality of life she has chosen is the embodiment of everything that Good Housekeeping has stood for –

the Magazine, the Seal, the Institute. Who else can speak to the New Traditionalist with that kind of authority and trust?

Who is more committed to helping her live the life she has chosen?

That's why there has never been a better time for Good Housekeeping.

AMERICA IS COMING HOME TO GOOD HOUSEKEEPING

Against reinscriptions like this one, other, less heavy-handed, versions (in films like *Fatal Attraction, Prizzi's Honor, Desperately Seeking Susan, The Good Mother, Aliens, Thelma and Louise,* to name only a few) figure the "new" woman's independence from husband, children, or housekeeping as "acceptable," even as this transgression is ultimately resecured within the structures of a reformed patriarchal order. Representations of feminism in the popular media often contribute to the containment of this revolutionary potential of the "new" woman by figuring feminism's "revolution" by way of a discourse which merely refuses the prevailing patriarchal inscriptions of women, this time from the liberal/ left rather than the conservative/right. Vivian Gornick's cover story "Who Says We Haven't Made A Revolution?" which appeared in the *New York Times Magazine* eighteen months after the revolutionary New Traditionalist, is a case in point. The feminist subject implicit in the cover photo for this essay—presumable the referent of the "we" in the essay's title—is at face value quite different from the New Traditionalist. The feminine/feminist subject of this portrait is a collective/group rather than an individual and is stripped of the codes of "proper" femininity (the domestic scene, the children, the [absent] husband). All of these women are public figures of varying renown: Alix Kates Shulman, Ann Snitow, Phyllis Chessler, Ellen Willis, Kate Millett. Wearing simple, somber blues and browns (no black and white nostalgia here), their clothes display few "feminine" markers—no lace, no flowers--none of the codes of allurement or submission. Two wear trousers, Kate Millett black boots. Shoulders back, chins up, arms on hips, they gaze boldly out at the viewer with expressions ranging from dignified confidence to glee. (This in marked contrast to the good housekeeping madonna whose glazed eyes, half-smile, and drooping posture suggest numb repose.)

Still, all of these women are white and recognizably middle class. If these components of the "we" in whose name revolution is claimed suspiciously link the feminist with the New Traditionalist, the frame for Gornick's text establishes their "sisterhood" through yet another set of common links. Here the feminist's struggle to re-engender the separate spheres of work and intimacy is implicitly defined through her relation to men. The essay opens with Gornick's narrative of a conversation with a male colleague who is interested and amused by her hunger for the larger world and announces that he has recently made his intimate relationships the top priority in his life. This neat reversal of the ideology of separate spheres is complemented by the image of the New Woman offered in the essay's final paragraphs. Here the article's utopian vision is couched in terms of a party someday in the future where the sexual charge might be generated by powerful women whom the men would hover around. While the roomful of Vivian's friends all agree this will never come to pass, one consoles her by adding, "You're a New Woman of the 70's and 80's. That means intermittent erotic connection, and the company of intelligent woman" (Gornick, 53). Clearly this New Woman has come a long way from the New Traditionalist! Or has she?

If we take the claims to new-ness here at less than face value we can recognize in them the strategy of transference. In fact, it works in both ad and essay and to a similar effect. This strategy acknowledges that certain dimensions of woman's place within capitalist and patriarchal arrangements have changed, but at the same time it keeps intact the preconstructed symbolic order on which they rely. Surely Gornick's feminist discourse on the New Woman endorses woman's new relation to work and the demise of an ideology of separate spheres, unlike the New Traditionalist's message which would recruit woman—at least ideologically—back into the home. But both the New Traditionalist's and the liberal feminist's claims for revolution meet ideologically on the common ground of the hegemonic culture's preconstructed and interdependent class and sex categories. The (liberal) feminist is still very much defined through an (invisible) hierarchy of social differences that takes for granted class privilege, values white over black, and sutures her as sexualized female firmly within a heterosexual symbolic order. While the feminist New Woman seems to be situated outside marriage and so "liberated" in that sense, her sexuality is still defined in terms of the heterosexual contract upon which that institution depends. Here the traditional patriarchal engendering of mind-vs.-body is reversed; sensuality and erotic connection are valorized in order to secure women's association with men, while "intelligent" company is the province of women together. This is, then, a classic instance of a counterdiscourse, one that merely re-arranges the prevailing paradigm without really challenging its terms. The claims to new-ness here merely transfer the symbolic anchors for "woman" from a more blatant and therefore now unsanctioned patriarchal order to an updated, (hetero)sexualized and perhaps more insidious, version of femininity whose many social privileges are never questioned.

Much of the work within white western feminist theory recently has been aimed at addressing—through various reassessments of who feminist history speaks for—just this sort of rearticulation of dominant ideology within feminism. And yet these efforts, too, often take up the discourse of the new and of the New Woman. To what extent has the emblem "New Woman" compromised the transformative potential of feminist interventions in historiography? In turning to what is thought of as more properly "women's history," I want to examine the ways in which the invocation of New Woman in feminist historiography has a bearing on feminism's oppositional claims. At issue here are several questions, among them, what is required to marshal the revolutionary face of the new for the subject of feminism, and what might be lost when feminist history represents its project in the name of the New Woman? Does the signature "New Woman" necessarily reinforce the preconstructed categories on which the hegemonic rearticulation of identity depends? And if so, why?

III

The New Women's History emerged in the early seventies in Britain and the U.S. as feminist work in the academy came to be shored up by the effects of the

Women's Movement in the larger culture. Earlier isolated efforts to insert women into historical narratives were displaced by a self-consciously politicized feminist movement in historical scholarship which questioned the assumptions underlying the very structure of the discipline.[11] The New Women's History claimed its newness not only on the strength of its insistence that women be included in the culture's otherwise phallocentric narratives, but also through its assertion that this inclusion would transform the very notion of history. Under the forceful critique of feminist historians, history was exposed as an interested narrative rather than a more or less objective—or lightly interpretive—record of the facts. Standards of selection and objects of historical inquiry were shown to be political choices. Feminist re-evaluation of the historical canon led to questioning schemes of periodization, assumptions of causation, and the prioritizing of particular topics as legitimate objects of analysis (Smith-Rosenberg, "New Woman," 185). Formerly uncharted areas of inquiry were opened up: sexuality, reproduction, domestic arrangements—to name a few. As the product of complex interactions between the political perspective of the Women's Movement and the New Left, the New Women's History shifted the focus of historiography from the notable and the public to the inconspicuous and inarticulate: the working classes, immigrants, slaves, and servants. In these respects it shared much in common with the New Social History which arose out of intersections between Marxist historiography and the *Annales* School. While these approaches for the most part ignored women, however, the New Women's History placed women at the center of its analytic schema. The effect, the New Women historians claimed, was to make institutions and processes central to women's lives the object of inquiry (Smith-Rosenberg, "New Woman," 188).

"The New Women's History" is a phrase coined by Caroll Smith-Rosenberg in one of the earliest assessments of feminist inroads in historiography, her essay, "The New Woman and the New History" (1975). Its women-centeredness is indicative of the theoretical framework informing the earliest phase of academic feminism, particularly in the U.S. As Joan Scott has argued in her genealogy of Women's History, the New Women's History assumed "women" to be a fixed and known entity. Taking "women" as its special charge in these terms, however, proved to be a mixed blessing. Perversely, these narratives tended to legitimize the nature and experiences of women as their domain but as a result any threat of a disruptive feminist critique was safely contained. The subject of the New Women's History could readily be perceived merely as an add-on to "real" history and confined to a minor place in an expanded canon.

The increasing circulation of postmodern theories by the mid-seventies and the concomitant pressures on academic feminists to attend to the implicit white, western, middle-class subject inscribed in the category "woman" began to shift the terms of inquiry in feminist scholarship from "woman" to "gender" and, by the next decade, to the even more diffuse category—"difference." The exclusive focus on gender is, however, specific to feminist history in the U.S., in part the effect of the articulation of the New Women's History onto the cultural feminist discourses increasingly central to Women's Studies here. In contrast, the New Women's History in Britain, emerging primarily out of British New Left alignments with labor, has tended to emphasize class (Newton, et al., 4).[12] The intersection of these two currents of work has occurred mostly in the past decade, in part the outcome of continued political pressures on the ideology of essential womanhood and on a gender-neutral category of class, and in part the effect of the intersection of feminist history with New Historicist and cultural materialist histories.[13] While feminist historians have pointed out that these categories are too exact—socialist, cultural, as well as radical feminist tendencies inform work on both sides of the Atlantic—the more salient issue for materialist feminist history now, I think, is the terms of their intersection.

In a recent essay in *Cultural Critique,* Judith Newton argues what might be seen as the *New* Women's History position. She claims that the invisibility of feminist contributions to the New Historicism re-enacts the nineteenth-century ideology of separate spheres. Newton argues that the New Women's History anticipates New Historicism and postmodernism in that feminism posits "a self which is at the same time multiple, contradictory and in process" (Newton, "History As Usual?" 99). Although Newton's point can be taken as an assertion of the effects of feminism's critique of the autonomous individual on the formation of the postmodern subject, I would argue that between a feminist self-in-process and a discursively constructed subject lies in the theoretical *difference* of postmodernism, a difference that feminism glosses over to its peril. For it is precisely this *untheorized difference* between self and subject that underlies the feminist historian's argument that feminist knowledge is grounded in women's experience (ibid., 93). But what is meant by an appeal to "women's experience"? In defending the New Women's History, Newton elides "women's experience" with "gender" as the distinguishing trait of new-ness: the difference of Women's History is "the degree to which gender relations, gender struggle, women, and women's activities and power are seen as being within "history" (ibid., 103). In the New Women's History, she contends, "subjectivity [is] gendered and often female and women [are] at the heart of historical study" (ibid., 100).[14] As this chain of signifiers indicates, gendered subjectivity turns out to be synonymous with the category "women." But if "gendered women" are the focus of historical study, what has happened to feminism's multiple and contradictory self? Multiplicity and contradiction here do not disrupt the center of liberal humanist history, they just re-engender it. Now women rather than men are at the heart of historical analysis. The ideology of the self which undergirds this center remains intact, the difference within "woman" and the social arrangements this "difference" depends upon remain undisrupted.

To a greater degree than Judith Newton, Joan Scott endorses the useful effects of postmodern theory for women's history, affirming the ways the shift from gender to "difference" problematizes women's experience as the basis for knowledge. For Scott, making history as much an object of attention as a method of analysis means that the categories a history invokes or takes for granted participate in the production of knowledge for the present (*Gender*, 2). She also argues that attending to historical narrative per se will relocate the historian's authority in her commitment to a certain kind of feminist political work and her ability to theorize it.[15] Scott cautions against a pluralist response to the critique of history's positivism—a response that would merely expand existing historical categories to include women. And she contests the circular logic in women's history in which "experience" explains gender difference and gender difference explains the asymmetries of male and female "experience" (ibid., 4). Instead she calls for "an analysis of discrimination that extend(s) to the categories themselves"— including man and woman. In these respects her work goes a long way toward wrenching the New Women's History out of an empiricist problematic. But the "more radical epistemology" she calls for is still bounded by gender. In the introduction to *Gender and the Politics of History* she asserts that

> my specific concern as a feminist is with knowledge about sexual difference, with gender. As a historian I am particularly interested in historicizing gender by pointing to the variable and contradictory meanings attributed to sexual difference, to the political processes by which those meanings are developed and contested, to the instability and malleability of the categories "women" and "men." . . . (10)

While Scott's work problematizes the opposition of women's history to history, gender emphatically constitutes the focus of her feminist history.

Although the compounded pressures from political discourses within feminism as well as postmodern theories of the subject have moved feminist historiography to affirm, in Judith Newton's words, "an enlarged feminist collectivity" ("History as Usual," 121), the relationship between this acknowledgement and the discourses of the historian is often incongruent. Nowhere is this incongruity more evident than in the invocation of the "holy trinity" of "class, race, and gender" as the requisite categories of historical analysis. The very same essays that posit gender as the central focus of historical analysis often also offer high praise for "the most politically inclusive scholars who invoke all three categories as crucial to the writing of a new history" (Scott, "Gender," 82; Newton, "History As Usual?" 120). Beyond this sort of affirming gesture, however, the narrative's emphasis almost invariably falls on gender or at most the intersection of gender and class.[16] More often than not, the category of race is no more than an afterthought.

This is not to say that white western feminism has been deaf to critiques from its marginalized voices—African-American, Lesbian, Chicana feminists, to name a few—and has failed to be to some degree refigured as a result. But, as Christina Crosby has argued, the emergent questions about theorizing difference which have now become so central to feminism, especially in the U.S., need to be explicitly discussed as questions of history and theories of history (154). Too often feminist analysis repeats the discourse of identity it is trying to displace when history is the issue. As Crosby puts it, "if the feminist problematic is to shift from the recognition of women in history, "history" must be posed as a theoretical problem" (155).

Joan Kelly's argument in "The Doubled Vision of Feminist Theory" (1979) is frequently referred to as an example of the sort of paradigm shift feminist historians need to advance, an important early call from a feminist historian for an overhaul of the theoretical framework on which feminist history depends. It seems to me, however, that the most radical implications of Kelly's proposals are often overlooked. Kelly argues that by the seventies feminist theory had already begun to supersede the dualistic view of social relations it inherited from the nineteenth century, a view which bifurcates history into the domains of class and sexuality, public and private. In order for feminist social thought to successfully overcome these dualisms, to account satisfactorily for sex, class, and race oppositions, Kelly argues, it can no longer focus exclusively on relations of class as marxism has, or of sexuality as psychoanalysis does. Instead, a "more complex pattern of sociosexual arrangements is called for," one that sees socioeconomic and sexual-familial relations "*in their systematic connectedness*" (59). Kelly's proposal for an alternative feminist history understands economic and sexual-familial relations as inextricably related while still maintaining their particularity in terms of class or race. (61). She contends that if feminism were to pursue this logic, the vision of society as split into two spheres would be replaced with a "unified doubled view," one that presents as interdependent the relations between public and private spheres. This view, she argues, should enable feminists to understand better the persistence of patriarchy which "has had as its strength an ability to assimilate itself so perfectly to socioeconomic, political and cultural structures as to be virtually invisible" (61).

The feature of Kelly's argument which to my mind is so crucial to feminist history now is the relationship she posits between the aims of feminist inquiry, or, as she puts it, "our conception of the scope of the women's movement . . . its relation to issues of race and class," and her call for a systemic analysis.[17] She understands patriarchy as ideological *and* as implicated in a network of other social structures. In this respect, Kelly's "unified doubled vision" is a *global* analytic, a way of thinking that does not privilege gender or women's self-evident experience, and yet allows for analysis of a highly differentiated and particularized subject in relation to a set of historically specific systemic relations. If it is taken seriously, Joan Kelly's vision implies a radical rewriting of the New Women's History. Not least of all, her proposal raises questions about the usefulness of the very category "New Women" as a way to signify feminist interventions in traditional historiography.

The pressures on this signature and their implications for feminist readings of the late nineteenth century in particular are played out in the series of essays subtitled "Writing History" in the anthology *Coming to Terms,* published by the Pembroke Center for Teaching and Research on Women (1989). The difference in emphasis in the titles of the first two essays—from Joan Scott's "Gender: A Useful Category of Historical Analysis" to Carroll Smith-Rosenberg's "The Body Politic"—is indicative of a theoretical shift in feminist history from "gender" to "the body" as the central category of analysis. As Smith-Rosenberg acknowledges, this move is at least partially indebted to the impact of Foucault upon feminist history. And it is precisely this recent "trend" in feminist work that I want to examine in terms of its bearing on the reconfiguration of the symbolic order under the guise of the new.

Carroll Smith-Rosenberg's essay "The Body Politic" is a useful index of how the New Women's History is being reformulated via Foucault. The essay acknowledges the changes her thinking has undergone since the publication over ten years ago of "The New Woman and the New History" and even since the inception of this piece in 1985. As in her earlier essay, Smith-Rosenberg frames her arguments for feminist history in the context of a reading of the nineteenth-century New Woman. In "The Body Politic," however, she announces at the outset that the focus of her inquiry will be "words and things . . . the processes by which our passions and desires assume meaning within historically specific discourses and ideologies" (101). She argues that the "female-rooted discourse" of a first generation of New Women which emerged at the end of the nineteenth century in Britain and the United States was displaced by the male-constructed metaphors of a second generation of New Women. This transformation, she contends, curtailed these younger women's expressive powers, identities, and political strength (120). The theoretical framework for this historical narrative combines Foucauldian genealogy with a cultural feminist notion of woman as expressive, experiential self. As a result, historical change is biologized—as the effect of succeeding generations of women—and psychologized within the terms of a feminized family alliance:

> In the generational differences that fractured the New Women and robbed them of their political power, we see fictive daughters struggle for independence from mothers who would not respond to their new voices. We hear fictive mothers mourn the loss of daughters who seem neither to understand nor appreciate the women who preceded them. (120)

Smith-Rosenberg's generational narrative posits history as an ominous repetition whose subject assumes mythic proportions. She invites feminist historians to ponder the parallels between these earlier generations of New Women and their own. And she cautions today's New Women who take up the post-structuralist "language of our times" against the dangers of forfeiting, as did "our" foremothers, "an identity as women" (121).

Denise Riley's "Commentary" on this essay and Evelyn Brooks-Higginbotham's piece on "The Problem of Race in Women's History" offer explicit and implicit critiques of the theory of history at work here. By insisting that "a feminist history can't afford to validate characterizations of 'women' however flattering they may look," Riley shifts the grounds for historicizing from "woman" to feminism (138). She argues that tracing the

> sexualized metaphoric constructions of the body politic and its political effects . . . becomes impracticable if the female as a historically weighted aberration slips by unchallenged, to re-enter triumphantly at the level of language. (138)

Riley's contention that Smith-Rosenberg's "female" has in some ways fallen out of history can, I think, be more usefully translated into a statement about the ideological effects of contesting historical narratives, contesting *versions* of history. For Smith-Rosenberg's narrative *is* historical, and its historicity lies in its power to shape how we make sense of the world now. She and Riley both insist that the "will to a female identity" is a historical problem. But the issue at stake between them is the effect of one telling of that history and identity over another.

Evelyn Brooks-Higgenbotham's argument for writing black women into history makes clear what some of these stakes are. She argues that "factors of class and race make any generalization of womanhood's common oppression impossible" (133). The implication of a "New Women's History" in a racist ideology is undeniable once we consider how a historical narrative which accounted for the intersections of race, gender, and class disrupts any invocation of a generic New Woman. As the work of Sharon Harley and Delores Janiewski has argued, the feminization of a new workforce which was so much a factor in the emergence of the nineteenth-century New Woman not only did not renew black women but in many ways depended upon their exploitation. Although white women outnumbered white men in the new clerical workforce, the reverse held true for blacks. The intersection of racism and sexism allowed black men into an increasingly feminized profession while black women were excluded from clerical work, the vast majority being confined to low paying, unskilled jobs (Harley). The New (white and middle-class) Woman's class mobility and independence was predicated on black women's continued subordination as farm laborers, charwomen, and factory or domestic workers (Janiewski, 35). Within the economy of the southern United States, the interaction of gender, race, and class relegated black women to the very bottom of the social hierarchy and subverted any potential for collective consciousness on the part of black and white women in the same "class" position, when "class" is defined strictly in terms of labor (ibid.).

As Robyn Wiegman has argued, historically the image of the (white middle-class heterosexual) woman "for whom gender is the only means of cultural disempowerment," has often rendered other forms of oppression invisible (310).[18] One of the most compelling issues for feminism now is the need to address the dynamics of this process, the ways in which patriarchal oppression exceeds the boundaries of gender difference. As a number of other feminists—among them Elsa Barkley Brown, Hazel Carby, Denise Riley, and Hortense Spillers—have affirmed, writing race into "Women's History" entails more than just adding black women; rather "it involves staking out and re-fashioning the entire problematic out of which the subject of history is theorized" (Riley, "Commentary," 137). These examples from *Coming to Terms* serve to demonstrate that the theoretical problematic out of which a historical narrative is drafted has everything to do with the subject of feminism. If the New Women's History is being displaced by a new historicism of bodies and politics, or of subjects fractured along multiple modalities of difference, Smith-Rosenberg's essay should instruct us to be suspicious of this new-ness. The point is not that the New Woman is no longer a worthy object of historical inquiry, but that the framework in which a particular social category is historicized can contain or enhance that history's oppositional force. If the interdiscourse into which Smith-Rosenberg articulates her New Woman helps resecure the obviousness of "woman" in terms of her visible biology, it also helps insure the obviousness of "history." The connection between the two is foregrounded in the closing paragraphs of the essay where she offers the conflicts among successive generations of New Women as an object lesson for feminist historians. Out of this parallel emerges the feminist historian's "other"—the theorists who threaten to disrupt and reject political alliances based on female identity just as the second generation of New Women did. The true New Woman (historian) turns out here to be the New Traditionalist after all. Her new-ness lies in a willingness to invoke the avant-garde discourses of postmodernism, but the implications of her critique of the centered subject are, finally, contained by a most reductive body politics. This new historian depends, too, upon a theory of history which holds on to an empiricist subject concealed within appeals to an asocial body which can "transcend discourse, surprise it with the unexpected, exert power" (Smith-Rosenberg, "The Body Politic," 121). Reverting to the empirical body as the ground for knowledge is in part the effect of Smith-Rosenberg's allegiance to Foucault, in particular his refusal to fully think through the relationship between the materiality of discourse and the materiality of the nondiscursive. Like Foucault, she simply describes them as "separate and inseparable" forces somewhere out there in history.

To the extent that the New Women's History articulates the discourses of postmodernism into an interdiscourse in which the subject of feminist practice is anchored in preconstructed categories which naturalize both "woman" and the historian's standpoint, it performs the conservative work of transference typical of hegemonic articulations of the new. In the guise of new-ness the New Women's History continues to shelter and nurture several of the mainstays of the cultural common sense. The persistence of this interdiscourse in historical narratives that claim new-ness should spark our suspicion about the degree to which the "New Women's" History is indeed a transformative feminist intervention in the social imaginary.

IV

If feminist theory is to construct historical narratives that do not just reinstall updated versions of the "New Woman," it will need to find ways to resist the conservative politics of the new and deploy instead its revolutionary possibilities. Understood not as a scientific theory outside ideology, but as a counterhegemonic discourse, materialist feminist history can offer a politically useful alternative to both traditional and new historicism. Basing its concept of history on a theory of ideology and a systemic logic of the social, materialist feminist history understands historical time as the effect of complex and differentially articulated structures that constitute the social formation, among them the ideological and discursive structures of meaning. The historian's construction of the theoretical object of her narrative is always ideological, and as ideology it has a very specific materiality and historicity. This means that the historical fact is no longer merely the empirically given archive, even as it is "mediated" by the historian's interpretation. Rather, a *historical* fact *becomes* a historical fact because it enters the discourses of culture and in so doing causes a mutation in the relations which that culture effects (Althusser, *Reading*, 102). As Christina Crosby has argued, to read history as a concept produced by a particular discourse is to belie the guarantee that history will provide the truth. It is to acknowledge that "history" is never simply grounded in empirical facts and that reading is not an innocent process of discovery (148).

Once we understand the narratives circulating in culture as ideologies—some articulated within the hegemonic culture, some circulating on its margins—all texts of culture can be read as having a claim on history, and "historical" narratives can be unhinged from the disciplinary boundaries set around them. "History proper" can then be seen as a particular mode of reading and writing which supports a specific regime of truth and disciplining of knowledge. If knowledge of the past is understood as ideological in the sense that it takes the form of narratives which arise out of and for the social real in the present, the rationale for writing history can be revised, too. No longer is the historian's driving impulse the desire to disclose or to express more accurate views of the way things once were, but rather an effort to produce or disrupt the discursive materiality of the present by renarrating the past. If historical narratives are no longer taken to be transparent vehicles of an empirical archive, the reasons for reading historical sources can be taken to lie in the ideological force which they—or their narration—(continue to) exert on the present. In some cases, the selection of a particular historical moment becomes urgent—whether the historian acknowledges this or not—because the discourses emerging in that particular social formation continue to exercise ideological pressures on the present. In other cases, the mode of reading the past, more than the discourses in the archive per se, has an urgency in the formation of reality in the contemporary social order. Reading historical discourse as a process which formulates certain objects (including history itself) and subjects means that history can be read for its social and political effects. Many of these effects are registered in the lines that striate the mirror of a history that purports to reflect reality. These traces are the marks of all that is excluded from the proper historical field, those other histories that the legitimate discursive formation suppresses.

This understanding of history has several far-reaching implications for feminist work. First of all, situating the problematic out of which historical narrative is constructed within the discursive field of the present encourages feminist history to account for its own historicity. This means that the subject of feminist history is itself always open to those forces which its narratives delineate and exclude. It is in this sense always provisional, and like the stories it emerges from, invariably contradictorily situated. In materialist feminist practice, historical narratives are both the object and vehicle of ideology critique. The historian's narrative reads in the texts of culture the various ways in which particular codes help maintain or subvert the hierarchical distributions of power and wealth. But because these texts, no matter now "historically remote," continue to circulate or are brought (back) into circulation by virtue of their inscription in the historian's narrative, they have an ideological force now, too, in the present.

It is from this understanding of the narrativity of history as always bound up in the contemporary historical situation that we can begin to draft a framework for explaining the relationship between the discourses produced in a particular historical moment in the past and the discursive positions from which they are read in the present—without lapsing into a totalizing or teleological historicism. The renarration of "woman" by twentieth-century feminists is a case in point. The particular archives we select, how we read "woman" in them, what of that archive we make visible and how we frame it—all of these and other "choices" are determined by the feminist historian's position in her own historical and ideological formation. The discourses on the New Woman in late *nineteenth-*century western culture, for example, and the discourses on the New Woman in the late *twentieth-*century emerge out of very different social formations, each with their own historically-specific conjunctural arrangements. They are in this respect *historically* distinct. But they are ideologically bound in that the New Woman has become *interesting* as an object of inquiry for the "new" feminist critic of the late twentieth century. One reason for this interest is the continued ideological force of the nexus of discourses out of which the New Woman emerged at the end of the nineteenth century, discourses which continue to shape both academic feminist theory and the common sense view of "woman."

V

Elizabeth Fox-Genovese's suggestion that women's history should not "substitute the chronicle of the female subject for that of the male but rather restore conflict, ambiguity, and tragedy to the center of the historical process" is one index of the recent shift in focus in much feminist history from "gender" to "difference" (29). But whether this shift signals an ideological intervention in the social order that proper history helps guarantee depends on how this "difference" is understood. Feminist history that puts difference at the center of the historical process has frequently drawn upon Foucault's work and the New Historicism it helped produce. Foucauldian history shares with traditional historicism an insistence on the empirical, but it also promotes postmodernism's pulverized vision of the social, critique of the centered subject, and rejection of systemic analysis. Much like Carroll Smith-Rosenberg's "The Body Politic," many feminist appropriations of Foucault have rearticulated the terms of his "New History" within an analytic framework that seems to install "woman" as the linchpin of a new hegemonic order. I want now to examine these terms, with an eye to the ways they effect the parameters and the politics of the intersecting new-nesses of Foucauldian New Historicism and a (new) New Women's History.

Heavily indebted to Nietzsche, Foucault's genealogy aims to question three dominant themes of western history—the notions of origin, subject, and implicit meaning (Foucault, "History, Discourse, Discontinuity," 237).[19] With Nietzsche, Foucault asserts that "what is found at the beginning of things is not the inviolable identity of their origin; it is the dissension of other things. It is disparity" (Foucault, "NGH," 142). Part of Foucault's extension of the Nietzschean historical project entails dismantling the structure of oppositions upon which the interdiscourse of Enlightenment historiography has been based. In its place Foucault would substitute "the analysis of the field of simultaneous differences and of successive differences" (Foucault, "HDD," 237).

However, at the same time Foucault's understanding of difference denies dialectic contestation, he construes his notion of genealogy in contestatory terms: his "general" history is defined in opposition to "global" history. As Foucault reads it, a global history would regroup all its elements around one principle or unique form, whereas general history describes "the peculiarity of practices, the play of relations, the form of dependencies" (ibid., 240). What emerges from Foucault's most succinct accounting of his theory of history in "Nietzsche, Genealogy, History" is a set of oppositions: plurality, difference, and systems are set against totality, unity, and system; history as an unbroken continuity is opposed to events maintained "in their proper dispersion" ("NGH," 146). Clearly, Foucault's critique of the oppositional logic of dialectics has not escaped that logic itself. Nonetheless, in arguing that it *does*, Foucault effects an important shift in the shape of the historical object. His "effective history" as opposed to both empiricist and global history "shortens its vision to those things closest to it—the body, the nervous system, nutrition, digestion, energies" (ibid., 155). In this shift to the local object of inquiry, the historian's standpoint is effaced, overwhelmed by the immediacy of his own archive and the accumulation of empirical detail (ibid., 140).[20] As a result, the narrativity of history is obscured and Foucault's arguments for difference and dispersion take on the character of empirical claims. Thus, while this new empirical history aims to dismantle the empiricist subject, the alternative subject it constructs bears many of the same features. Autonomous, disengaged, transcendent, it beckons the empirical to speak for itself.

This separation of theoretical subject from historical object which underlies Foucault's discontinuous, effective history makes it impossible for Foucault to answer challenges to the usefulness of his history to a progressive political agenda. The essay "History, Discourse, Discontinuity" is built around Foucault's response to this very challenge as posed to him by the editors of the French journal *Esprit*. They question whether Foucault's history suggests either acceptance of the social system or appeal to an uncontrolled event to disrupt the system. Foucault admits that he has been preoccupied by this very question, but the answer he offers finally renders the terms of the question moot. There is no system, he replies, only systems; no progression, only difference. In such a schema, the writing of history can never *intervene* in social arrangements because intervention is not possible. The most history can offer is an empirical archive which describes. As a result, one of the most banal but important challenges to the historian's account—the question, "So what?"—a question which goes to the heart of the political vision implied in any historical narrative, is suppressed.

The most established appropriation of Foucault in cultural studies—the New Historicism—has not, for the most part, addressed these problems with Foucault's analytic. Likewise, feminists have only to a very limited extent critiqued the particular shape Foucauldian historiography assumes in the newest versions of New Women's History.[21] The conception of power and the inattention to "gender" in the New Historicism tend to distinguish it from the New Women's History. But both share a notion of the relationship between "theory" and "history" and an emphasis on empirical analysis. And ultimately both pose difficulties for a materialist feminist political agenda.

As one of the leading scholarly movements attempting to redress the entrenchment of formalism in literary studies by a call for a return to history, New Historicism has also been one of the prime forces at work in the transformation of literary criticism into cultural studies. Itself an eclectic grouping, New Historicism is associated primarily with a distinctly American and predominantly Foucauldian historiography promoted by the journal *Representations* under the editorship of Stephan Greenblatt. New Historicism in the U.S. is also loosely allied with British "cultural materialism" which has a longer history in the cultural analysis of postwar British marxists, chief among them the late Raymond Williams.[22] Although critiques of the reductive historicism of a class-based analysis fueled the emergence of postmodernism in Europe, in the U.S. during the eighties the rediscovery of history in literary studies has often been played out as an effort to contain the intellectual turmoil precipitated by the advent of postmodernism into the academy. In some quarters "history" has become a way to manage the crisis of representation; for some, a return to positivist historiography seems to offer indeterminate texts a firm and safe ground in factual, historical "contexts."

The New Historicism's role in this crisis management is distinct from a reactionary return to positivism in that it engages in debates over exactly what constitutes history and the workings of power, and embraces postmodern theories of the subject and of language. Nonetheless, while the New Historicism opens texts to their social uses in ways that implicate language and power in the production of cultural meanings, in a crucial respect it shares with more overtly neo-positivist narratives a separation of "theory" from "history." While acknowledging that "explanations about one's methodology become inevitable in materialist criticism" (Dollimore, 13), to the extent that the New Historicism presents itself as "method" it tends to make invisible the theoretical problematic which informs its narrative. New Historicist readings can cordon off an area of inquiry without accounting for the ways their own discursive constructions of history contribute to the materiality of the real right now. This implicit location of the historical object outside of its production in a historical narrative contradicts the *materialist* theory of discourse and of the subject the New Historicism espouses.

Feminists who have turned to the work of Foucault have often celebrated this suppression of "theory" in his analytic as compatible with feminism's critique of "master narratives" and preference for decentered, localized paradigms (Chevigny; Gallagher).[23] This resistance to "theory" is a shared interdiscourse that binds the New Historicist and cultural materialist feminisms of the eighties and the New Women's History. The separation of "theory" from "history" which makes Foucauldian analysis so appealing to some feminist scholars is, however, one of its most pernicious features for a transformative feminist praxis. For the suppression of theory—that is, critical attention to the historian's problematic— underlies the elision of Foucauldian empirical New Historicism into a neo-liberal historiography. Equating localized narrative with non-theoretical narrative assumes that theoretical frameworks can be evaded. Of course, they never can. Making these frameworks "disappear" merely conceals their continuing ideological work.

It is precisely this naturalizing of historical narrative that invites the mere addition of new identities to make narratives of history more "inclusive." This addition may be couched in terms of a concession that identities—whether lesbian, gay, African-American, or Chicana—are discursively produced; but the inclusion of new groups, like the addition of new empirical data, does not necessarily guarantee the transformation of the subject of history. On the contrary, this way of framing the celebration of difference merely re-forms the humanist self by articulating it as a more plural postmodern diversity of selves. What is forfeited in an insistence on micro-analysis is the possibility of forging connections between and among multiple constructions of any identity—woman, say—within and between social formations and historical moments, including the historian's own. Judith Walkowitz's work on sexuality and prostitution in Victorian England, for example, adds a wealth of information to a feminist archive on relations between the law, the popular press, and the discourses of sexuality and class relations in nineteenth-century Britain. But like Carroll Smith-Rosenberg's work on the New Woman in the U.S., the local perimeters of her empirical, Foucauldian-inflected history make invisible the far-reaching political and economic arrangements— the relations of monopoly capitalism and imperialism—in which the nineteenth-century sexualization of the feminine was entangled. Nancy Armstrong's study of *Desire in Domestic Fiction* makes even more explicit that a Foucauldian historical analysis reinforces a pluralist subject. Her argument that the formation of the modern political state was accomplished mainly through bourgeois cultural hegemony so divorces culture from economic change as to dismiss it altogether. The devastating feature of this localized reading of culture for feminist analysis is not that the economy is left out, but that isolating cultural practice in nineteenth-century Britain from its overdetermined production by and through economic as well as cultural and political practices unhinges an emerging discourse of feminine individualism from social arrangements which imbricate the construction of the feminine subject in the west in capital's expanding markets and imperial policy. As a result, analysis of the production of western subjectivities is disengaged from its wide-reaching effects upon and determination by oppressive or exploitative practices in other social formations.

The negative effects of a Foucauldian-inflected ludic postmodernism on feminist history are also evident in Joan Scott's work. For Scott, poststructuralist theory (by way of Foucault and Derrida in particular) offers feminist history a way to address the "play of force" involved in society's construction and implementation of meanings. And it is this play that constitutes both "politics" and textuality. Reducing social relations to language is problematic for feminist history, however, because it closes off signification and discourse from the nondiscursive—from relations of property, of labor, state control.[24] Scott's feminist history is ultimately a regional analytic—a study of "rhetoric or discourse rather than ideology or consciousness" (*Gender*, 4). This emphasis on discourse as rhetoric underscores that the social space for Scott is thoroughly textualized. In her words, "interest is discursively produced" and objects of study like "economics, industrialization, relations of production, factories, families, classes, genders," etc., are "epistemological phenomena" (ibid., 5).

The point is not for feminists to become orthodox marxists and insist on the economic as the prime mover of history, but to suggest that a historical narrative that frames its reading of culture within a regional analytic—whether that region is defined as a particular metropolitan or subaltern social formation or the domains of ideology, culture or representation—will read the discourses and subjectivities circulating within that social formation (the New Woman in Britain or in the northeastern U.S., for example) in isolation. This way of reading history closes off the possibility of addressing the material links which bind various modalities of difference to nondiscursive relations within and across cultures. In that it contributes to the further atomization of social relations, this sort of local reading helps to keep invisible and so sustain the broad-reaching exploitative social relations in which the production of western subjectivities circulates.

Gayatri Spivak asserts that "feminism within the social relations and institutions of the metropolis has something like a relationship with the fight for individualism in the upwardly middle-class mobile bourgeois cultural politics of the European nineteenth century" ("Imperialism and Sexual Difference," 226). Spivak's analogy between contemporary feminism's place within western cultural politics and the function of the discourses of individualism in the re-formation of subjectivities in the nineteenth century is suggestive for the connection it implies between the discourses of Women's History in the west now and the continued ideological force of the discourses out of which the nineteenth-century middle-class subject was articulated. She hints not only of a relationship between the objects of inquiry and the theoretical frameworks of feminist historiography but also of their mutual implication in a broader global political economy. A historical framework that would address these connections without falling into the epistemological trap of a vulgar historicism must be able to explain the relationship between its historical object—the discourses on woman from the late nineteenth century, for example—and its historical subject—the particular feminist standpoint it speaks from.

The work of exploring the relationships among the discourses through which western feminism constructs its history, the conditions of their emergence and redeployment, and the subject of feminist praxis now has barely begun. Moreover, feminist development of a global analytic along the lines suggested in Joan Kelly's essay on the doubled vision of feminist theory is already contending with the powerful reactionary claims made on history by traditional empiricist and neo-Nietzschean discourses, both of which contest systemic analysis. Rather than rush to reinstate woman's agency, feminists need to develop historical narratives whose readings of particular historical conjunctures can also account for the far-reaching economic and political effects of the historian's own frame of intelligibility and the subjectivities it produces. Only in this way can we help make certain that feminist history is not a yet newer New Women's History whose concerns for historical agency merely rearrange rather than revamp the social relations that traditional western historiography has managed so well to sustain.

VI

By way of addressing how materialist feminism might supersede some of the problems in the New Women's History and the New Historicism by reading history from the standpoint of a theory of ideology, I want to look at another set of historical narratives—the spate of feminist readings of Freud's *Dora* which has appeared in a publishing flurry over the past ten years. I have chosen these texts which would not typically be classified as "history" in order to make several points. First of all, reading them as "history" troubles from another angle than the New Women's History the conventional academic divisions between "theory" and its "other," signified variously as "(case) history," "application," or "data." Within this binary structure, these feminist revisions and critiques of *Dora* would most likely be considered more "theory" than "history"—whether feminist, literary, or psychoanalytic. Yet they are in the broadest sense histories.[25]

They read an archive, albeit a very small one, from the past and often make the same empirical claims for their readings as traditional/empiricist history does—professing to offer a more accurate accounting of events as they really happened. But they are also histories in the ideological sense in which I used it earlier. As narratives of the past circulating in culture now they take up a place among the many discourses contesting for the status of truth and in so doing, to whatever degree, they help to shape the social imaginary.

A sustained materialist history of the emergence of psychoanalysis at the turn of the century has yet to be done. But the ground has been prepared from several quarters.[26] Foucault's analysis of the function of sexuality in the formation and disciplining of new subjectivities has been, of course, an enormous contribution. Although in itself a regional analytic, Foucault's work on sexuality as a discourse and a disciplinary apparatus can be articulated within a systemic account of the ideological function and historical emergence of psychoanalysis under capitalism, its effect on the re-formation of western subjectivities, and the wide-ranging economic and political practices it helped install and support. Post-Althusserian marxist and materialist feminist theory in the seventies has also produced indispensable contributions to the formulation of this history. Theorists working across these discourses have aimed to disarticulate the transformative contributions of psychoanalysis from the universalizing and ahistorical assumptions inscribed in its theoretical framework, and to rearticulate them within a materialist and historical problematic.[27] Drawing upon this work, a materialist history of psychoanalysis would have to account for the double-edged effects of the intervention of psychoanalysis in western culture—its tremendously powerful disruption of the centered subject of liberal humanism, as well as its articulation within a set of institutional practices which tamed that disruptive potential.

Psychoanalytic feminist discourses, drawing primarily upon French feminist theory, have been shaped by this uneven legacy. Both feminist and psychoanalytic frameworks are informed by critiques of empiricism, challenging observable givens and the cult of common sense.[28] Jacqueline Rose has often argued that the radical nature of Freud's work for feminism lies in its challenge to the empiricist bourgeois subject. It is this shared subversive ground that constitutes feminism's affinity with psychoanalysis, that is, their mutual recognition that at the very heart of psychic life, lies a resistance to the symbolic order. However, the oppositional position which psychoanalysis takes vis-à-vis the centered subject has been undermined by the bourgeois family romance on which psychoanalytic theory is founded, and by its accompanying notion of an autonomous sexuality. While they have called into question the patriarchal assumptions in this heuristic, more often than not psychoanalytic feminist theories have continued to treat sexuality as autonomous. They have generally not incorporated into their analytic frameworks the cultural materialist's recognition that the drama of sexuality in the middle-class family was played out and made possible by the political econo-mies of race and class, nor have they investigated the shifting ideological force of this notion of sexuality in relation to changes in the configuration of "family" in the west.[29] One effect of these "blindnesses" in psychoanalytic feminist theory is that the preconstructed nodal points by which the discourses of psychoanalysis were articulated within the hegemonic ideology often continue to underwrite the subject—even the unstable postmodern subject—the theory constructs.

Because psychoanalytic feminism is increasingly coming to occupy a promi-nent position within the emerging canon of feminist theory, feminists need to take very seriously the relationship between its subject and the re-formed (postmodern) subject currently being inserted in the dominant discourses of western culture.[30] In various guises and in a range of muted versions, feminist appropriations of the psychoanalytic framework are increasingly buttressing the conservative re-formation of the cultural center, particularly in the humanities. For this reason, feminist theory that draws heavily upon psychoanalysis cannot simply be dismissed by materialist feminists. Furthermore, as the genealogy of materialist feminism indicates, overlaps between the two problematics make a critical engagement between them useful to the elaboration and strengthening of postmodern materialist feminist critique.

Despite their problems, feminist rereadings of *Dora* have offered an important critical wedge in to the reception of Freud's work and have constituted a produc-tive arena for the elaboration of psychoanalytic feminist inquiry. They make visible the patriarchal and phallocentric assumptions written into psychoanalysis. They stress the inscription of patriarchal power in Freud's reading of Dora's hysterical symptoms, especially his insistence on constructing feminine sexuality in terms of genital sensation and desire for the phallus.[31] Feminist have decons-tructed Freud's analysis, reading in the riddles he cannot solve and the conclusions he literally marginalizes in the footnotes of the text clues to Dora's resistance to the subjectivity produced for her by the psychoanalytic treatment. They locate in that resistance a female sexuality—the single simple factor of Dora's deep-rooted homosexual love for Frau K.—which challenges the text's phallocentric normalization of feminine desire. In making visible the patriarchal assumptions in Freud's sexualization of the middle-class woman and in substituting for that reading of woman a narrative of feminine resistance, these feminist critiques offer a significant counterdiscourse to the reigning psychoanalytic paradigm.

Read from the standpoint of a materialist feminist understanding of history, however, they can be seen to pose many problems of their own. First of all, they are written, almost without exception, from within a framework which individualizes the subject. Despite the potential for psychoanalysis to decenter the humanist individual, it is not out of keeping with the incipient individualism in its "psychic" focus for the patriarchal assumptions through which Dora is constructed to be ascribed to Freud, the individual. In some instances the contradictions in the text of *Dora* and their effect on the notion of femininity it posits are read as the product of Freud's fears, unconscious motives, or psycho-sexual past.

Madelon Sprengnether's essay in *The (M)other Tongue* (1985), for example, reads *Dora* as "an attempted seduction via interpretation" (60). The essay proceeds along these lines, analyzing *Dora* as an expression of Freud's anxiety, a "product of his unconscious needs and wishes" (60). Similarly, an essay by Collins, et al. in the special issue of *Diacritics* on *Dora* (1983), argues that Freud's narrative is subject to his own unconscious determinants and therefore open to analysis by the same stratagem. In this respect, these "later" re-visions are much like Steven Marcus' earlier reconsideration of *Dora* (1975). Although Marcus' piece takes an appreciative rather than a critical tack—for Marcus *Dora* is a model of modernist "literary" narrative—he, too, reads the text's contradictory fragmentariness through the unifying device of Freud's consciousness. Issuing their critiques from within a psychoanalytic logic leads several of the essays to locate the text's contradictions in the dynamics of an unsuccessful transference. Collins, et al., for example, conclude that the gaps and contradictions in the narrative are a function of Freud's own refusal to accept Dora's identification of him with Frau K.—that is, his refusal to be identified with the object of Dora's homosexual love (40). The unquestioned acceptance of psychoanalytic transference as a model for change typifies the dominant thematic in all of these readings.

For all that they contest the patriarchal hierarchy implicit in the Oedipal model of sexual development, nonetheless, these essays articulate that criticism in terms of the very same model. The limits this strategy poses are most evident in the overriding emphasis in many of these essays on displacing Freud's phallocentric Oedipal narrative with a pre-Oedipal reading of Dora's actions and symptoms.[32] Exemplified most emphatically in the essays by Mary Jacobus (1986) and Maria Ramas (1980), the pre-Oedipal reading of *Dora* begins, as Freud's does, with the question, "What does Dora want?" This time, however, the answer is that she yearns for her mother and, moreover, that this yearning isn't just to assume the mother's role but to fuse with her. The father's installation as the regulating force of sexual relations is replaced by an argument for the mother's primacy in the prehistory of the gendered subject. This argument takes Freud's dismissal of Dora's mother as symptomatic of the repression of the mother at the root of western civilization. While Mary Jacobus acknowledges her debt to Kristeva, others draw more generally upon the development of this line of thinking in the

French feminist critique of psychoanalysis. In its ideological effects, however, this reading of *Dora* is finally not much different from the one that ascribes her rejection of Freud's analysis to problems in his handling of the transference process. Both keep intact the preconstructed categories that sustain patriarchal oppression in its broadest sense. Among them is an "obvious" binary gender division which equates femininity with femaleness and masculinity with maleness, an accompanying universal notion of woman and of patriarchy, and the natural kinship arrangement of the middle-class heterosexual nuclear family.

Jacqueline Rose has critiqued this "desire to validate the pre-oedipal instance as resistance to the oedipal structure itself" in French feminist thought for leading to a " 'materialization' of the *bodily* relation so that the body of the mother, or more properly, the girl's relation to it, is then placed as being somehow outside repression" (28). While Rose's point is well taken, and has been made by feminists elsewhere, her reading of *Dora* does not provide an alternative materialist understanding of the text and its construction of femininity and sexuality. Rose argues for treating femininity not, as she contends the French feminists do, as a *content*, or even as a discourse, but as a relationship *to* discourse (ibid., 41). The "essence" of that relationship is desire. While Rose's suggestion has the positive effect of destabilizing sexuality as a content or a substance, it is not clear how an insistence on desire per se helps further an understanding either of the operations of the discourse of sexuality in the construction of the feminine or of feminism as a political agenda for social change.[33]

In this respect, Rose places Dora in a transhistorical dimension much like Catherine Clement's analysis of her as the typical hysteric. According to Clement's reading, the hysteric is a mythic figure like the sorceress or witch. As Clement reads her, the hysteric's confinement within the private space of the family ultimately reinforces the family's hold upon her and bars her from full entry into the symbolic. In this way she is emblematic of the foiled desire of all women. The hysteric can take up a place in history only when her desire is underwritten by the twentieth-century feminist (Clement or the feminist press *des femmes*) who displaces Dora and her sisters by calling for the emergence of a "newly born woman" (Gallop, 133). For Clement, "desire" and resistance only attain their materiality in feminist cultural practice. However, this formulation does not account for the circulation of the figure of the hysteric in western culture since the nineteenth century and its effects on the construction of woman. The mythic notion of femininity in Clement's apology for sorceress and hysteric presents these figures as timeless—dislocated from any particular social formation and outside the symbolic order. Much like Rose's paean to desire, this appeal to myth unhinges the hysteric from her discursive construction in a symbolic order whose articulation is always historically specific.

In seeming contrast, Nancy Armstrong reads *Dora* in terms of the cultural context of the late nineteenth century. Despite the overtly "historicist" frame of her study, however, Armstrong does not very thoroughly rearticulate her appropriations from psychoanalysis within a historicist paradigm. The easy mingling of Foucault and French feminism in Armstrong's reading indicates the popularity of these analytics in feminist cultural studies now and points to some of the difficulties in the theory of history their conjuncture implies. Like Marcus, Armstrong reads *Dora* as participating in the larger modernist effort to enclose cultural materials within a structure of consciousness which removes them from history. However, she also reads this strategy as co-operating with an assumption of sexual difference as the basis for human identity, an assumption that underlies and undermines any radical alternative. Armstrong pursues this argument in terms of the historical specificity of Freud's text, which she presents from the vantage point of the contest between the new social sciences and an older tradition of female knowledge circulating in domestic fiction. In part as the effect of shifts in the formation of subjectivities incurred through the emergence of a dominant class of new professionals and bureaucrats and the accompanying development of the position of disinterested technical "knower," new forms of knowledge and of individuality emerged in the late nineteenth century. Knowledges that had belonged to the housewife and mother came under professional scrutiny and a "body of female knowledge" that had once permeated the discourses of both the common sense and middle-class fiction was displaced by literature's special function as "art," alienated from national, race, or gender affiliations. Freud's case studies, she argues, are paradigmatic modernist texts in that domestic categories are dissolved within the self, setting the stage for further penetration, mapping, and *control* of the individual (Armstrong, 229).

This notion of "controlling" the individual seems quite at odds with Foucault's theory of the discursive construction of subjects upon which Armstrong ostensibly draws. However, the concept of a subversive identity prior to the mechanisms of social control *is* in keeping with the French feminist theories which also inform Armstrong's concepts of gender, feminine resistance, and desire. For Armstrong, the space for feminine identity is the "unzoned female body" (ibid., 230). It is there "that one finds a kind of desire not controlled by the phallus" (ibid.). Much older than the Freudian sexualized consciousness, this desire is encapsulated in the history of sexuality recorded in the tradition of domestic fiction. And it is this tradition which serves as the utopian moment of Armstrong's argument. The effect is to make female bodily desire the motivating cause of historical change (ibid.). Although Armstrong critiques the dynamics of Freud's narrative which establish gender on the one-sided fact of the male's biological nature, she, too, posits gender as biologically defined, but in terms that merely reverse the Freudian paradigm. In this curious blend of Foucauldian and French feminist theories, the *discursivity* of Freud's narrative becomes the "struggle between male and female modes of representation for the authority to define female desire" (ibid., 237). This biologizing of femininity effaces the specific class and national interests inscribed in the construction of feminine sexuality in *Dora*, and locates the agency for historical change and resistance in an ahistorical, asocial "female desire."

As in the more overtly psychoanalytic readings, eclectic accounts of *Dora* like Armstrong's remove the discursive or ideological materiality of the "histories" they offer from any connection to economic or political practices. Consequently, readings like this that gesture toward history tend to lapse into formalism. The text's "symptoms" are read as Freud reads symptoms—through the lens of the family romance or its extension in the transference relationship—and "overdetermination" remains, as it is for Freud, a matter of individual psychic cathexis. Sharon Willis, for example, examines the overdetermined analytic scene in terms of the relationship between the analyst's unconscious desires and a collective unconscious which she calls "idealogy." Without working through the contesting analytics through which these concepts are drawn, however, it is difficult to develop a coherent theoretical understanding of the relationships among the text of *Dora*, the analytic scene it "represents," the feminine sexuality it promotes, and its bearing on the discursive construction of subjectivity.

Nonetheless, these feminist readings of *Dora* are significant as histories because they underscore how the interpretation/renarration of texts from a prior historical moment intervenes in the construction of subjectivities in the present. The "gaps" in them—between theories of gender grounded in social discourse or biology, between anti-patriarchal critique or a framework that merely reverses the terms of a patriarchal hierarchy—are all produced out of western feminism's contemporary ideological moment. While they intervene in the phallocentric assumptions in psychoanalysis, the alternatives they project tend to construct a notion of woman that reinforces the prevailing ideology of the feminine: a monolithic and universal category which privileges gender over other modes of difference, often invoking an umproblematized notion of sexuality as a prediscursive substance. While some feminists, like Sharon Willis, indicate that the bourgeois social structures out of which *Dora* emerged maintained an unequal distribution of power along sexual lines "among others, of course" (58), scant mention is made of these "others" and how their construction intersects with the hysteric. Coming to terms with the material relation between the hysteric and these "others," however, would require, at the very least, unravelling the intersection between the sexualization of the feminine and the preconstructed categories of difference it is entangled with, its ideological effects, and the economic and political forces that it sustains and disrupts.

When it does arise in these readings, the question of the "other" tends to circle around the unsettling figures of the lesbian and the nurse/governess, and in a manner that often disrupts the coherence of the analyses. Feminist critics have quite confidently pointed out Freud's marginalization of Dora's love for Frau K. and his inability to imagine female genital sex.[34] However, while several critics have read Freud's failure of imagination as the projection of a male-centered sexuality upon Dora, the problem of how to make sense of the heterosexual assumptions in this projection and of how Dora's resistance to it is discursively inscribed is more troublesome. Moreover, when these issues are addressed in these readings they tend to be dealt with exclusively in terms of the Oedipal drama. Interpretations that aim to displace the Oedipal version of feminine sexuality with a pre-Oedipal feminine sexuality actually rely upon and help reinforce the suturing of sexuality to a binary notion of gender difference. It is this unquestioned equation that allows Maria Ramas to argue that Dora's pre-Oedipal love for a woman underlies Ida Bauer's "identification with masculinity" and her emphasis on oral sexuality (478). Construing a woman's sexual desire for another woman as "masculine" articulates feminine sexuality within a gender system that depends on a preconstructed heterosexual division of the sexes into opposites. By allowing the preconstructed heterosexual organization of gender to go unexamined we perpetuate its status as "normal" and "natural," beyond history or critical inquiry, and so mystify its ideological force and the alternatives it obscures.

In a more subtle way, the heteronormative articulation of sexuality also underscores Nancy Armstrong's objection to Freud's equation of true identity with genital sexuality and of genital sexuality with desire for the penis.[35] She acknowledges that Freud opposes the construction of sexuality as instinctual/genital to an "other" sexuality—Dora's "gynaecophilic" love for Frau K.—which he can only acknowledge in the margins of the text. But Armstrong translates this "gynaecophilia" into "women's knowledge" (240). Through this sleight of hand, the regulation of sexuality by a heterosexual gender system is taken for granted and the possibility of an "other" sexuality is dismissed.[36] One need not read between the lines of Armstrong's argument to come to this conclusion. Her text is quite explicit: "That Freud should insist upon Dora's lesbian desires in the face of the outcome of her narrative is peculiar indeed" (240). Stunningly, the authority for this declaration is Freud's "proof" of Dora's heterosexuality: " 'Years have gone by since her visit. In the meantime the girl has married' " (240). If it were not for the clear seriousness of this remark, the invocation of marriage here to settle the case on Dora's questionable heterosexuality might be read as a tongue in cheek reference to the classic comic ending, a cunning lesbian joke. However, the appeal to marriage to guarantee sexuality seems to be indeed, *straight*forward. In the best tradition of domestic fiction, it closes off a host of questions the construction of feminine sexuality in *Dora* so symptomatically leaves open: the relationships among sexual knowledge, "genital sexuality," resistance to heterosexuality, and lesbian desire—their intersection by gender as well as class differences and their traversal by the discourses of imperialism—as well as the question of how all of them affect and are affected by the reader's historical standpoint.

Armstrong is not alone in leaving the category of heterosexuality unquestioned. Maria Ramas, for example, assumes that Dora and Frau K.'s discussions "were unquestionably of heterosexual phantasies which mediated the sexual relation between the two women . . . The man is necessary because desire viewed through the Oedipal complex is always a triangular affair" (491). On the "other " hand, declarations of Dora's lesbianism—like Cixous' celebration of Dora's "beautiful, staggering homosexuality" (148), or Gallop's endorsement of her ambiguous bisexuality—tend to merely redress an unproblematized sexuality by a counter-invocation of the obvious or the indeterminate. If we are to develop ways of reading the function of the discourses of sexuality in the formation of subjectivities as a crucial element in historical narrative, we cannot afford to fall back on assumptions or accolades which take for granted the very categories we are setting out to examine. To do so—even from a counterhegemonic discourse—only serves to keep in place, unquestioned, the modalities of difference across which the discourses of sexuality range, both as they emerged in the late nineteenth century and as they circulate in the present. Before feminist critical practice can fully come to terms with the hysteric's "bisexuality" and leave behind the roles she helplessly denounced, as Clement would have the "newly born woman" do, we must understand more fully the materiality of sexuality and its function in the reproduction of the feminine subject across the modes of alterity inscribed in the social imaginary in a particular historical moment.

The gaps in this recent feminist archive on *Dora* around the question of sexuality are complemented by the critical reception of the figure of the govern-ess.[37] Although feminist readings of this case study often take up an analysis of Freud's sexualization of Dora's relation to her governess, particularly in terms of their shared sexual knowledge, their critique of the text's equation of active, even aggressive, sexuality with the "lower classes" does not disrupt the otherwise homogeneous category of the feminine. In fact, quite the contrary. Jane Gallop, for example, indicates that the figure of the nurse is crucial to the particular way in which the family came to be sexualized in the development of psychoanalysis. In Freud's reformulation of the seduction theory into the Oedipal complex, the father can no longer be blamed as the perpetrator of the seduction. Even the mother, to the extent that she is the child's primary caretaker, only seduces her son unwittingly. The role of actual intentional seducer falls to the nurse or servant.[38] In this way, the *agent provocateur* for sexualizing the family defines a liminal position between the private sphere of the family and the workplace. As Gallop sees it, the nurse represents an alterity which is inassimilable to the laws of endogamy and exogamy. "She is there at the heart of the family, in the cell nucleus" (145). But at the same time, she is a threshold figure existing between "within the family" and "outside the family" (146). While the nurse/governess' class position establishes her alterity, as Gallop indicates, this alterity is underscored by her defeminization, and it is this defeminization which prob-lematizes Gallop's ready equation of the positions of mother, wife, and servant under the umbrella of "woman's" subordination in a patriarchal economy (148).

How, then, can the text's identification of Dora with the nurse/governess be read? The answer is, I would argue, ideologically. If the sexualization of Dora by way of an oblique identification with the figure of the nurse/governess and the text's management of the contradictions this identification poses are read ideologically, the historical conditions which this construction helped manage would be made visible. The daughter's sexualization by way of the figure of the governess hints of shifts in economic and political arrangements in the west that will require new relations between private and public spheres, new disciplinary mechanisms, and new subjectivities. Dora can be read as a product of this ideological shift, her sexualization related to her historical position as middle-class woman. From this standpoint the particular sexualization of a Viennese middle-class daughter by way of the working-class servant in her home could be seen as one facet of a broad reconfiguration of the feminine subject in the late nineteenth century, a reconfiguration brought on by an overdetermined crisis in capital's relations of production as it moved into its monopoly phase.

As middle-class women were increasingly recruited into the marketplace, the ideology of separate spheres and the notion of the sexless angel in the house was put under pressure. The figure of the governess as working woman inside the home—potential threat to the sexual and property rights marriage secured—had already served as a site of ideological contest since early in the nineteenth century. As caretaker and model for the young, she was simultaneously linked to the chaste decorum of middle-class ideals and to the unregulated sexuality and sexual aggression associated with working-class women (Poovey, *Uneven Develop-ments*, 128–33). By the later part of the century, however, the middle-class daughter, increasingly being recruited into the job market and the professions, displaced the governess as a site of ideological concern and as the preeminent threatening figure of feminine excess.

If the place of this New Woman within renegotiated bourgeois social arrange-ments is read only from the vantage point of Austrian, British, or U.S. middle-class culture, the implication of these shifts in more far-reaching economic and political arrangements is easily occluded and a western middle-class feminist standpoint readily reinforced. Freud's framework for reading the hysteric belies these local boundaries through its inscription of the feminine object of inquiry in the discourse of colonialism. In one of his early lectures on the aetiology of hysteria delivered to the Psychiatric and Neurological Association in 1896, Freud launches his controversial argument against Charcot's theory of the hereditary origins of hysteria, proposing instead to elaborate on Breuer's thesis that hysteria is caused by traumatic experiences in the patient's life. Freud's contribution in this lecture is the contention that the experiential origins of hysteria can make themselves known through the patient's symptoms if they are "heard as witnesses to the history of the origin of the illness" ("Aetiology," 192). In order to explain this notion, which defies not just credibility but intelligibility for his audience, Freud employs an analogy that would be more familiar to them, one "taken from an advance that has in fact been made in another field of work" (ibid.). In the long passage that follows, Freud spins out his metaphor, inviting his audience to identify with the position of investigator in this "new" and unnamed endeavor: "Imagine that an explorer arrives in a little-known region where his interest is aroused by an expanse of ruins . . . with half effaced and unreadable inscriptions" (ibid.). Faced with these indecipherable ruins, he may question the inhabitants, "perhaps semi-barbaric peoples," about what tradition tells them of these stones or he may set them to work to uncover what is buried. If successful, the discoveries are self-explanatory; the inscriptions may be deciphered and translated: presto— "*Saxa loquantur!*" (ibid., 191–92).[39]

Jacqueline Rose has argued that Freud's "discoveries" here pose a forceful challenge to empiricism in that for the first time the hysterical woman was not judged by being looked at or examined; instead "she was allowed to *speak*" (98). However, once we read this challenge in terms of the analogy in which it is framed, we can see that like the speaking stones of the ancient culture which the European explorer "discovers," the hysteric does not "speak" for herself. In fact, as Freud's own text unconsciously reveals, her historical emergence as the object of scientific inquiry places her speech immediately within the nexus of discursive and nondiscursive relations upon which the European explorer's "discoveries" depends.

I cite this example to make the point that reading/writing the history of psycho-analysis has to take into account the ways that psychoanalysis inscribes the hysteric in a Eurocentric symbolic order whose categories remain unaltered. That Freud's explanation of hysteria couches it in terms of the analyst's reading practice, which in turn relies upon the conceptual framework of anthropology and imperial conquest, troubles any simple equation of his object of inquiry with an obvious "woman"—old or new. Freud's analogy indicates very forcefully the metonymic relations between the subject of psychoanalysis and the subjects of the emergent social sciences. It also suggests that their shared interdiscourse might well collaborate in the suppression of a more radical narrative of the re-formation of western subjectivities, a narrative which the hysteric's history continues to shelter.

As Jacqueline Rose has argued, perhaps the most productive response to the charge that psychoanalysis has no sense of history is not to dismiss it as a useful analytic framework but to both acknowledge how it has functioned as history and to rewrite that history, including its reinforcement of western imperialism and the interventions it has continually made into the institutions which control women's lives. Rose's brief sketch of those interventions hints of the complex articulations of class and sexuality upon which the founding of the discipline depended: the hysteric is both the overeducated and the under-class woman who indulges in uncontrolled or nonproductive sexuality. Recognizing, as Rose does, that Freud's earliest investigations on hysteria took place not in the parlors of Vienna but in the Salpetriere Clinic in Paris, suggests that further work remains to be done to read the complex negotiations of social difference that psychoanalysis managed in the sexualization of the western woman. A materialist feminist history of psychoanalysis and its function in the sexualization of the new western woman needs to attend to the ways its discourse relies upon an array of preconstructed categories—like heterosexuality and colonial conquest—often deploying and intersecting with the discourse of the "new" to transfer these subterranean anchors for value and normativity from one site to another.

VII

I agree with Carroll Smith-Rosenberg's argument that "the New Woman is critically important to new feminist scholars" ("The Body Politic," 120), but for a very different reason than hers. To my mind, the figure of the New Woman is interesting for feminists now because the discourses out of which she emerged continue to intervene in contemporary ideologies of the feminine. How we read this figure—as instance of generational difference among feminists, as ideological containment of feminine excess, or as one of many interlinked sexualized subjects serving the new relations of empire—is in part the effect of debates over history and the social which emerged in the late nineteenth century.[40] Reading the New Woman from the standpoint of a theory of history as ideology challenges some of the central categories and assumptions of recent feminist thought. Chief among them is the notion of identity. A global historical logic explodes the remnants of identity thinking harbored in the micro-analytics of a New Historicism that limits its view of history to the conjunctural relations within a single social formation. Perhaps most importantly, reading the New Woman within a global historical narrative situates the threatening other within the fabric of a particular social arrangement, in the preconstructed categories of difference and value which anchor the subjectivities it requires. In this way a global history offers a theoretical framework that in Maria Lugones' phrase, puts plurality "in the very structure of a theory" (13). That it is a systemic plurality means that while the particularities of colonialism, racism, and heterosexism can be articulated in their fullest historical specificity, the connections between them are not lost to a celebration of difference as play or diversity.

In order to rewrite history "otherwise," the identity politics that underscores the New Women's History will have to be dismantled. As A. Sivanandan has commented,

> if black and third world feminism has meant anything, it has meant, on the one hand, a corrective to the personalization of politics and the individualization of power in the white women's movement and, on the other, an attempt to forge a unity between race, gender, and class. ("RAT," 31)

A feminist theory genuinely interested in moving beyond the "white women's movement" or the "straight women's movement" must pursue a commitment to thinking through the connections between modalities of difference. It can not rely on problematics that reinforce personalization or that disallow the formulation of links among practices and social formations. Nor can it afford to fall back on the logic of pluralism and eclecticism. Taken to their fullest implications, critiques of western feminism like those of Maria Lugones, Evelyn Brooks-Higgenbotham, Hazel Carby, Chandra Mohanty, and others indicate that, in Carby's words, "the process of accounting for the historical and contemporary position of black women challenges the use of some of the central categories and assumptions of recent mainstream feminist thought" ("White Woman, Listen!," 213).[41] The narratives out of which the New Women's History have been written indicate that "woman," "history," and their increasingly troublesome "other"—"theory"—might well be some of those categories. As Elizabeth Weed has argued in the introduction to *Coming To Terms*, theoretical inquiry into these categories is urgent for those concerned with social change. The historian's critique of identity in this sense is not an effort to deny agency as

> necessary for political action but to resist what is dangerously seductive because familiar. It is the politics which ask "what is to be done?" rather than "who am I?" which attempt to avoid the identificatory structures available everywhere, those structures which enable us to see women of color but not race, blacks but not whites. (xxi)

While identity politics helps, provisionally at least, to overcome the alienation and paranoia that capital visits differently on various groups, it ultimately fragments struggle by sending "groups" off in search of their sectional identities, leaving the system of relations upon which they rely itself unscathed.[42] Jenny Bourne underscores this point in her critique of identity politics as the new fashion of the liberal left.

> Identity politics is all the rage. Exploitation is out (it is extrinsically determinist). Oppression is in (it is intrinsically personal). What Is To Be Done has been replaced by Who Am I. Political culture has ceded to cultural politics. The material world has passed into the metaphysical. The Blacks, the Women, the Gays have all searched for themselves. (1)

If feminist history is to address the ways exploitation and oppression shape the social construction of difference, it cannot be a narrative that clings to identity politics.[43] Putting "plurality in the very structure of our theory" means we will have to radically *re*-structure that theory to make connections between and among domains of the social. Making these connections has the disruptive potential not only to challenge but also to reimagine the subject of feminist praxis, from an identity or a coalition of identities—which keeps the boundaries between groups, regions, social formations intact—to a collective global standpoint. At the very least this collective subject rewrites "New Women's History" as "Feminist History," a narrative whose revolutionary power lies in its potential to transform the interdiscourse of hegemonic culture.

VIII

History is a culture's narrative of itself. It appears wherever a people's stories circulate. The disciplining of history "proper" in schools and universities tends to legitimize certain narratives as "real history" and delegitimize or suppress others as propaganda, fiction, folk lore, or popular culture. Feminist historiography tells one version of this suppression. And in the telling it helps clear the space for histories from the "other" side. As feminists have long recognized, the task of rewriting history spills outside of disciplinary boundaries and resists easy relegation to one department or program. More than that, it exceeds the confines of the academy itself, appearing wherever feminist narratives circulate—in the home and in the streets, in community centers, movie theatres, clinics, conference rooms . . .

Within feminist critical inquiry there is a strong discursive "community" which has been and continues to speak from the limits of proper discipline. One of these limits is, of course, the academic institution itself. The relationship between the production of feminist history in the academy (whether a "proper" history or not) and in the larger culture is complex and highly mediated. The density of these mediations is such that the academy is perhaps not the site where revolutionary histories will be written. But how feminist scholars write history, and the extent to which their texts comply with the demands of well disciplined academic professionalism, does have an impact— however indirect—on how the culture's narratives of itself are told anew, and on the possibilities for social change that reinvention enables.

As feminism's crisis of authority unfolds, materialist feminists working in the academy are making use of postmodernism's powerful counterhegemonic theories of the subject-in-language in order to renarrate their cultures, particularly the social construction of woman as a multiply-differentiated and historically-specific subject position. The radical effectiveness of this appropriation depends to a great extent on the counterhegemonic coherence of our materialist feminist problematic. It is because eclectic appropriations "overlook" the materiality of discourse that they do not establish this coherence. As a result, the radical potential of the discourses they draw upon is readily recuperated into a familiar liberal pluralism. Much of the argument of this book has been aimed at explaining how ideology critique as a mode of reading might allow materialist feminism to appropriate postmodern knowledges in such a way as to make visible the contesting interests at stake in their social analytics and rearticulate them within a theoretical framework that is congruent with feminism's political agenda.

One of the positive consequences of opening up "woman" as feminism's subject is that in the process the aims of feminism as a political movement have also been re-examined. Recognizing "woman" as spread across multiple modalities of difference has pushed many feminists to address the ways in which the interests of feminism as a political movement for social change are entangled in the hierarchical structuring of racial, class, sexual, and gendered subject positions. And this recognition has in turn entailed rewriting the subject of feminism. Reading the history of the New Woman should teach us that merely claiming to be new is not enough for a radical discourse. In itself, *the new* is neither progressive nor conservative. Its oppositionality is determined by the frame of intelligibility in which it is deployed, the social logic and the values encoded in it, and their effects on social reality. Throughout the preceding chapters I have argued that the collective subject of a materialist feminist standpoint seizes upon the transformative and utopian potential of the new by virtue of the aims of its systemic analysis: the equal distribution of social resources and power, the end of exploitation, and the dismantling of patriarchy. Materialist feminism can make claims for the radical force of its practice and "new" collective subject on the basis of this revolutionary vision—the telos—of our analytic.

Doing this, however, is not the same as writing a historical master narrative. It does not mean devising a theoretical framework that solves the problems of a collective emancipatory movement once and for all. Materialist feminist theory embraces the authority of its narratives in the knowledge that its mode of reading, like any revolutionary practice, is *in* history and so provisional, always circulating in a field of contesting discourses that challenge and redefine its horizons. Through a reciprocal and ongoing process of disarticulation and rearticulation, materialist feminism forges alliances with other political discourses which oppose capitalism and patriarchy. And like any narrative, it harbors an "other" within. The task of writing history from a materialist feminist standpoint is to labor continually to release that "other," the unsaid of feminist praxis, and through this process of ongoing critique, strengthen the oppositional power of feminism's collective subject and emancipatory aims.

Notes

1. Feminism in the Postmodern Academy: Toward a Global Social Analytic

1. Discussions of various reform efforts in response to the crisis in the humanities can be found in Brantlinger; Cain; Morton and Zavarzadeh, *Theory/Pedagogy/Politics;* Gless; and Widdowson.

2. Feminism shares this distinguishing feature with post-colonial and anti-racist discourses. It is by now a commonplace that the relationship of these political movements to postmodernism is highly contested. See for instance, Hooks, "Postmodern Blackness"; West, "Specificity"; and Spivak, "Subaltern."

3. Although by now treatments of the relationship of feminism to postmodernism are too numerous to cite exhaustively, the following texts address some of the key issues raised by their intersection: Ebert; Flax; Giroux; "The 'Difference' of Postmodern Feminism," Harding, *Whose Science? Whose Knowledge?*; Kipnis; Moi, "Feminism, Postmodernism, and Style"; Hooks, "Postmodern Blackness"; Newton, "History As Usual"; Fraser and Nicholson; Paul Smith; and Suleiman.

4. Ebert's succinct formulation of the distinction between ludic and resistance postmodernism ("The 'Difference' of Postmodern Feminism") is notable for the materialist feminist position it argues from. Other differentiations among postmodern discourses along similar lines include Giroux; Huyssen; Morton and Zavarzadeh, *Theory/Pedagogy/Politics* and *Theory, (Post)modernity, Opposition;* Mohan "Modernity and Imperialism"; and Norris.

5. Versions of this argument can be found in Ebert, "The 'Difference' of Postmodern Feminism"; Moi, "Feminism, Postmodernism, and Style"; and Rooney, "Discipline."

6. See for example Derrida's *of Grammatology,* or "Structure, Sign and Play in the Discourse of the Human Sciences," in *Writing and Difference.*

7. See Hall, "Brave New World" and Hebdige for an analysis of the requirements for

139

the emergence of "new identities" in the "new times" of late capitalism. For a critique of the left's attention to identities as itself a function of economic upheavals which have shifted capital's center of gravity from the center to the periphery and within the center to peripheral workers, see Sivanandan, *Communities of Resistance*.

8. For a summary sketch of the development of the globalized economy after World War II, see Shor or Robins; for a more detailed elaboration see Mandel.

9. "Late capitalism" as an object of inquiry has been theorized from a range of philosophical positions. My use the concept here is drawn from Mandel's division of the capitalist mode of production into three phases: market capitalism, the monopoly stage, and multinational or "late" capital. Emerging from a global crisis generally traced to the transformation in relations of production following World War II, late capitalism constitutes the most saturated form of capitalism, colonizing in its sweep nature and the unconscious through strategies like the Green Revolution and the increasingly pervasive media and advertising industries.

10. For an analysis of the role of one prestigious university in these arrangements see Trumpbour.

11. In this capacity, Gayatri Spivak has called teachers of the humanities the "discjockeys of an advanced capitalist technocracy" ("Explanation and Culture," 208).

12. The professionalization of western middle-class women in the eighties and the related retrenchment among western and especially academic feminists from a political agenda aimed at wide-ranging social transformation has begun to be addressed critically by feminists on the left. See for example Breines et al.; Ehrenreich et al.; Pollitt; and Stacey. However, these critiques of post-feminism fail to demonstrate the ways the simultaneous professionalization of western women and the increased emphasis on marriage and the nuclear family are possible because of the shift onto "third-world" women of modes of exploitation under which "first-world" women had previously suffered. The conditions of exploitation have not disappeared, they have simply been displaced. The privilege of postfeminism, however, depends on the invisibility of this displacement. For a global analysis of post-industrialism's impact on women in the electronics industry in particular, see Hennessy and Mohan, "Postindustrial Feminism"; Nash and Fernandez-Kelly; Ong; and Sivanandan, "Imperialism and Disorganic Development." For a description of women's position in western post-industrial society under the "informatics of domination," see Haraway's "Manifesto."

13. See Mohan, "Modernity," 6ff. for an elaboration of these points.

14. A glance at the business pages of any major newspaper will confirm this. To name only two examples—in 1991 Coke launched its new global advertising campaign and Colgate Palmolive placed oversized ads recruiting consultants on diversity.

15. The diversity movement is not the only instructive backdrop for this renewed emphasis on the necessary critical force to cultural studies. The history of the disciplining of American Studies serves as a cautionary example of uncritical interdisciplinarity. See Brantlinger; and Rooney, "Discipline and Vanish" on this.

16. The word "historicity" here is meant to convey that the circulation of materialist

feminism as a discourse in history is always subject to the ongoing contest over differently interested claims to truth.

17. Examples of eclecticism in materialist feminist work will be offered in some detail in chapters 3 and 4.

18. For a critique of eclecticism, see Rooney, *Seductive Reasoning*. A succinct treatment of its effects on materialist feminist practice can be found in Glazer.

19. For an interesting treatment of the late capitalist "era of globalization" and its relation to calls for "localism" in western politics and culture see Robins.

20. Examples of feminist arguments *for* this kind of eclectic appropriation of Foucault include Walkowitz et al.; Armstrong, "Introduction"; and Diamond and Quinby, "Introduction."

21. Among those who have found Laclau and Mouffe's arguments important for the development of a resistance postmodernism are Aronowitz, "Postmodernism and Politics"; Giroux; and Paul Smith.

22. Foucault, *Power/Knowledge,* 53; hereafter abbreviated as *P/K*.

23. Several critics of post-marxism have commented on the tendency in these discourses to reduce marxism to one single theory or to conflate Marx and marxism. See, for example, Geras; Wolff and Cullenberg.

24. Foucault, *History of Sexuality*, vol. 1, 92–93; hereafter abbreviated as *HS*. Other instances of Foucault's hints at a global frame of reference can be found in *Power/ Knowledge*. In his essay on "Truth and Power," for example, he refers to the internal regimes of power that affect a science and which at certain points undergo a global modification (113). In discussing the function of the specific intellectual he cites as one of the risks of this activity the inability to develop struggles because of the lack of a global strategy (130). To what extent Foucault endorses this global strategy and how it intersects with the intellectual's intervention in regimes of truth is not entirely clear.

25. For feminist critiques which address the consequences of the normative vacuum in Foucault, see Fraser, "Foucault on Modern Power"; and Hartsock, "Foucault On Power: A Theory for Women?" For a feminist critique of the problem of power in Foucault for theorizing oppression see Alcoff, "Feminist Politics and Foucault."

26. See Aronowitz, "Socialist Strategy," and Geras for positive and negative critiques of Laclau and Mouffe. For a succinct summary of Laclau's post-marxism, its contest with the logic of the dialectic, and its coincidence with a psychoanalysis based on a logic of the signifier, see his "Psychoanalysis and Marxism."

27. Laclau and Mouffe are quite explicit about this two-pronged social order and its bearing on their own position. As they see it, the plurality of contemporary struggles has given rise to a theoretical crisis, and "it is at the middle point of this two-way movement between the theoretical and the political that our own discourse will be located" (2).

28. For analysis of Laclau and Mouffe as an instance of ludic postmodern social theory see Zavarzadeh and Morton, *Theory/(Post)modernity/Opposition*.

29. See Callinicos; and Hall, "Marxism Without Guarantees." For other arguments along these lines see Tony Bennett; and Resnick and Wolff.

30. For a rereading of "totality" as a framework in which various knowledges are positioned rather than as a Hegelian unity, see Jameson, "History as Class Consciousness," 58–63, and *The Political Unconscious,* 50–57, 190–94. For a history of the concept of totality in western marxism, see Jay.

31. In addition to Laclau and Mouffe's analysis, bibliographies on recent critiques of Althusser can be found in Boswell; and the Student Marxist Collective.

32. Laclau and Mouffe argue that the intuition of the materiality of discourse within marxist theory, the notion that ideologies are more than ideas but are embodied in institutions and rituals, reached an impasse in Althusser and Gramsci because it "was referred to the field of *ideologies,* that is, to the formation that was thought under the concept of 'superstructure' " as an *a priori* unity (109). Likewise, Foucault posits ideology as a flawed concept because necessarily secondary to an economic infrastructure (*P/K,* 118).

33. See Omvedt on rethinking the construction of gender at this level.

34. As I have indicated already, post-marxist theories locate their analysis at this level. Many of the impasses of so-called "totalizing" marxist or materialist feminist theories can be understood in terms of a failure to differentiate distinct levels of analysis. In fact, few marxist theorists emphasize the importance of distinguishing levels of analysis. For a discussion of this point in a range of contexts and suggestions for theorizing at all three levels, see Pat and Hugh Armstrong, 210–11; Thompson, 134–35; and Wright, 7–12.

35. My treatment of the global analytic in this section is indebted to collaborative work with Rajeswari Mohan and with the Student Marxist Collective at Syracuse University.

36. As much of the recent work on class and ideology has indicated, rethinking the category "class" from its reified construction as "proletariat" in classic marxism to include a range of subjectivities need not require abandoning the dialectic. See Hamilton and Barrett; Haug; Omvedt; Resnick and Wolff; and Wright.

37. See Rosalind Delmar, "What Is Feminism?" for an assessment of the crisis in feminism which links the problematic signifier "woman" to a general political crisis of representation. While Delmar questions a feminist political agenda based on the interests of "woman" as a self-evident social category, she does not advance an alternative. Denise Riley, in *Am I that Name?: Feminism and the Category of "Women" in History,* treats the relation between "woman" and "women" as dependent on the historical specificities of a hierarchical distinction between the sexes. In exploring the implications of the category "woman" as ultimately an indeterminate effect, however, Riley recommends a situational praxis for feminism—claiming the category "woman" when it is strategically useful. Such a practice can serve to mystify the ways these shifting articulations of "woman" and the sexual hierarchy they maintain are related to larger productive forces. Although it does not engage with postmodernism, Elizabeth Spelman's analysis of "inessential woman" is an

important critique of the white, western, middle-class privilege that informs the category "woman" in feminist thought.

38. For examples of the first sort see Kristeva; Irigaray; Cixous and their appropriators, especially Jardine; and Moi, *Sexual/Textual Politics*. For examples of the second see Armstrong; Nussbaum and Brown, "Introduction"; Poovey, "Introduction" to *Uneven Developments*.

39. For a critique of Jardine which develops this point further see Moi, "Feminism, Postmodernism, and Style."

40. For a discussion of the intersections of feminism, modernity and postmodernity, see Giroux.

41. For a summary of the debate on dual systems theory, see Sargent.

2. The Materiality of Discourse: Feminism and Post-Marxism

1. The strongest feminist criticisms of the Foucauldian problematic have been those of Nancy Fraser and Linda Alcoff. Both point to problems in Foucault's concept of power for an emancipatory politics that addresses patriarchal as well as other modes of oppression.

2. For further critiques of Foucault's notion of discursive practice see Lecourt; and Callinicos.

3. Foucault has explicitly denied the discourse of his own analysis the status of material practice. His opening remarks in "The Order of Discourse" are probably one of the most bald admissions of the desire that underlies this evasion: "Desire says: 'I should not like to have to enter this risky order of discourse; I should like it to be all around me like a calm,, deep transparence, infinitely open, where others would fit in with my expectations, and from which truths would emerge one by one; I should only have to let myself be carried, within it and by it, like a happy wreck' " (51).

4. See *HS* for an example: "Just as the network of power relations ends by forming a dense web that passes through apparatuses and institutions, without being exactly localized in them, so, too, the swarm of points of resistance traverses social stratifications and individual unities" (96). Critiques of Foucault's theory of power and the problems it raises for theorizing resistance can be found in Alcoff, "Feminist Politics"; Callinicos; Cavallari; and Fraser, "Foucault on Modern Power".

5. There is an ideological similarity between this Foucauldian notion of subjectivity and the concept of oppositionality in some feminist standpoint theory, for example Dorothy Smith's notion of an "insider's sociology" which begins in a "locally embodied site of knowledge . . . where the subject is actually located" ("Sociological Theory," 6–7). In both cases the oppositional knowledge or subject is ambiguously linked to the relations of ruling which regulate, organize, govern, and otherwise control our societies.

6. For Foucault's fullest elaboration of the materiality of the body see "Nietzsche, Genealogy, History," hereafter referred to as "NGH."

7. See Fraser, "Foucault's Body Language" on how Foucault's politics of negation is

tempered by his turn to a metaphysics of bodies which may be no less subject to co-optation and mystification than Foucault claims humanist critique has been. For further critiques of Foucault's conception of bodies and pleasures, see Alcoff, "Feminist Politics"; Habermas, "Genealogical Writing"; and Zinner.

8. For an example of the former see Poovey, "Scenes," and of the latter see Laqueur. Susan Bordo's essay on "The Body and the Reproduction of Femininity" is an interesting instance of both. In treating the body as the inscribed surface on which culture's rules are etched, she emphasizes its discursivity; at other times, however, she presents the body as speaking an inchoate protest from beyond or outside of discourse.

9. Additional critiques of the historical conditions out of which the New Philosophers were formed and the important influence of Foucault on their work may be found in Ferry and Renaut; Jameson, "Periodizing"; and Spivak and Ryan.

10. For analysis of Kristeva's critique of Saussurean linguistics see Moi, *Sexual/Textual Politics;* on her intervention into Lacan's theory of the subject, see Silverman; for her contribution to a materialist theory of the subject, see Pajaczkowska.

11. *Revolution in Poetic Language,* 25. All other quotes from *Revolution in Poetic Language* will be included simply as page numbers in the text.

12. This is exactly Marx's point in the sixth thesis on Feuerbach where he traces Feuerbach's "natural" subject to the presupposition of "an abstract—isolated—human individual" (*Collected Works,* vol. 5, 8).

13. Many feminist critics of Kristeva have made this point. See, for example, Adams and Brown; Jones, "Julia Kristeva on Femininity," Rose; Moi, *Sexual/Textual Politics;* Stanton; and Spivak, "French Feminism."

14. In this respect, Kristeva's theory of discourse is similar to other feminist theories that ground women's knowledge in the body. For critiques of this sort of corporeal epistemology see Ebert "(Body) Politics"; Spivak, "French Feminism"; and Morton, "The Body."

15. For summaries of Kristeva's work that divided it into phases, see Moi "Introduction," *Kristeva Reader;* and Jardine, "Opaque Texts." Ann Rosalind Jones, on the other hand, sees Kristeva's rejection of politics in the eighties not as a turnabout, but as coherent with the disciplines of psychoanalysis and literary criticism she has consistently worked within, "disciplines that privilege the individual subject while analyzing its dissolution" (80).

16. Dana Polan contends that Foucault's project is firmly situated within a romantic-modernist aestheticism, in which literary texts serve a key part in the general figure of the marginal. (Laura Kipnis makes a similar point about Kristeva). Foucault's own writing, Polan argues, becomes most poetic when he talks of writers he admires (369). See especially the essays on literature in *Language, Counter-Memory Practice.*

17. On the relation between the emergence of the New Right in the west and the New Philosophy in France, see Spivak and Ryan; Dews; and Jones "Julia Kristeva on Femininity".

18. See for instance Rajchman; and Jardine, *Gynesis.*

19. For examples see Jameson, *The Political Unconscious;* and West, "Ethics and Action."

20. For an example of the former see Gilligan; for an example of the latter see Addleson. See also Jardine, "Opaque Texts," on the feminist critique of ethics and its intersection with the discourses of modernity.

21. Wayne Booth's recent book, *An Ethics of Criticism,* exemplifies one form of the recuperation of liberal formalist reading practices in the name of "ethics"; Booth's anxiety over use of the word "ethics" inadvertently indicates the kind of alliance being formed between the political right and center under the name of ethics. He points out that the category "ethical" makes some of "us" (liberals?) nervous because it has the negative connotations of morality and censorship, but then proceeds to use it (otherwise uncritically) as a category to define the evaluative function of form in narrative.

22. As Kristeva herself puts it, this is an ethics which is "not a repressive force but an almost marginal individual unveiling of pleasure and of violence" ("Interview," 8).

23. Foucault identifies the construction of "the kind of being to which we aspire when we behave in a moral way" as "what I call the telos" ("Genealogy of Ethics," 239).

24. Brief elaborations of Derrida's concept of *différance* can be found in the essay "Différance" in *Speech and Phenomena,* and the translator's preface in *Of Grammatology* (lxx–lxxi).

25. In contrast to Foley, Gayatri Spivak has argued again and again for the potential political uses of deconstruction. In her highly suggestive discussion of the textuality of the value form in Marx, Spivak gestures toward the possibilities of appropriating deconstruction's critique of the sign for a materialist understanding of textuality as it operates within a global analytic ("Scattered Speculations"). However, Spivak's strategy is to bring Derrida and Marx into tension and stop there—a position she describes as a "politically interested refusal to push to the limit the founding presuppositions of [her] desires" ("Subaltern Studies," 271). This "refusal" perhaps has to be judged both in terms of the historical and cultural determinants of the position of post-colonial intellectual woman working in the west and the effectivity of this ultimately ambivalent position for feminist political praxis.

26. Mohan's elaboration of a materialist theory of *differánce* offers both a sustained ideology critique of Derridean deconstruction and a reworking of *différance* within a postmodern problematic. In doing so she draws upon Volosinov's insights into the "multi-accentuality" of the ideological sign as a function of the class struggle and Althusser's arguments in "Philosophy As a Revolutionary Weapon" that the ambiguities in the meanings of words are the effect of the contest over meaning. In this way she understands the slippage of signification in terms of ongoing battles over the construction of the social real that are always both decisive and undecided.

27. Henry Giroux's invocation of Laclau and Mouffe's work in his argument for a feminism that draws upon the most progressive aspects of modernism and postmodernism is one example of the ways their postmodernized liberalism is being aligned with feminism now.

3. The Feminist Standpoint, Discourse, and Authority: From Women's Lives to Ideology Critique

1. As a critique of the empiricist subject, feminist standpoint theory shares its historical importance with other feminist epistemologies—cultural, empiricist, and postmodern. In various ways, all of these feminist knowledges have called into question claims to truth in the discourses of modernity. While cultural and empiricist feminists tend to offer a *description* of reality as it transparently appears to women, however, feminist standpoint theorists typically present a systematic *explanation* of reality as socially constructed and emphasize the function of women's position in its reproduction (Jaggar, 381).

2. See for example Jaggar, 387; and Smith, *The Everyday World as Problematic*.

3. In her critique of experiential feminism, Grant makes an important argument for reclaiming reason for feminism: "It is reason which makes discourse possible. . . . It is faith and intuition which cannot be challenged" (113). While I think this particular formulation tends to reinscribe the opposition between reason = social vs. intuition = asocial rather than refiguring so-called "irrational" ways of knowing in relation to counterhegemonic knowledges, still, Grant's essay is a provocative contribution to the debates on experience in feminist epistemology now.

4. Although Smith does not fully elaborate how ideological practices are related to other social practices, she does posit a social analytic which supersedes the marxist base-superstructure model. In discussing the discourse of femininity, she envisions the relationship between discourse and other productive relations as a "web or cats-cradle of texts, stringing together and co-ordinating the multiple local and particular sites of the everyday worlds of women and men with the market processes of the fashion, cosmetic, garment and publishing industries" ("Femininity As A Discourse," 167). She does not, however, move beyond analysis at the level of social formation to situate the discourses of femininity in the west within the larger sphere of productive relations that comprise multinational capitalism.

5. In "Sociological Theory As Methods of Writing Patriarchy into Feminist Texts," Smith critiques the privileging of the "textual order of discourse"—the discourse of the ruling social sciences—as the object of traditional sociological work for being based on "the realization of the actual as the discursive." She argues for an alternative sociology that begins in a knowledge community outside the discipline, in the "experiences" of those who have formerly been the objects of study. However, it is the troubling relationship between the actual and the discursive that remains unexplained in her critique of the oppressive effects of ruling knowledges.

6. See *Lenin and Philosophy* and *Reading Capital* for the fullest developments of Althusser's theory of ideology.

7. The upper and lower case distinctions here are meant to convey the difference between the actual Real, which, like the Real in Lacan, is categorically unknown, and the socially produced real. Unlike Lacan's Real, however, this real is located within a problematic which posits it not in terms of an individualized metaphysical emptiness or fullness—death or *jouissance*—but as a limit space to history, marking that which cannot be known historically except in its mediation through discourse.

For more on the debates over the distinction between these terms see Ebert, "The Romance of Patriarchy"; Jardine, *Gynesis;* Jameson, *Political Unconscious;* and Zavarzadeh *Reading.*

8. For elaborations on this point see Giroux; Hall, "Marxism Without Guarantees"; and Zavarzadeh and Morton, *Theory/(Post) Modernity/Opposition.*

9. For analysis of Gramsci's contribution to neo-marxist epistemology, see Mouffe, "Hegemony"; and Wolff. For an elaboration of the uses of this epistemology for an emancipatory politics see Giroux; and West, "Specificity of Afro-American Oppression."

10. For further theoretical development of this point see Hall, "Toad in the Garden"; and Pecheux, "Ideology."

11. For examples of these critiques see Bartkowski; de Lauretis, *Technologies,* 31–33; Fuss; Jardine, "Pretexts"; and Poovey, "Feminism and Deconstruction." Relevant texts of Derrida's include "Choreographies," *Spurs,* and "Women in the Beehive."

12. For critiques of French feminism that pursue this line of argument see Jones, "Writing the Body"; Poovey, "Feminism and Deconstruction"; and Stanton.

13. As Fredric Jameson has suggested, "what the marxist theory of capitalist society has taught us . . . is the way in which the very possibility of conceiving of a certain passionate value or of being capable of feeling a certain unique emotion is dependent on the labor of other people and on a social differentiation of production within which those particular human possibilities are available or on the other hand excluded" ("History and Class Consciousness," 54).

14. This phrase is taken from Judith Butler's very suggestive critique of heterosexual coherence in *Gender Trouble.*

15. Some of the more blatant examples can be found in the flourishing discourse of sociobiology. The publication in scholarly and popular presses of studies on the relationship between "stress" and early menarche are only one instance of the vitality of these preconstructed equations. The latest theory, supported by a host of child development studies, explains teenage pregnancy as the effect of early menarche brought on by an exacerbated genetic urge to reproduce under "stressful" circumstances. What counts as stressful circumstances is the crux of the claim here. Girls undergo menarche earlier, the argument goes, in a "stressful" family arrangement where parents are negotiating divorce or the father is absent.

16. Michelle Barrett's definition of ideology as "a generic term for the processes by which meaning is produced, challenged, reproduced, transformed" (97) is one example of what I mean by "reading" here.

17. For overviews of marxian critique see Benhabib; Held; Stillman; and Thompson.

18. A theory of the discursive construction of the subject supersedes the contradiction Seyla Benhabib points to in Marx between systemic analysis and the perspective of lived experience. While Benhabib suggests that Habermas' theory of communicative interaction offers the best way to theorize the mediation between these two perspectives, the theory of the subject on which Habermas' notion of intersubjectivity is

premised retains problematic empiricist assumptions in its understanding of the relationship between representation and subjectivity.

19. See, for example, de Man's notion of textual crisis as a separation between intent and execution, which leads him to privilege literature as a demystifying discourse, or Derrida's concept of the supplement, which posits the slippage of signification as the exclusive property of the text.

20. For feminist arguments on this point see Butler, *Gender Trouble;* Fuss; and Poovey, "Feminism and Deconstruction."

21. For some theorists these challenges to the integrity of the liberal subject are inherent in the condition of modernity, an argument that posits postmodernity as the fulfillment of the Enlightenment rather than a break from it. For debates on this issue see Habermas, *Philosophical Discourses;* Foucault, "What Is Enlightenment?"; Lyotard; and Mouffe, "Hegemony."

22. For a critique of the contradictions in Marx's theory of the collective singular subject, see Benhabib.

23. Denise Riley's work offers some of the most succinct formulations of the issues at stake in the strategic use of "woman."

24. Similar pressures from within marxism have made visible the inadequacy of its subject. The mode of politics called for by the class subject of history where one group or organization acts in the name of the whole poses the same kinds of representational problems as any liberal identity politics.

25. Cornel West's analysis of the specificity of Afro-American oppression is a useful model of how to theorize the specificity of a political and ideological standpoint within a systemic analytic. In suggesting that the particular terms of Afro-American oppression are inextricably linked both to a particular problematic and to the systemic reach of capitalist arrangements, his analysis implies ways to consider how the "specificity" of various critiques might intersect.

26. The list of those who have addressed this issue is a long one. Stephen Heath's "Difference" (1978) is often cited as one of the first to launch the proposal. More recently, several contributors to the *Men in Feminism* collection (1987) (Jardine, Kamuf, Schor) and the special issue of *differences* on "Another Look At Essentialism" (1989) (especially de Lauretis, Schor, Fuss) have taken various positions on the question. Fuss's booklength study (1989) is an extended exploration of the consequences of the binary opposition of the constructed and the essential. Gayatri Spivak's name more than any other is associated with the call for taking the risk of essence—a suggestion she proposed in relation to the work of the Subaltern Studies Group. For a discussion of her skeptical response to the ready appropriation of this idea and of some shifts in her position on the strategic use of essentialism see "In A Word."

4. New Woman, New History

1. See Descombes and Habermas (*Philosophical Discourses*) for a discussion of the debates around the problem of history in contemporary European philosophy. Peter

Novick's study of the pressures of an empiricist historiography in American Studies indicates that the disruption of traditional historiography predates poststructuralism and has been building throughout the twentieth century.

2. Gregor Mc Lennan gives a useful overview of various versions of empiricism, which he distinguishes from historical realism. Mc Lennan's argument for a "scientific realism" (which includes feminism) is problematic, however, in that it does not fully theorize the relationship between theory's structuring role in historical narratives and empirical evidence.

3. Postmodern historiography is itself a highly contested terrain. For both White and Jameson, for example, because historical accounts are narratives, the historical past is only accessible by way of its prior textualization. However, unlike Jameson's marxist challenge to empiricism, which conceptualizes the textuality of history in terms of the material interests encoded in historical narrative, White reads the narrativity of history as primarily a matter of tropes. John Toews' review of several publications in the eighties offers a useful overview of some of the issues at stake for intellectual history "after the linguistic turn."

4. In mapping out this argument, I am endorsing a view of the relationship between modernity and the feminine that deserves a much fuller development in terms of its place within contemporary debates on modernity. As a reading that comes out of the articulation of feminist and neo-marxist problematics, the following sketch implicitly questions the negative notion of modernity posed by the post-marxism of Foucault, Lyotard, Baudrillard, and others. In contending that the discourses of the new circulating in contemporary western capitalist culture are a continuation of the fascination with the new which underlies the capitalist mode of production, I am offering a view of postmodernity as continuous with rather than distinct from the political economy of modernity.

5. See for example, Marx's comment in *The Communist Manifesto* that constant revolutionalizing of production, uninterrupted disturbance of all social conditions, everlasting uncertainty and agitation distinguish the bourgeois epoch from all earlier ones (92). For further discussion of these issues see Berman; Lefort, 156ff.

6. Adorno reads the cult of the new as it found expression in Poe and Baudelaire exclusively in these terms, as a rebellion against the alienating impulse toward repetition in the industrial age, a rebellion, moreover, which promises no transformative innovation. For Adorno this rebellion takes the form of a dream of novelty that remains chained to the sickness it aims to compensate for (235).

7. See Zavarzadeh, *Seeing Films Politically* for an elaboration of this notion of the new and its application to a reading of *Prizzi's Honor*.

8. For analyses of the effects of these shifts in economic and political arrangements on the position of women and the ideology of femininity see Dyhouse; Holcombe; Lewis; and Frances Widdowson.

9. These "Character Notes" by H. S. Scott and E. B. Hall helped shape other "new" subjectivities as well. Included in the series were "The Beauty," "The School Girl," and "The Laborer."

10. This chapter was already completed when Marcy Darnovsky's excellent essay ap-

peared in *Social Text.* Her analysis offers a much fuller history and critique of the New Traditionalist campaign as well as readings of its first six ads. I am indebted to several of the points she raises.

11. In addition to Scott's overview of this archive, see Lerner; Newton; and Smith-Rosenberg, "New Woman."

12. This difference in emphasis is evident in Terry Lovell's recent anthology of *British Feminist Thought* which includes two essays (by Sally Alexander and Catherine Hall) representative of "Feminism and the Historians," as well as a brief overview of recent developments in feminist history in Britain.

13. For feminist scholarship which derives from this intersection, see Armstrong; Davidoff and Hall; Newton et al.; Poovey, *Uneven Developments;* and Walkowitz, *Prostitution.*

14. See also Judith Newton's review of Davidoff and Hall's *Family Fortunes,* which she praises for "plac[ing] gender and women at the heart of their investigation" (8).

15. Examples of this kind of analysis which Scott cites include Carby, *Reconstructing Womanhood;* Poovey, *Uneven Developments;* and Walkowitz, *Prostitution.*

16. Newton's review of Armstrong's and Poovey's work—both of which treat the ways in which class relied on gender for its articulation ("History As Usual?")—and Smith-Rosenberg's review of Davidoff and Hall both make this point clear. This focus is of course explicit in studies like Newton et al.'s *Sex and Class.*

17. Although Kelly generally uses the term "unified" to describe her proposal for feminist theory, the mode of analysis she describes could more accurately be labelled "systemic." The totalized, Hegelian notion of history implied by the term "unified" is quite at odds with the materialist analysis of "woman" in "systematically unified terms" across relations of sex, class, and race that Kelly calls for.

18. This point has been made again and again in the writings of "women of color," (see, for example, Alarcon; Brook-Higgenbotham; Carby; Davis; Hooks; Lorde; Sandoval). However, its impact on "white" feminist history has not been widespread, to say the least, as the *Coming to Terms* anthology demonstrates. Robyn Wiegman's work is one noteworthy exception.

19. Hereafter cited as "HDD."

20. See Lentricchia for a critique of Foucault on this point.

21. In addition to the feminist critiques of Foucault I have mentioned in chapters 1 and 2, Judith Newton's essay on "Historicisms New and Old" points to the problems Foucault's theory of power poses for a feminist history that insists power operates hierarchically and progressive human agency is possible. Newton cautions white (materialist) feminists not to be seduced by the possible "theoretical dodges employed by white western men," among them Foucault (466).

22. For overviews and evaluations of New Historicism, see Howard; Porter; and Veeser.

23. Although Joan Scott contends that it goes without saying feminism needs theory, the fact that "it has been said so often" has not quelled the ongoing debate over "theory" within feminist discourse. Feminist critiques of theory still often homogenize all of postmodernism and equate it with "theoreticism" and an elitism associated

with class and race oppression. (Barbara Christian's now famous essay, "The Race for Theory," is the most often cited formulation of this position). While these arguments make visible the ways theoretical discourses in the academy can be used to police those who have recently gained access to this privileged site, they rely on the notion that some writing is naturally accessible and "clear." Whenever some discourses are treated as transparent or naturally pleasurable or intelligible, writing gets dehistoricized. It is this appeal to the natural that has, of course, been used so brutally in the academy and elsewhere to suppress oppositional knowledges.

24. For a critique of Scott along these lines, see Genovese, *Feminism Without Illusions,* 157ff.

25. Several of these texts are catalogued with Library of Congress numbers that place them with feminist studies, others with literary criticism, still others with science.

26. Although the general critique of the ahistorical treatment of sexuality in the psychoanalytic problematic has been made frequently, renarrations of the emergence of psychoanalysis which situate it in the nexus of cultural, political, and economic forces in the late nineteenth century are few. Jameson offers a brief historical account of the isolation of sexual experience as the outcome of a general process of social development which includes the atomization of the family (*Political Unconscious,* 65–66). For additional historicizing work on the emergence of psychoanalysis see Coward; Foreman, 64–69; and Rose, 94–99.

27. Some of this work includes that of Barrett; Coward; Henriques et al.; and the *m/f* group.

28. Juliet Mitchell's defense of Freud (1974) was one of the first feminist arguments to be developed along these lines. See also Rose.

29. For a critique of feminist psychoanalysis along these lines, see Wilson.

30. In *Gender Trouble* Judith Butler offers a strong critique of psychoanalytic feminism which points in particular to its "binary heterosexist framework that carves up genders into masculine and feminine" (66).

31. Freud reads Dora's symptoms as displays of a pathological lack of desire for the penis and of a veiled incestuous desire for her father and his stand-in, Herr K., the husband of her father's mistress. According to Freud's narrative, Herr K. propositioned Dora, perhaps as the result of an agreement between the two men that she was to be given Herr K. in exchange for his wife.

32. In addition to the essays by Jacobus and Ramas, Collins et al., Sprengnether, and Willis also rewrite *Dora* in terms of a pre-Oedipal narrative.

33. Nor does this argument seem much different from Mary Jacobus' contention that the discourse of maternity is another name for the ambiguities of sexual difference (42). In both cases the "grounds" for social and historical change are located in an asocial space.

34. This critique is aimed at Freud's supposition that Dora's impotent father must have had Frau K. engage in fellatio, an assumption that suppresses the more "obvious" but ideologically dangerous conclusion that cunnilingus would have been their more probable sexual practice. This argument can be found in Willis; and Hertz.

35. In his introduction to *Herculine Barbin,* Foucault addresses the historical development of the notion of a "true sex" during the nineteenth century, its place in the emergence of psychology and psychoanalysis, and its continued hold on current opinion (viii).

36. A similar "slip" occurs in Hertz's essay. Hertz argues that Freud wanted to maintain distinctions between the analyst's knowledge which comes from books and his female patients' knowledge which was oral. By framing his argument in an insistence that Freud was not "squeamish" about lesbian love, Hertz closes off the *question* of how the text constructs the lesbian, and also avoids discussion of the relation between the discourse of psychoanalysis and the maintenance of a preconstructed heterosexual paradigm in the developing science of sexology.

37. Several critics have remarked on the ways the genealogy of the name "Dora" links her with the nurse/governess. Freud himself wrote that he chose the name "Dora" because it had been given to his sister's governess who, like her charge, was named "Rosa." But since the same name couldn't apply to the sister's nursemaid as well as her charge (!) the servant had to be given a new name, Dora. (see Sprengnether, 52.) Sprengnether and Marcus both remark on the patriarchal assumptions in this choice of pseudonyms.

38. The foundation of Freud's equation of sexuality with the lower classes is put forward in his "Aetiology of Hysteria," where he argues that "everything goes to show that the injunction for the sexual safeguarding of childhood is far more frequently transgressed in the case of the children of the proletariat" than in the middle classes (207). From here it is an easy step to postulate that middle-class children are more frequently exposed to sexual assaults than we realize—"by their nurses and nursery maids" (207). When a girl child is sexually assaulted by a boy, the boy's knowledge of these behaviors is traced to his own subjection to sexual practices by "some female servant or governess—which on account of their origin were often of a disgusting sort" (152). However, Freud admits that his study doesn't solve the riddle of why hysteria is not more common among the lower classes. The contradiction this admission poses is resolved by linking the discourse of sexuality to the discourse of heredity: the fact that hysteria is so much rarer in the lower classes than its aetiology would warrant is no longer incomprehensible once "the ego's efforts at defence" are seen to depend upon the subject's total moral and intellectual development—a development presumably much more refined in the middle classes. However, the riddle is not entirely solved by recourse to heredity since, in Freud's own admission, Charcot reported a surprisingly large incidence of hysteria among working class *men.*

39. ('Trans. "Stones Speak!") A similar passage appears in the opening pages of *Dora,* where Freud again invokes the analogy of "those discoverers whose good fortune it is to bring to the light of day after their long burial the priceless though mutilated relics of antiquity." He compares his work of reconstruction to that of "the conscientious archaeologist" who "does not omit to mention in each case where the authentic parts end and my constructions begin" (27). The hermeneutic problem of authenticity vs interpretation which Freud raises here as well as its bearing on an imperialist political economy continues to haunt historiography.

40. Treatments of the New Woman in late nineteenth-century Britain have primarily addressed her as a cultural phenomena. See for example Cunningham; Dowling; Fernando; Mac Pike; Showalter; and Stubbs. Penny Boumelha's study reads the New Woman as ideology. While Boumelha aims to include gender within a marxist/ materialist theory of ideology, in fact she brackets off economic and political determinants from cultural representations. John Goode's essays are valuable readings of the disruptive effects of the New Woman on the production of the real; but here textual constructions of sexuality are separated from other subject positions traversing the category "woman." While Gilbert and Gubar's reading of the New Woman addresses the construction of this figure in a range of literary texts, the theoretical framework of their study—tracing "sexchanges" in terms of changing roles, analyzing themes that collect around the concepts of "male" and "female," and locating texts in their sociocultural context—assumes a problematic in which the materiality of subjectivities, of texts as ideology, and of textuality as social signification are unquestioned. While they relate the figure of the New Woman to constructions of racial otherness and to imperialism, the exclusively cultural emphasis of their analysis mystifies the interests at stake in the reconfiguration of femininity—for instance, the relation between the reformation of the western feminine subject and capital's exploitation of colonial and working-class women.

41. For other critiques of feminism's implicitly white subject see Combahee River Collective; Mc Dowell; Moraga; Sandoval; and Valerie Smith.

42. A Sivanandan's history of the (British) state's appropriation of progressive identity-based anti-racist movements offers an instructive critique of the divisive effects of an identity discourse issuing from just this sort of liberal/progressive movement. He sees in the state's promotion and support for cultural diversity programs based on identity politics and aimed at black communities in Britain a long-term project aimed at breaking up a potentially insurgent black and anti-racist solidarity forming in Britain in the seventies. The success of this project depended in large part on the denial of the systemic connection between race and class, racism and imperialism, and the substitution in its place of the notion that identity is all. Institutional racism, in this logic, is reduced to black or white prejudice. Racism *is* made a "white problem," but one that is severed from exploitative power structures.

43. The argument for experience as a starting point for critique is not the same as an argument for identity politics. Theorists like Mae Henderson, for example, have contended that experience can be used as a critical effort to open up ideological contradictions—as in the African-American ritual of testifying. This rewriting of "experience" in fact refuses the identity politics usually associated with "experience" and contests the notion of individuality. As Henderson explains it, testifying is "not the product of a self-authenticating individual but a critical commentary on ideological formations" (Weed, xxv). In this sense the appeal to experience in a counterhegemonic discourse can serve as an inaugural step toward the systemic logic I am arguing for.

Bibliography

Adams, Parveen, and Beverly Brown. "The Feminine Body and Feminist Politics." *m/f* 3 (1979): 35–50.

Addleson, Kathryn Pyne. "Moral Revolution." *Women and Values: Readings in Recent Feminist Philosophy*. Ed. Marilyn Pearsnel. Belmont, Cal.: Wadsworth, 1986.

Adorno, Theodor. *Minima Moralia: Reflections From A Damaged Life*. Trans. E. F. N. Jephcott. London: Verso, 1974.

Alarcón, Norma. "The Theoretical Subject(s) of *This Bridge Called My Back* and Anglo-American Feminism." In *Making Face, Making Soul/Hacienda Caras: Creative and Critical Perspectives by Women of Color*. Ed. Gloria Anzaldúa. 356–369. San Francisco: Aunt Lute, 1990.

Alcoff, Linda. "Cultural Feminism versus Post-Structuralism: The Identity Crisis in Feminist Theory." *Signs* 13, no. 3 (1988): 405–36.

———. "Feminist Politics and Foucault: The Limits to a Collaboration." In *Crises in Continental Philosophy*. Ed. Arlene Dallery and Charles Scott. 69–86. Albany: SUNY, 1990.

Alexander, Sally. "Women, Class and Sexual Differences in the 1830's and 1840's: Some Reflections on the Writing of a Feminist History." *History Workshop Journal* 17 (1984): 123–49.

Althusser, Louis. *For Marx*. Trans. Ben Brewster. London: NLB, 1977.

———. "Is It Simple To Be A Marxist In Philosophy?" *Essays in Self-Criticism*. Trans. Grahame Lock. 163–207. London: NLB, 1976.

———. *Lenin and Philosophy and Other Essays*. Trans. Ben Brewster. New York: Monthly Review, 1971.

———. "Philosophy As A Revolutionary Weapon." *Lenin and Philosophy*. 11–22.

———, and Etienne Balibar. *Reading Capital*. Trans. Ben Brewster. London: NLB, 1970.

Armstrong, Nancy. *Desire in Domestic Fiction: A Political Reading of the Novel.* New York: Oxford University Press, 1987.

Armstrong, Pat, and Hugh Armstrong. "Beyond Sexless Class and Classless Sex." In *The Politics of Diversity: Feminism, Marxism and Nationalism.* Ed. Roberta Hamilton and Michele Barrett. 208–239. London: Verso, 1986.

Aronowitz, Stanley. *The Crisis in Historical Materialism: Class, Politics, and Culture in Marxist Theory.* New York: Praeger, 1981.

———. "Postmodernism and Politics." Ross, 46–62.

———. "Theory and Socialist Strategy." *Social Text* (Winter 1986–87): 1–16.

Avling, Nat. "What Is the Role of the 'New Woman'?" *Westminster Review.* 150 (1898): 576–87.

Baldick, Chris. *The Social Mission of English Criticism: 1548–1932.* Oxford: Oxford University Press, 1983.

Barrett, Michele. *Women's Oppression Today: Problems in Marxist Feminist Analysis.* London: Verso, 1980.

———. and Mary McIntosh. "Christine Delphy: Towards A Materialist Feminism?" *Feminist Review* (Jan. 1979): 95–106.

Bartkowski, Frances. "Feminism and Deconstruction: A Union Forever Deferred." *Enclitic* 4, no. 2 (1980): 70–76.

Belsey, Catherine. *Critical Practice.* New York: Methuen, 1980.

Benhabib, Seyla. *Critique, Norm, Utopia: A Study of the Foundations of Critical Theory.* New York: Columbia University Press, 1986.

Bennett, Tony. "Texts in History: The Determinations of Readings and Their Texts." In *Post-Structuralism and the Question of History.* Ed. Derek Attridge, Geoff Bennington, and Robert Young. 63–81. Cambridge: Cambridge University Press, 1987.

Benveniste, Emile. *Problems in General Linguistics.* Coral Gables, Fla.: University of Miami Press, 1971.

Berman, Marshall. *All That Is Solid Melts Into Air: The Experience of Modernity.* New York: Simon and Schuster, 1982.

Bhabha, Homi. "The Other Question." *Screen* 24, no. 6 (1983): 18–36.

Booth, Wayne C. *The Company We Keep: An Ethics of Fiction.* Berkeley: University of California Press, 1988.

Bordo, Susan R. "Anorexia Nervosa: Psychopathology as the Crystallization of Culture." Diamond and Quinby, 87–118.

———. "The Body and the Reproduction of Femininity: A Feminist Appropriation of Foucault." In *Gender/Body/Knowledge: Feminist Reconstructions of Being and Knowing.* Ed. Alison Jaggar and Susan Bordo. 13–33. New Brunswick, N.J.: Rutgers University Press, 1989.

Boswell, Terry E., Edgar V. Kiser, and Kathryn Baker. "Recent Developments in Marxist Theories of Ideology." *Insurgent Sociologist* 13, no. 4 (1986): 5–22.

Boumelha, Penny. *Thomas Hardy and Women: Sexual Ideology in Narrative Form.* Sussex: Harvester, 1982.

Bourne, Jenny. "Homelands of the Mind: Jewish Feminism and Identity Politics." *Race and Class* 29, no. 1 (1987): 1–24.

Brantlinger, Patrick. *Crusoe's Footprints: Cultural Studies in Britain and America.* New York: Routledge, 1990.

Breines, Winnie, et al. "Social Biology, Family Studies and the Anti-Feminist Backlash." *Feminist Studies* 4, no. 1 (1978): 43–67.

Brooks-Higgenbotham, Evelyn. "African-American Women's History and the Metalanguage of Race." *Signs* 17, no. 2 (1992): 251–74.

———. "Beyond the Sound of Silence: Afro-American Women in History." *Gender and History* 1, no. 1 (1989): 50–67.

———. "The Problem of Race in Women's History." Weed, 122–33.

Brown, Elsa Barkeley. "Womanist Consciousness: Maggie Lena Walker and the Independent Order of St. Luke." *Signs* 14, no. 3 (1989): 610–33.

Butler, Judith. *Gender Trouble: Feminism and the Subversion of Identity.* New York: Routledge, 1990.

———. "Gender Trouble, Feminist Theory, and Psychoanalytic Discourse." In *Feminism/Postmodernism.* Ed. Linda Nicholson. 324–40. New York: Routledge, 1990.

Cain, William E. *The Crisis in Criticism: Theory, Literature and Reform in English Studies.* Baltimore: Johns Hopkins University Press, 1984.

Callinicos, Alex. *Is There A Future For Marxism?* London: Macmillan, 1982.

Carby, Hazel V. *Reconstructing Womanhood: The Emergence of the Afro-American Woman Novelist.* New York: Oxford University Press, 1987.

———. "White Women Listen!: Black Feminism and the Boundaries of Sisterhood." *The Empire Strikes Back: Race and Racism in 70's Britain.* Educational Center For Contemporary Cultural Studies. 212–35. London: Hutchinson, 1982.

Cavallari, Hector Mario. "*Savoir and Pouvoir:* Michel Foucault's Theory of Discursive Practice." *Humanities and Society* (1980): 55–72.

Chevigny, Bell, et al. "Patrolling the Borders: Feminist Historiography and the New Historicism." *Radical History Review* 43 (1989): 3–43.

Christ, Carol. "Victorian Masculinity and the Angel in the House." In *A Widening Sphere: Changing Roles of Victorian Women.* Ed. Martha Vicinus. 13–27. Bloomington: Indiana University Press, 1983.

Christian, Barbara. "The Race for Theory." *Cultural Critique* 6 (Spring 1981): 51–63.

Cixous, Hélène, and Catherine Clément. *The Newly Born Woman.* Trans. Betsy Wing. Minneapolis: University of Minnesota Press, 1986.

Collins, Jerre et al. "Questioning the Unconscious: The *Dora* Archive." *Diacritics* (Spring 1983): 37–41.

Combahee River Collective. "A Black Feminist Statement." In *This Bridge Called My*

Back: Writings of Radical Women of Color. Ed. Gloria Anzaldúa and Cherrie Moraga. 210–18. New York: Kitchen Table Press, 1983.

Cornell, Drucilla, and Adam Thurschwell. "Feminism, Negativity and Intersubjectivity." In *Feminism As Critique*. Ed. Seyla Benhabib and Drucilla Cornell. 143–62. Minneapolis: University of Minnesota Press, 1987.

Coward, Rosalind. *Patriarchal Precedents: Sexuality and Social Relations*. London: Routledge, 1983.

Crosby, Christina. *The Ends of History: Victorians and "The Woman Question."* New York: Routledge, 1991.

Culler, Jonathan. *On Deconstruction: Theory and Criticism After Structuralism*. Ithaca: Cornell University Press, 1982.

Cunningham, Gail. *The "New Woman" and the Victorian Novel*. New York: Barnes and Noble, 1979.

Darnovsky, Marcy. "The New Traditionalism: Repackaging Ms. Consumer." *Social Text* 29 (1991): 72–94.

Davidoff, Lenore, and Catherine Hall. *Family Fortunes: Men and Women of the English Middle Class, 1780–1850*. Chicago: University of Chicago Press, 1987.

Davin, Anna. "Imperialism and Motherhood." *History Workshop Journal* 5 (1978): 9–65.

Davis, Angela. *Women, Race, and Class*. New York: Random House, 1981.

de Lauretis, Teresa. *Alice Doesn't: Feminism, Semiotics, Cinema*. Bloomington: Indiana University Press, 1984.

———. "Eccentric Subjects: Feminist Theory and Historical Consciousness." *Feminist Studies* 16, no. 1 (Spring 1990): 115–50.

———. "The Essence of the Triangle or, Taking the Risk of Essentialism Seriously: Feminist Theory in Italy, the U.S. and Britain." *differences* 1, no. 2 (1989): 3–37.

———. "Feminist Studies/Critical Studies: Issues, Terms and Contexts." In *Feminist Studies/Critical Studies*. Ed. Teresa de Lauretis. 1–19. Bloomington: Indiana University Press, 1986.

———. "Sexual Indifference and Lesbian Representation." *Theatre Journal* 40, no. 2 (1988): 155–77.

———. *Technologies of Gender: Essays on Theory, Film, and Fiction*. Bloomington: Indiana University Press, 1987.

de Man, Paul. *Blindness and Insight: Essays in the Rhetoric of Contemporary Criticism*. Minneapolis: University of Minnesota Press, 1971.

Deleuze, Gilles. *Foucault*. Trans. Sean Hand. Minneapolis: University of Minnesota Press, 1986.

Delmar, Rosalind. "What Is Feminism?" In *What Is Feminism?* Ed. Juliet Mitchell and Ann Oakley. 8–33. New York: Pantheon, 1986.

Delphy, Christine. *Close To Home: A Materialist Analysis of Women's Oppression*. London: Hutchinson, 1984.

Derrida, Jacques. *Of Grammatology*. Trans. Gayatri Chakravorty Spivak. Baltimore: Johns Hopkins, 1974.

————. *Speech and Phenomena And Other Essays on Husserl's Theory of Signs*. Trans. David B. Allison. Evanston: Northwestern University Press, 1973.

————. *Spurs*. Trans. Barbara Harlow. Chicago: University of Chicago Press, 1979.

————. "Women in the Beehive: A Seminar with Jacques Derrida." In *Men in Feminism*. Ed. Alice Jardine and Paul Smith. 189–201. New York: Methuen, 1987.

————. *Writing and Difference*. Chicago: University of Chicago Press, 1978.

————, and Christie Mac Donald. "Choreographies." *Diacritics* 12 (1982): 66–76.

Descombes, Vincent. *Modern French Philosophy*. Trans. L. Scott-Fox and J. M. Harding. Cambridge University Press, 1979.

Dews, Peter. "The *Nouvelle Philosophie* and Foucault." *Economy and Society* 8 (1979): 127–71.

Diamond, Irene, and Lee Quinby, eds. *Feminism and Foucault: Reflections on Resistance*. Boston: Northeastern University Press, 1988.

Dollimore, Jonathan, and Alan Sinfield, eds. *Political Shakespeare: New Essays in Cultural Materialism*. Ithaca: Cornell University Press, 1985.

Dowling, Linda. "The Decadent and the New Woman in the 1890s." *Nineteenth Century Fiction* 33 (1979): 434–53.

Dyhouse, Carol. *Girls Growing Up in Late Victorian and Edwardian England*. London: Routledge and Kegan Paul, 1981.

Eagleton, Terry. "Frère Jacques: The Politics of Deconstruction." In *Against the Grain: Selected Essays 1975–1985*. 79–88. London: Verso, 1986.

Eastwood, M. "The New Woman in Fiction and in Fact." *The Humanitarian* 5 (1894): 375–79.

Ebert, Teresa. "The (Body) Politics of Feminist Theory." *Phoebe* 3, no. 2 (1991): 56–63.

————. "The 'Difference' of Postmodern Feminism." *College English* 53, no. 8 (1991): 886–904.

————. "The Romance of Patriarchy: Ideology, Subjectivity, and Postmodern Feminist Cultural Theory." *Cultural Critique* 10 (Fall 1988): 19–58.

Ehrenreich, Barbara et al. *Remaking Love: The Feminization of Sex*. New York: Anchor, 1986.

Felman, Shoshana. *Writing and Madness*. Trans. Martha Noel Evans and the author. Ithaca: Cornell University Press, 1985.

Fernando, Lloyd. *The New Woman in the Late Victorian Novel*. University Park: Penn State University Press, 1977.

Ferry, Luc, and Alain Renaut. *French Philosophy of the Sixties: An Essay on Anti-Humanism*. Trans. Mary Schnackenberg Cattani. Amherst: University of Massachusetts Press, 1985.

Flax, Jane. "Postmodernism and Gender Relations in Feminist Theory." Nicholson, 39–62.

Nancy Folbre and Heidi Hartmann. "The Persistence of Patriarchal Capitalism." *Rethinking Marxism*. 2, no. 4 (1989): 90–96.

Foley, Barbara. "The Politics of Deconstruction." In *Deconstruction At Yale*. Ed. Robert Con Davis and Ronald Schleifer. 113–34. Norman: University of Oklahoma Press, 1985.

Foreman, Ann. *Femininity As Alienation: Women and the Family in Marxism and Psychoanalysis*. London: Pluto, 1977.

Foucault, Michel. *The Archaeology of Knowledge*. Trans. A. M. Sheridan Smith. New York: Pantheon, 1972.

———. *Discipline and Punish: The Birth of the Prison*. Trans. Alan Sheridan. New York: Vintage, 1979.

———. *Herculine Barbin: Being the Recently Discovered Memoirs of a Nineteenth Century French Hermaphrodite*. New York: Pantheon, 1980.

———. "History, Discourse and Discontinuity." *Salmagundi* 20 (1972): 225–48.

———. *The History of Sexuality*. Vol. 1. Trans. Robert Hurley. New York: Vintage, 1980.

———. "Nietzsche, Genealogy, History." In *Language, Counter-Memory, Practice: Selected Essays and Interviews*. Trans. Donald F. Bouchard and Sherry Simon. 139–64. Ithaca: Cornell University Press, 1977.

———. "On the Genealogy of Ethics: An Overview of Work in Progress." In *Michel Foucault: Beyond Structuralism and Hermeneutics*. Hubert Dreyfus and Paul Rabinow. 229–259. University of Chicago Press, 1983.

———. "The Order of Discourse." In *Untying the Text: A Post-Structuralist Reader*. Ed. Robert Young. 51–77. Boston: Routledge, 1981.

———. *The Order of Things: An Archaeology of the Human Sciences*. New York: Random House, 1973.

———. "Polemics, Politics, and Problematizations." In *The Foucault Reader*. Ed. Paul Rabinow. 381–90. New York: Pantheon, 1984.

———. "Politics and Ethics: An Interview." In *The Foucault Reader*. 373–79.

———. "Politics and the Study of Discourse." *Ideology and Consciousness* 3 (1978): 7–26.

———. *Power/Knowledge: Selected Interviews and Other Writings: 1972–1977*. Trans. Colin Gordon, Leo Marshall, John Mepham, and Kate Soper. New York: Pantheon, 1980.

———. *The Use of Pleasure. The History of Sexuality*. Vol. 2. Trans. Robert Hurley. New York: Vintage, 1986.

———. "What Is Enlightenment?" In *The Foucault Reader*. 32–50.

Fox-Genovese, Elizabeth. *Feminism Without Illusions: A Critique of Individualism*. Chapel Hill: University of North Carolina Press, 1991.

———. "Placing Women's History in History." *New Left Review* 133 (1982): 5–29.

Fraser, Nancy. "Foucault's Body Language: A Post Humanist Political Rhetoric?" *Salmagundi* 61 (1983): 55–70.

———. "Foucault on Modern Power: Empirical Insights and Normative Confusions." *Praxis International* (Oct. 1981): 272–87.

———. "Michel Foucault: A Young Conservative?" *Ethics* (Oct. 1985): 165–84.

———. "The Uses and Abuses of French Discourse Theories for Feminist Politics" *boundary 2* 17, no. 2 (Summer 1990): 82–101.

———, and Linda Nicholson. "Social Criticism Without Philosophy: An Encounter Between Feminism and Postmodernism." Nicholson, 19–38.

Freud, Sigmund. "The Aetiology of Hysteria." In *The Complete Works*. Vol. 3. Trans. James Strachey and Anna Freud. 191–224. London: Hogarth, 1962.

———. *Dora: An Analysis of A Case of Hysteria*. New York: Macmillan, 1963.

Fuss, Diana. *Essentially Speaking: Feminism, Nature and Difference*. New York: Routledge, 1989.

Gallagher, Catherine. "Marxism and the New Historicism." Veeser, 37–48.

Gallop, Jane. *The Daughter's Seduction: Feminism and Psychoanalysis*. Ithaca: Cornell University Press, 1982.

Geras, Norman. "Post-Marxism?" *New Left Review* 163 (1987): 40–82.

Gilbert, Sandra M., and Susan Gubar. *No Man's Land: The Place of the Woman Writer in the Twentieth Century*. Vol. 2. New Haven: Yale University Press, 1989.

Gilligan, Carol. "Concepts of Self and of Morality." *Harvard Educational Review* 47 (1977): 481–513.

Giroux, Henry, ed. *Postmodernism, Feminism, and Cultural Politics: Redrawing Educational Boundaries*. Albany: SUNY Press, 1991.

Glazer, Nona. "Questioning Eclectic Practice in Curriculum Change: A Marxist Perspective." *Signs* 12, no. 2 (1987): 293–304.

Gless, Darryl J., and Barbara Herrnstein Smith, ed. *The Politics of Liberal Education*. Durham: Duke University Press, 1992.

Goode, John. "Sue Bridehead and the New Woman." In *Women Writing and Writing About Women*. Ed. Mary Jacobus. 100–113. London: Croom Helm, 1979.

———. *Thomas Hardy: The Offensive Truth*. Oxford: Blackwell, 1988.

Gornick, Vivian. "Who Says We Haven't Made A Revolution?" *New York Times Magazine* (15 Apr. 1990): 24ff.

Grant, Judith. "I Feel Therefore I am: A Critique of Experience as A Basis for Feminist Epistemology." In *Feminism and Epistemology: Approaches to Research in Women and Politics*. Ed. Maria J. Falco. 99–127. New York: Haworth, 1987.

Gramsci, Antonio. *Selections from the Prison Notebooks*. Trans. Quentin Hoare and Geoffrey Nowell Smith. Newark: International, 1971.

Habermas, Jurgen. "Genealogical Writing of History: On Some Aporias in Foucault's Theory of Power." *Canadian Journal of Political and Social Theory* 10, nos. 1–2 (1986): 1–9.

————. *The Philosophical Discourses of Modernity*. Trans. Frederick Lawrence. Cambridge: MIT Press, 1987.

Hall, Stuart. "Brave New World." *Marxism Today* (Oct. 1988): 24–29.

————. "The Emergence of Cultural Studies and the Crisis of the Humanities." *October* 53 (1990): 11–23.

————. "The Problem of Ideology—Marxism Without Guarantees." *Journal of Communication Inquiry* 10, no. 2 (1986): 28–43.

————. "The Toad in the Garden: Thatcherism Among the Theorists." Nelson and Grossberg, 35–57.

Hamilton, Roberta, and Michele Barrett, eds. *The Politics of Diversity: Feminism, Marxism, and Nationalism*. London: Verso, 1986.

Hammerton, A. James. *Emmigrant Gentlewomen: Genteel Poverty and Female Emmigration 1830–1914*. London: Croom Helm, 1979.

Haraway, Donna. "A Manifesto for Cyborgs: Science, Technology, and Socialist Feminism in the 1980s." *Socialist Review* 80: 65–105.

————. "Reading Bucci Emecheta: Contests for Women's Experience in Women's Studies." *Inscriptions* 3–4 (1988): 107–23.

————. "Situated Knowledges: The Science Question in Feminism and the Privilege of Partial Perspective." *Feminist Studies* 14 (Fall 1988): 575–96.

Harding, Sandra. "The Instability of the Analytical Categories of Feminist Theory." *Signs* 11, no. 4 (1986): 654–64.

————. "Reinventing Ourselves As Others." Lecture. Syracuse University, April 1990.

————. *Whose Science? Whose Knowledge? Thinking From Women's Lives*. Ithaca: Cornell University Press, 1991.

————. "Subjectivity, Experience and Knowledge: An Epistemology from/for Rainbow Coalition Politics." In *Who Can Speak? Authority and Critical Discourse*. Ed. Judith Roof and Robyn Wiegman. University of Illinois Press, forthcoming.

Harley, Sharon. "Black Women in A Southern City." Hawkes and Skemp, 57–74.

Hartsock, Nancy C. "The Feminist Standpoint: Developing the Ground for a Specifically Feminist Historical Materialism." In *Feminism and Methodology*. Ed. Sandra Harding. 157–80. Bloomington: Indiana University Press, 1987.

————. "Foucault on Power: A Theory for Women?" Nicholson, 157–75.

————. "Rethinking Modernism: Minority vs. Majority Theories." *Cultural Critique* (Fall 1987): 187–205.

Haug, Frigga, ed. *Female Sexualization: A Collective Work of Memory*. Trans. Erica Carter. London: Verso, 1987.

Hawkes, Joanne V., and Sheila L. Skemp, eds. *Sex, Race, and the Role of Women in the South*. Jackson: University of Mississippi Press, 1983.

Hawkesworth, Mary E. "Knowers, Knowing, Known: Feminist Theory and Claims of Truth." *Signs* 14, no. 3 (1989): 533–57.

Heath, Stephen. "Difference." *Screen* 19, no. 3 (Autumn 1978): 50–112.

———. "Narrative Space." In *Narrative, Apparatus, Ideology: A Film Theory Reader*. Ed. Philip Rosen. 379–419. New York: Columbia University Press, 1986.

Hebdige, Dick. "After the Masses." *Marxism Today* (January 1989): 50–55.

Held, David. *Introduction to Critical Theory: Horkheimer to Habermas*. Berkeley: University of California Press, 1980.

Hennessy, Rosemary, and Rajeswari Mohan. "The Construction of Woman in Three Popular Texts of Empire: Towards a Critique of Materialist Feminism." *Textual Practice* 3, no. 3 (1989): 323–59.

———. "Postindustrial Feminism." Letter. *Socialist Review* 18, no. 2 (1988): 161–63.

Henriques, Julian, et al., eds. *Changing The Subject: Psychology, Social Regulation, and Subjectivity*. New York: Methuen, 1984.

Hertz, Neil. "Dora's Secrets, Freud's Techniques." *Diacritics* (Spring 1983): 65–76.

Hindess, Barry, and Paul Hirst. *Pre-Capitalist Modes of Production*. London: Routledge, 1975.

Holcombe, Lee. *Wives and Property: Reform of the Married Women's Property Law in Nineteenth Century England*. Toronto: University of Toronto Press, 1983.

Hooks, Bell. "Postmodern Blackness." In *Yearning*. 23–32.

———. *Yearning: Race, Gender and Cultural Politics*. Boston: South End, 1990.

Howard, Dick. *The Politics of Critique*. Minneapolis: University of Minnesota Press, 1988.

Howard, Jean E. "The New Historicism in Renaissance Studies." *English Literary Renaissance* 16, no. 1 (1986): 13–43.

Hull, Gloria T., et al., eds. *All the Women Are White, All the Blacks Are Male, But Some of Us Are Brave: Black Women's Studies*. Old Westbury, N.Y.: The Feminist Press, 1982.

Huyssen, Andreas. "Mapping the Postmodern." Nicholson, 234–77.

Irigaray, Luce. *This Sex Which Is Not One*. Trans. Catherine Porter. Ithaca: Cornell University Press, 1985.

———. *Speculum of the Other Woman*. Trans. Gillian C. Gill. Ithaca: Cornell University Press, 1985.

Jaggar, Alison M. *Feminist Politics and Human Nature*. Sussex: Harvester, 1983.

Jacobus, Mary. "*Dora* and the Pregnant Madonna." In *Reading Woman: Essays in Feminist Criticism*. 137–96. New York: Columbia University Press, 1986.

Jameson, Fredric. "*History and Class Consciousness* As An Unfinished Project." *Rethinking Marxism* 1, no. 1 (1988): 49–72.

———. "Periodizing the 60s." In *The Ideologies of Theory: Essays 1971–1986*. Vol. 2. 178–208. Minneapolis: University of Minnesota Press, 1988.

———. *The Political Unconscious: Narrative As A Socially Symbolic Act*. Ithaca: Cornell University Press, 1981.

————. "Postmodernism, or the Cultural Logic of Late Capitalism." *New Left Review* 146 (1984): 53–92.

Janiewski, Delores. "Sisters Under Their Skins: Southern Working Women, 1880–1950." Hawkes and Skemp, 13–35.

JanMohamed, Abdul and David Lloyd. "Minority Discourse: What Is To Be Done?" *Cultural Critique* (Fall 1987): 5–17.

Jardine, Alice. *Gynesis: Configurations of Woman and Modernity.* Ithaca: Cornell University Press, 1985.

————. "Pre-Texts for the Trans-Atlantic Feminist." *Yale French Studies* 62 (1981): 220–36.

————. "Opaque Texts and Transparent Contexts: The Political Difference of Julia Kristeva." In *The Poetics of Gender.* Ed. Nancy K. Miller. New York: 96–109. Columbia University Press, 1986.

————, and Paul Smith, eds. *Men in Feminism.* New York: Methuen, 1987.

Jay, Martin. *Marxism and Totality: The Adventures of A Concept from Lukacs to Habermas.* Berkeley: University of California Press, 1984.

Jones, Ann Rosalind. "Julia Kristeva on Femininity: The Limits of a Semiotic Politic." *Feminist Review* 18 (1984): 80–97.

————. "Writing the Body: Toward an Understanding of l'Ecriture Feminine." *Feminist Studies* 7, no. 2 (1981): 247–63.

Kaplan, Cora. "Like Any Other Rebel Slave." Lecture. Syracuse University, March 1990.

————. *Sea Changes: Culture and Feminism.* London: Verso, 1987.

Kelly, Joan. *Women, History and Theory.* Chicago: University of Chicago Press, 1984.

————. "The Doubled Vision of Feminist Theory." *Women, History, Theory.* 51–64.

Kipnis, Laura. "Feminism: The Political Conscience of Postmodernism?" In *Universal Abandon?* Ed. Andrew Ross. 149–66. Minneapolis: University of Minnesota Press, 1988.

Kristeva, Julia. *Desire in Language: A Semiotic Approach to Literature and Art.* Trans. Thomas Gora, Alice Jardine, and Leon S. Roudiez. New York: Columbia University Press, 1980.

————. "Interview with Julia Kristeva." *Critical Texts* 3, no. 3 (1986): 5–13.

————. *In the Beginning Was Love: Psychoanalysis and Faith.* Trans. Arthur Goldhammer. New York: Columbia University Press, 1987.

————. "Psychoanalysis and the Polis." Trans. Margaret Waller. *Critical Inquiry* 9 (1982): 77–92.

————. *Revolution in Poetic Language.* Trans. Margaret Waller. New York: Columbia University Press, 1984.

————. "Woman Can Never Be Defined." Trans. Marilyn August. In *New French Feminisms.* Ed. Elaine Marks and Isabelle de Courtivron. 137–41. Amherst: University of Massachusetts Press, 1980.

————. "Women's Time." Trans. Alice Jardine and Harry Blake. In *Feminist Theory: A*

Critique of Ideology. Ed. Claire Keohane, Michele Rosaldo, and Barbara Gelpi. 31–53. Chicago: University of Chicago Press, 1982.

Kuhn, Annette, and Ann Marie Wolpe. "Feminism and Materialism." In *Feminism and Materialism.* 1–10. London: Routledge and Kegan Paul, 1978.

La Capra, Dominick. *Rethinking Intellectual History: Texts, Contexts, Language.* Ithaca: Cornell University Press, 1983.

Laclau, Ernesto. "Psychoanalysis and Marxism." Trans. Amy G. Reiter-Mc Intosh. *Critical Inquiry* 13 (Winter 1987): 330–33.

———, and Chantal Mouffe. *Hegemony and Socialist Strategy.* London: Verso, 1985.

———. "Post-Marxism Without Apologies." *New Left Review* 166 (Nov.–Dec. 1987): 79–106.

Landry, Donna. "The World According to Moi: Politics and Feminist Literary Theory." *Criticism* 29, no. 1 (1987): 119–32.

Laqueur, Thomas. "Orgasm, Generation and the Politics of Reproductive Biology." *Representations* 14 (1986): 1–41.

Lecourt, Dominique. *Marxism and Epistemology: Bachelard, Conguilhem, Foucault.* Trans. Ben Brewster. London: NLB, 1975.

Lefort, Claude. *The Political Forms of Modern Society: Bureaucracy, Democracy, Totalitarianism.* Cambridge, Mass.: MIT Press, 1986.

Lemert, Charles and Garth Gillan. "The New Alternative in Critical Sociology: Foucault's Discursive Analysis." *Cultural Hermeneutics* 4 (1977): 309–20.

Lentricchia, Frank. *After The New Criticism.* Chicago: University of Chicago Press, 1980.

Lerner, Gerda. "Placing Women in Women's History: Definitions and Challenges." *Feminist Studies* 3 (1975): 1–14.

Lewis, Jane. *Women in England 1870–1950: Sexual Divisions and Social Change.* Bloomington: Indiana University Press, 1984.

Lorde, Audre. *Sister Outsider: Essays and Speeches.* Trumansberg, N.Y.: Crossing Press, 1984.

Lovell, Terry, ed. *British Feminist Thought: A Reader.* Oxford: Blackwell, 1990.

Lugones, Maria. "On the Logic of Pluralist Feminism." Lecture. Syracuse University, 1989.

Lydon, Mary. "Foucault and Feminism: A Romance of Many Dimensions." *Humanities in Society* 5 (1982): 245–53.

Lyotard, Jean Francois. *The Postmodern Condition: A Report on Knowledge.* Trans. Geoff Bennington and Brian Massumi. Minneapolis: University of Minnesota Press, 1984.

Macdonnell, Diane. *Theories of Discourse: An Introduction.* New York: Blackwell, 1986.

Macherey, Pierre. *A Theory of Literary Production.* Trans. Geoffrey Wall. London: Routledge, 1978.

Mac Pike, Loralee. "The New Woman, Childbearing, and the Reconstruction of Gender, 1840–1900." *NWSA Journal* 1, no. 3 (1989): 368–97.

Mandel, Ernest. *Late Capitalism*. Trans. Joris de Bres. London: Verso, 1972.

Marcus, Steven. "Freud and Dora: History, Case History." In *Representations: Essays on Literature and Society*. 247–310. New York: Random House, 1975.

Martin, Biddy. "Feminism, Criticism and Foucault." Diamond and Quinby, 3–20.

——, and Chandra Talpade Mohanty. "Feminist Politics: What's Home Got To Do With It?" In *Feminist Studies, Critical Studies*. Ed. Teresa de Lauretis. 191–212. Bloomington: Indiana University Press, 1986.

Marx, Karl. *The Communist Manifesto*. New York: Norton, 1988.

——. *The Eighteenth Brumaire of Louis Bonaparte*. New York: International, 1963.

——, and Frederick Engels. *Collected Works*. Vol. 5. New York: International, 1976.

Mc Dowell, Deborah. "New Directions for Black Feminist Criticism." In *The New Feminist Literary Criticism: Essays on Women, Literature, Theory*. Ed. Elaine Showalter. 186–99. New York: Pantheon, 1985.

Mc Lennan, Gregor. "History and Theory: Contemporary Debates and Directions." *Literature and History* 10, no. 2 (Autumn 1984): 139–64.

Merk, Mandy. "Difference and Its Discontents." *Screen* 28, no. 1 (1987): 2–9.

Mies, Maria. *Patriarchy and Accumulation on a World Scale: Women and the International Division of Labor*. London: Zed, 1986.

Mitchell, Juliet. *Psychoanalysis and Feminism*. New York: Random House, 1974.

Mohan, Rajeswari. "Modernity and Imperialism: A Critique of Literary Modernism." Diss. Syracuse University, 1990.

——. Rev. of *The Political Forms of Modern Society*, by Claude Lefort. *Rethinking Marxism* 2, no. 1 (1989): 141–57.

Mohanty, Chandra Talpade. "Under Western Eyes: Feminist Scholarship and Colonial Discourses." *Feminist Review* 30 (1988): 61–88.

Moi, Toril. "Feminism, Postmodernism, and Style: Recent Feminist Criticism in the United States." *Cultural Critique* 9 (Spring 1988): 3–24.

——. *French Feminist Thought: A Reader*. New York: Blackwell, 1987.

——. *The Kristeva Reader*. New York: Columbia University Press, 1986.

——. *Sexual/Textual Politics: Feminist Literary Theory*. London: Methuen, 1985.

Moraga, Cherrie. "From A Long Line of Vendidas: Chicanas and Feminism." In *Feminist Studies/Critical Studies*. Ed. Teresa de Lauretis. 173–90. Bloomington: Indiana University Press, 1986.

Morton, Donald. "The Body in/and the Text: The Politics of Clitoral Theoretics." Unpublished essay.

——, and Mas'ud Zavarzadeh. "The Nostalgia for Law and Order and the Policing of Knowledge: The Politics of Contemporary Literary Theory." *Syracuse Scholar Supplement* (Spring 1987): 25–71.

——, and Mas'ud Zavarzadeh, eds. *Theory/Pedagogy/Politics: Texts for Change*. Urbana: University of Illinois Press, 1991.

————, and Mas'ud Zavarzadeh. "War of the Words: the Battle of and for English." *In These Times* (28 Oct.–3 Nov. 1987): 18–19.

Mouffe, Chantal. "Between Philosophy and Politics: Democracy and the Decentering of the Subject." Lecture. Syracuse University, 1990.

————. *Gramsci and Marxist Theory*. London: Routledge, 1979.

————. "Hegemony and Ideology in Gramsci." In *Gramsci and Marxist Theory*. 168–204.

————. "Radical Democracy: Modern or Postmodern?" Ross, 31–45.

————. "The Sex-Gender System and the Discursive Construction of Women's Subordination." *Rethinking Ideology: A Marxist Debate*. Ed. Sakari Hanninen and Leena Paldan. 139–43. New York: International, 1983.

Mouzelis, Nicos. "Marxism or Post-Marxism?" *New Left Review* 167 (1988): 107–23.

Mullet, Sheila. "Shifting Perspectives: A New Approach to Ethics." *Feminist Perspectives: Philosophical Essays on Method and Morals*. Eds. Lorraine Code, et al. 109–26. Toronto: University of Toronto Press, 1988.

Nash, June, and Maria Patricia Fernandez Kelly, eds. *Women, Men, and the International Division of Labor*. Albany: SUNY Press, 1983.

Nelson, Cary, and Lawrence Grossberg, eds. *Marxism and the Interpretation of Culture*. Urbana and Chicago: University of Illinois Press, 1988.

Newton, Judith. *"Family Fortunes:* "New History" and "New Historicism." *Radical History Review* 43 (1989): 5–22.

————. "Historicisms New and Old: Charles Dickens Meets Marxism, Feminism, and West Coast Foucault." *Feminist Studies* 16, no. 3 (1990): 449–70.

————. "History As Usual?: Feminism and the New Historicism." *Cultural Critique* 9 (1988): 87–121.

————, Mary P. Ryan, and Judith R. Walkowitz, eds. *Sex and Class in Women's History*. London: Routledge and Kegan Paul, 1983.

Nicholson, Linda J. *Gender in History: The Limits of Social Theory in the Age of the Family*. New York: Columbia University Press, 1986.

————, ed. *Feminism/Postmodernism*. New York: Routledge, 1990.

Norris, Christopher. *What's Wrong With Postmodernism?: Critical Theory and the Ends of Philosophy*. Baltimore: Johns Hopkins, 1990.

Novick, Peter. *That Noble Dream: The "Objectivity Question" and the American Historical Profession*. Cambridge: Cambridge University Press, 1988.

Nussbaum, Felicity, and Laura Brown, eds. *The New Eighteenth Century: Theory, Politics, English Literature*. New York: Methuen, 1987.

Omvedt, Gail. "Patriarchy: The Analysis of Women's Oppression." *Insurgent Sociologist* 13, no. 3 (1986): 30–50.

Ong, Aihwa. "Disassembling Gender in the Electronics Age: A Review Essay." *Feminist Studies* 13, no. 3 (1987): 609–22.

Owens, Craig. "The Discourse of Others: Feminists and Postmodernism." In *The Anti-*

Aesthetic: Essays on Postmodern Culture. Ed. Hal Foster. 57–82. Port Townsend, Wash.: Bay Press, 1983.

Pajaczkowska, Claire. "Introduction to Kristeva." *m/f* 5–6 (1981): 149–57.

Palmer, D. J. *The Rise of English Studies*. London: Oxford University Press, 1965.

Pecheux, Michel. "Ideology: Fortress or Paradoxical Space?" In *Rethinking Ideology: A Marxist Debate*. Ed. Sakari Hanninen and Leena Paldan. 31–34. New York: International.

———. *Language, Semantics and Ideology*. New York: St. Martin's, 1975.

Plaza, Monique. "Our Damages and Their Compensation: Rape: The Will Not to Know of Michel Foucault." *Feminist Issues* 1, no. 3 (1981): 25–35.

———. "Phallomorphic Power and the Psychology of Women." *Ideology and Consciousness* 4 (1978): 4–36.

Polan, Dana. "Fables of Transgression: The Reading of Politics and the Politics of Reading in Foucauldian Discourse." *boundary 2* 10 (1982): 361–81.

Pollitt, Katha. "Being Wedded Is Not Always Bliss." *Nation* (20 Sept. 1986): 239–242.

Poovey, Mary. "Feminism and Deconstruction." *Feminist Studies* 14, no. 1 (1988): 51–65.

———. "Scenes of An Indelicate Character: the Medical 'Treatment' of Victorian Women." *Representations* 14 (Spring 1986): 137–68.

———. *Uneven Developments: The Ideological Work of Gender in Mid-Victorian England*. Chicago: University of Chicago Press, 1988.

Porter, Carolyn. "Are We Being Historical Yet?" *South Atlantic Quarterly* 87, no. 4 (1988): 742–86.

Poster, Mark. *Foucault, Marxism and History: Mode of Production vs. Mode of Information*. Cambridge: Polity Press, 1984.

Poulantzas, Nicos. *State, Power, Socialism*. Trans. Patrick Camiller. London: Verso, 1980.

Pratt, Minnie Bruce. "Identity: Skin, Blood, Heart." In *Yours in Struggle: Three Feminist Perspectives on Anti-Semitism and Racism*. 11–63. Brooklyn, NY: Long Haul Press, 1984.

Rajchman, John. "Ethics After Foucault." *Social Text* (Fall 1986): 165–83.

———. *Michel Foucault: The Freedom of Philosophy*. New York: Columbia University Press, 1985.

Ramas, Maria. "Freud's Dora, Dora's Hysteria: The Negation of a Woman's Rebellion." *Feminist Studies* 6 (1980): 472–510.

Resnick, Stephen A., and Richard D. Wolff. "Marxist Epistemology: The Critique of Economic Determinism." *Social Text* (Fall 1982): 31–72.

Riley, Denise. *"Am I that Name?" : Feminism and the Category of 'Women' in History*. Minneapolis: University of Minnesota Press, 1988.

———. "Commentary: Feminism and the Consolidation of 'Women' in History." Weed, 134–39.

Robins, Kevin. "Global Times." *Marxism Today* (December 1989): 20–24.

Robinson, Ben. "Making Students Safe For Democracy: The Core Curriculum and Intellectual Management." Trumpbour, 361–75.

Rooney, Ellen. "Discipline and Vanish: Feminism, the Resistance to Theory, and the Politics of Cultural Studies." *differences* 2, no. 5 (1990): 14–28.

———. *Seductive Reasoning: Pluralism As The Problematic of Contemporary Literary Theory*. Ithaca: Cornell University Press, 1989.

Rose, Jacqueline. *Sexuality in the Field of Vision*. London: Verso, 1986.

Said, Edward. *The World, the Text, and the Critic*. Cambridge, Mass.: Harvard University Press, 1983.

Sandoval Cheyla. "U.S. Third World Feminism: The Theory and Method of Oppositional Consciousness in the Postmodern World." *Genders* 10 (Spring 1991): 1–24.

Sargent, Lydia. *Women and Revolution: A Discussion of the Unhappy Marriage of Marxism and Feminism*. Boston: South End, 1981.

Sawicki, Jana. *Disciplining Foucault: Feminism, Power, and the Body*. New York: Routledge, 1991.

———. "Identity Politics and Sexual Freedom: Foucault and Feminism." Diamond and Quinby, 177–92.

Schor, Naomi. "Dreaming Dissymmetry: Barthes, Foucault, and Sexual Difference." Jardine and Smith, 98–110.

———. "The Essentialism Which Is Not One: Coming To Grips With Irigaray." *differences* 1, no. 2 (1989): 38–58.

———. *Reading in Detail: Aesthetics and the Feminine*. New York: Methuen, 1987.

Scott, H. S., and E. B. Hall. "Character Note." *Cornhill* 23 (1984): 174–78, 365–68, 486–89, 593–97.

Scott, Joan W. "Commentary: Cyborgian Socialists?" Weed, 215–17.

———. "Deconstructing Equality versus Difference: or, the Uses of Post-Structuralist Theory for Feminism." *Feminist Studies* 14, no. 1 (1988): 33–50.

———. *Gender and the Politics of History*. New York: Columbia University Pres, 1988.

———. "Gender: A Useful Category of Historical Analysis." Weed, 81–100.

Shapiro, Michael. *Language and Political Understanding: The Politics of Discursive Practices*. New Haven: Yale University Press, 1981.

Shor, Juliet. "Trials and Tribulations." *Zeta* 1, no. 1 (1988): 15–18.

Showalter, Elaine. *Sexual Anarchy: Gender and Culture at the Fin de Siecle*. New York: Penguin, 1990.

Siebers, Tobin. *The Ethics of Criticism*. Ithaca: Cornell University Press, 1988.

Silverman, Kaja. *The Acoustic Mirror: The Female Voice in Psychoanalysis and Cinema*. Bloomington: Indiana University Press, 1988.

Sivanandan, A. *Communities of Resistance: Writings on Black Struggles for Socialism*. London: Verso, 1990.

————. "Imperialism and Disorganic Development in the Silicon Age." *Race and Class* 21, no. 2 (1979): 111–26.

————. "RAT and the Degradation of Black Struggle." *Race and Class* 24 (1985): 1–33.

Smart, Barry. *Foucault, Marxism and Critique*. London: Routledge, 1983.

Smith, Dorothy E. *The Everyday World As Problematic: A Feminist Sociology*. Boston: Northeastern University Press, 1987.

————. "Femininity As Discourse." *Texts, Facts, and Femininity: Exploring the Relations of Ruling*. New York: Routledge, 1990.

————. "Sociological Theory As Methods of Writing Patriarchy into Feminist Texts." Lecture. Syracuse University, 1988.

————. "The Woman's Perspective As A Radical Critique of Sociology." Harding, 84–96.

Smith, Paul. *Discerning the Subject*. University of Minnesota Press, 1988.

Smith, Valerie. "Split Affinities: The Case of Interracial Rape." In *Conflicts in Feminism*. Ed. Marianne Hirsch and Evelyn Fox Keller. 271–87. New York: Routledge. 1990.

Smith-Rosenberg, Carroll. "The Body Politic." Weed, 101–21.

————. "Misprisoning Pamela." *Michigan Quarterly Review* 26, no. 1 (1987): 9–29.

————. "The New Woman and the New History." *Feminist Studies* 3, nos. 1–2 (1975): 185–98.

Spelman, Elizabeth V. *Inessential Woman: Problems of Exclusion in Feminist Thought*. Boston: Beacon Press, 1989.

Spillers, Hortense J. *Comparative American Identities: Race, Sex, and Nationality in the Modern Text*. New York: Routledge, 1991.

————. "Mama's Baby, Papa's Maybe: An American Grammar Book." *Diacritics* 17, no. 2 (1987): 65–81.

Spivak, Gayatri Chakravorty. "Can the Subaltern Speak?" Nelson and Grossberg, 271–316.

————. "Explanation and Culture: Marginalia." *Humanities in Society* 2, no. 3 (1979): 201–21.

————. "Feminism and Critical Theory." In *For Alma Mater*. Ed. Paula Treichler, Chris Kramarae, and Beth Stafford. 119–42. Chicago: University of Illinois Press, 1985.

————. "French Feminism in An International Frame." In *In Other Worlds: Essays in Cultural Politics*. 134–53. New York: Methuen, 1987.

————. "Imperialism and Sexual Difference." *Oxford Literary Review* 8, nos. 1–2 (1986): 225–41.

————. "The Politics of Interpretations." *Critical Inquiry* 9 (1982): 259–78.

————. "Scattered Speculations on the Question of Value." *Diacritics* (Winter 1985): 73–93.

————. "Subaltern Studies: Deconstructing Historiography." In *Selected Subaltern Stud-*

ies. Ed. Ranajit Guha and Gayatri Spivak. 3–32. New York: Oxford University Press, 1988.

————, and Michael Ryan. "Anarchism Revisited: A New Philosophy?" *Diacritics* 8, no. 2 (1978): 66–79.

————, with Ellen Rooney. "In A Word." Interview. *differences* 1, no. 2 (Summer 1989): 124–54.

Sprengnether, Madelon. "Enforcing Oedipus: Freud and Dora." In *The (M)other Tongue*. Ed. Shirley Nelson Garner, Claire Keohane, and Madelon Sprengnether. 51–71. Ithaca: Cornell University Press, 1985.

Stacey, Judith. "Sexism By A Subtler Name? Postindustrial Conditions and Post-feminist Unconsciousness in the Silicon Valley." *Socialist Review* 17, no. 4 (1987): 7–28.

Stansell, Christine. "A Response to Joan Scott." *International Working Class History* 31 (1987): 24–29.

Stanton, Domna. "Difference on Trial: A Critique of the Maternal Metaphor in Cixous, Irigaray, and Kristeva." In *The Poetics of Gender*. Ed. Nancy K. Miller. 157–61. New York: Columbia University Press, 1986.

————. "Language and Revolution: The Franco-American Revolution." In *The Future of Difference*. Ed. Hester Eisenstein and Alice Jardine. 157–82. New Brunswick: Rutgers University Press, 1985.

Starn, Rudolph. "Seance and Suicide: The Media of Somatic History: Forward." *Representations* 22 (Spring 1988): 1–2.

Stillman, Peter G. "Marx's Enterprise of Critique." In *Marxism*. Ed. Roland J. Pennock and John W. Chapman. 252–55. New York: New York University Press, 1983.

Stubbs, Patricia. *Women and Fiction: Feminism and the Novel: 1880–1920*. New York: Barnes and Noble, 1979.

Student Marxist Collective. "Texts on Ideology: A Critical Bibliography." In *Theories of Ideology: Althusser and After*. Ed. Teresa Ebert and Mas'ud Zavarzadeh. University of Illinois Press, forthcoming.

Suleiman, Susan Rubin. *Subversive Intent: Gender, Politics, and the Avant-Garde*. Cambridge, Mass.: Harvard University Press, 1990.

Thompson, John B. *Studies in the Theory of Ideology*. Berkeley: University of California Press, 1984.

Toews, John E. "International History After the Linguistic Turn." *American Historical Review* 92, no. 4 (1987): 879–907.

Torton-Beck, Evelyn. "Asking For the Future." *Women's Review of Books* 6, no. 5 (1989): 21–22.

Trumpbour, John, ed. *How Harvard Rules: Reason in the Service of the Empire*. Boston: South End, 1989.

Veeser, H. Aram, ed. *The New Historicism*. New York: Routledge, 1989.

Vicinus, Martha. "Sexuality and Power: A Review of Current Work in the History of Sexuality." *Feminist Studies* 8, no. 1 (1982): 133–56.

Volosinov, V. N. *Marxism and the Philosophy of Language*. Trans. Ladislaw Matejka and I. R. Titunik. New York: Seminar Press, 1973.

Walby, Sylvia. *Theorizing Patriarchy*. Oxford: Blackwell, 1990.

Walkowitz, Judith R. *Prostitution and Victorian Sexuality: Women, Class, and the State*. Cambridge: Cambridge University Press, 1980.

———, Myra Jehlen, and Bill Chevigny. "Patrolling the Borders: Feminist Historiography and the New Historicism." *Radical History* 43 (Winter 1989): 23–43.

Walzer, Michael. "The Politics of Michel Foucault." In *Foucault: A Critical Reader*. Ed. David Couzens Hoy. 51–68. London: Blackwell, 1986.

Weed, Elizabeth, ed. *Coming To Terms: Feminism, Theory, Politics*. New York: Routledge, 1989.

Weedon, Chris. *Feminist Practice and Poststructuralist Theory*. Oxford: Blackwell, 1987.

West, Cornel. "Ethics and Action in Fredric Jameson's Marxist Hermeneutics." In *Postmodernism and Politics*. Ed. Jonathan Arac. 123–44. Minneapolis: University of Minnesota Press, 1986.

———. "Marxist Theory and the Specificity of Afro-American Oppression." *Marxism and the Interpretation of Culture*. Ed. Lawrence Grossberg and Cary Nelson. Chicago: University of Illinois Press, 17–29.

White, Hayden. *Tropics of Discourse: Essays in Cultural Criticism*. Baltimore: Johns Hopkins University Press, 1978.

Widdowson, Frances. *Going Up Into the Next Class: Women and Elementary School Training, 1840–1914*. London: Women's Research and Resources Center, 1980.

Widdowson, Peter. *Re-Reading English*. London: Methuen, 1982.

Wiegman, Robyn. "Black Bodies/American Commodities: Gender, Race, and the Bourgeois Ideal in Contemporary Film." In *Unspeakable Images: Ethnicity and the American Cinema*. Ed. Lester Friedman. 308–28. Urbana: University of Illinois Press, 1991.

Williams, Raymond. *Politics and Letters: Interviews With New Left Review*. London: New Left Books, 1979.

Willis, Sharon. "A Symptomatic Narrative." *Diacritics* (1983): 46–60.

Wilson, Elizabeth. "Psychoanalysis: Psychic Law and Order?" In *Sexuality: A Reader*. Ed. Feminist Review. 157–76. London: Virago, 1987.

Wittig, Monique. *The Straight Mind*. New York: Beacon, 1992.

Wolff, Richard, D. "Gramsci, Marxism and Philosophy." *Rethinking Marxism* 2, no. 2 (Summer 1989): 41–54.

———, and Stephen Cullenberg. "Marxism and Post-Marxism." *Social Text* (Fall 1986): 126–35.

Wright, Erik Olin. *Classes*. London: Verso, 1985.

Zavarzadeh, Mas'ud. *Seeing Films Politically*. Albany, N.Y.: State University Press, 1991.

————, and Donald Morton. *Theory, (Post)modernity, Opposition*. Washington, D.C. Maisonneuve Press, 1991.

Zinner, (Zita) Jacqueline. "Michel Foucault, *La Volunte de Savoir*." *Telos* 11 (1978): 215–26.

Index